NATIONALISM AND NATIONALITIES IN THE NEW EUROPE

NATIONALISM
AND NATIONALITIES
IN THE NEW EUROPE

EDITED BY **CHARLES A. KUPCHAN**

A COUNCIL ON FOREIGN RELATIONS BOOK

CORNELL UNIVERSITY PRESS · ITHACA AND LONDON

First published 1995 by Cornell University Press.

Printed in the United States of America

⊚ The paper in this book meets the minimum requirements of the American National Standard for Information Sciences—Permanence of Paper for Printed Library Materials, ANSI Z39.48-1984.

Library of Congress Cataloging-in-Publication Data

Nationalism and nationalism in the New Europe / edited by Charles Kupchan.
    p.   cm.
   Collection of discussion papers originally given during a series of seminars at the Council on Foreign Relations.
   "A Council on Foreign Relations book."
   Includes bibliographical references and index.
   Contents: Introduction; nationalism resurgent / Charles Kupchan—Reflections on the idea of the nation-state / David P. Calleo—Nationalism and ethnicity in Europe, East and West / George Schöpflin—Is democratic supranationalism a danger? / Ezra Suleiman—Fear thy neighbor: the breakup of Yugoslavia / Aleksa Djilas—Nationalism in southeastern Europe / Ivo Banac—Three faces of nationalism in the former Soviet Union / Paul A. Goble—Hypotheses on nationalism and the causes of war / Stephen van Evera—Ethnic nationalisms and implications for U.S. foreign policy / Henry Bienen.
   ISBN 0-8014-3162-X—ISBN 0-8014-8276-3 (pbk.)
   1. Europe—Politics   and   government—1989-   —Congresses.   2. Nationalism—Europe—History—20th century—Congresses. I. Kupchan, Charles. II. Council on Foreign Relations.
D2009.N36   1995
320.5'4'094—dc20   95-13351

Contents

Contributors

Ivo Banac is professor of history at Yale University.

Henry Bienen is president of Northwestern University.

David P. Calleo is professor at the School of Advanced International Studies of Johns Hopkins University in Washington, D.C.

Aleksa Djilas is an independent scholar in Belgrade.

Paul A. Goble is Senior Associate at the Carnegie Endowment for International Peace in Washington, D.C.

Charles A. Kupchan is Senior Fellow for Europe at the Council on Foreign Relations, New York, and teaches at Georgetown University.

George Schöpflin teaches at the University of London.

Ezra Suleiman is professor of politics at Princeton University.

Stephen Van Evera is assistant professor of political science at the Massachusetts Institute of Technology.

Preface

Nationalism and nationality are slippery concepts. For some, nationality connotes ethnicity; for others, it is synonymous with citizenship. In some parts of postcommunist Europe, nationalism is a critical source of social cohesion, in others, a source of fragmentation and violence.

This volume reflects the varied nature of nationalism in contemporary Europe as well as ongoing confusion within both academic and policymaking circles about what nationalism is and how it affects Europe's landscape. Some of the chapters have primarily conceptual objectives; they seek to clarify our understanding of nationalism and of how it affects societies, states, and interstate relations. Other chapters focus on specific regions in Europe and study the causes and effects of nationalism in those areas. Still others focus explicitly on policy and ask how the international community can channel toward constructive ends the resurgence of nationalism associated with the Cold War's end.

In the introductory chapter, I define nationalism, set forth a typology of nationalist ideologies which distinguishes between their content and their intensity, and generate hypotheses about why the content and intensity of nationalism change over time. I also ask what policy instruments can be used to affect the trajectory of contemporary nationalism. The chapter provides a conceptual foundation for the book, and I intend it to make an analytic contribution to the study of nationalism more generally.

In the second chapter, David Calleo examines the intellectual roots of European nationalism and reflects on how the idea of the nation-state evolved during the past century. Calleo not only puts contemporary nationalism in a historical context, but he also examines how nationalist ideology has both shaped and been shaped by geopolitics and the international system. George Schöpflin then contrasts national identities in Europe's west with those in Europe's east, offering a compelling explanation for why nation-states west and east have followed such different trajectories. Schöpflin's analysis sheds considerable light on the causes and likely course of nationalist sentiments in Europe's new democracies. In his chapter, Ezra Suleiman argues that the European Union needs to democratize to win popular legitimacy and drive forward the process of integration, despite the persistence of strong national identities that impair such democratization. Suleiman studies how the Union might address this important tension lurking within the enterprise of European integration.

Next, Aleksa Djilas examines the breakup of Yugoslavia. Weaving together nationalist tendencies left by the country's communist leaders, the role played by irresponsible elites and intellectuals, and the failure of the international community to react with appropriate vigor and purpose, Djilas both tells an important story and offers new insights into how and why nationalism triggered bloodshed in the Balkans. Ivo Banac follows with a more conceptual examination of the Yugoslav conflict. By comparing Balkan nationalisms with those in other parts of Europe and tracing their evolution over time, Banac puts the most recent round of violence in the region in historical perspective. In the seventh chapter, Paul Goble studies the national question in the former Soviet Union. Goble argues that Soviet leaders unwittingly fueled nationalist movements in the Soviet Union, setting the stage for the breakup of the USSR. He offers a useful typology of national movements in the region and suggests innovative ways to channel these movements toward peaceful and constructive ends.

In chapter 8, Stephen Van Evera analyzes why and how nationalism causes war. Although many scholars have alluded to the connection between nationalism and war, few have systematically examined this relationship. Van Evera significantly advances understanding of nationalism and its international effects by explicitly studying the causal links between nationalist sentiment and conflict. Henry Bienen outlines specific recommendations for U.S. policy in chapter 9. Mindful of domestic political constraints, doubtful that the destabilizing effects of nationalism in Europe threaten U.S. national security, and skeptical that U.S. intervention can dramatically change outcomes, Bienen cautions U.S. decision-makers against direct involvement in nationalist conflict in Europe's east. In the concluding chapter, I address the broader analytic questions raised in the introduction concerning how and why the content and intensity of nationalism change over time and offer general policy recommendations.

THIS book began life in late 1991, when Nicholas Rizopoulos, then director of studies at the Council on Foreign Relations, asked me to organize a research project on the evolution of post–Cold War Europe. At that time, few topics seemed more worthy of consideration than nationalism and its effects on Europe's changing landscape. Despite the unpredictable fluidity of developments since the collapse of communism, the assessment proved correct: nationalism continues to be one of the most potent forces shaping both the character of old and new European states and the relationships emerging among them.

I thank the Council on Foreign Relations for supporting this project. Funding for the research came in part from a grant made to the Council by the Rockefeller Foundation. The Pew Charitable Trusts Program on States, Reforms, and Conflicts in Eastern Europe also provided support.

The chapters in this volume were originally presented as discussion papers in seminars at the Council. I express my deep appreciation to the following participants in the seminar series, all of whom provided useful criticism and advice as the project moved forward and rough drafts were crafted into more polished chapters: Suzanne Berger, Thompson Bradley, David Cannadine, James Chace, Richard Cohen, Jean-Marc Coicaud, Mark Danner, Wolfgang Danspeckgruber, John Fox, Gidon Gottlieb, Shafiq Islam, Miles Kahler, Kenneth Keller, George Kenney, Elizabeth Kiss, Alexander Kitroeff, Ivo Lederer, Charles Maier, Kenneth Maxwell, Karl Meyer, Marguerite Michaels, Alexander Motyl, Diane Orentlicher, Adamantia Pollis, Elizabeth Prodomon, David Remnick, Nicholas Rizopoulos, Leon Sigal, Tony Smith, Jack Snyder, Ronald Steel, John Temple Swing, David Unger, Nicholas Wahl, and William Wohlforth. I am especially indebted to Michael Haltzel, who served as chairman of the seminar series and always kept the discussion sharp and on track.

An earlier version of Stephen Van Evera's chapter was published in *International Security* 18 (1994). I am grateful to the journal and to the MIT Press for permission to use this material here.

CHARLES A. KUPCHAN

New York City

NATIONALISM AND NATIONALITIES IN THE NEW EUROPE

1

Introduction: Nationalism Resurgent

Charles A. Kupchan

Nationalism is back. Across Europe, the Cold War's end has unleashed nationalist sentiments long suppressed by bipolar competition and, in the east, by communist coercion. The resurgence of nationalism is having dizzying effects. In Europe's west, the European Union is running up against strong national identities as it seeks to deepen integration and to extend membership northward and eastward. Not only is the traditional realm of sovereignty threatened as EU institutions grow stronger; if supranational bodies come to fulfill functions formerly provided by the state, minority groups such as the Catalans, Basques, Corsicans, Irish, Scots, and Flemish may seek greater levels of autonomy. In Europe's east, nationalism is in many instances providing a critical source of social cohesion for states in the midst of profound transformation. In countries that are more or less ethnically homogeneous—such as Poland—a common national identity and a shared national project provide momentum for the difficult process of state-building. But in more multiethnic states—such as the former Yugoslavia—nationalism is fueling violent fragmentation.

Scholars and policymakers alike are scrambling to understand where this new wave of nationalism has come from and how best to react to it. The stakes are extremely high. The future of the European Union, the course of reform in the new democracies, the viability of multiethnic states, the dampening of national rivalries, the moderation of Russian nationalism—these are all key determinants of whether Europe is headed toward an unprecedented period of peace or toward decades of ethnic strife and interstate war.

The international community is particularly ill-prepared to cope with the different strains of nationalism gaining potency in Europe. This inadequacy is not surprising. The Cold War presented challenges that differed dramatically from those emerging today. The failure to orchestrate a more coordinated response to events in Yugoslavia has all too clearly illustrated the pressing need to think through more systematically the causes and effects of the resurgence of nationalism in Europe.

The principal goal of this book is to contribute to this search for new concepts and policy mechanisms, and to push forward the debate emerging within the United States and the international community more generally over how to accommodate the forces of nationalism while preserving stability and preventing conflict across Europe. In this introductory chapter, I provide an analytic framework for thinking about nationalism—one intended to help focus and direct the emerging research agenda. Although numerous books have been written on nationalism,[1] the concept remains poorly defined and hypotheses about its contemporary forms have not been fully developed.[2] In this sense, the scholarly community is at a relatively early stage in its examination of nationalism in today's Europe. My primary aim is therefore to clarify what nationalism is, to develop a typology for studying its different forms, and to identify a set of questions for examining its contemporary causes and effects.

DEFINING NATIONALISM

Nationalism is an ideology that calls for the merging of the sentimental nation with the functional state. The state is purely administrative; it provides goods and services to its citizens. The nation is purely emotive; it provides a sense of belonging and community to its members. Nationalism thus engenders among a specified population a common political identity. This communal identity is rooted in a shared ethnicity, lineage, language, culture, religion, or citizenship. Drawing on existing common attributes and generating shared historical experiences and myths, nationalism elevates the nation-state to a place of primacy—one that transcends class, kinship, or regional affiliations in commanding popular loyalty. Nationalism is central to the process of transforming disparate and politically weak ethnic and cultural groupings into modern states. It also transforms the administrative state into the sentimental nation—a political community which, because of its emotional appeal, is capable of extracting far more devotion from its members. At its core, then, nationalism is about identity. In a world in which individuals can choose among many competing affiliations, nationalism posits that affiliation with the nation-state should serve as the defining element of political identification.[3]

Two assumptions guide the analysis in this introduction and the following chapters. First, nationalism and the concept of nationality are not primordial—that is, they were not dormant elements of a universal political dialogue which finally manifested themselves in Europe in the eighteenth century and then spread globally thereafter. Rather, nationalism was and continues to be socially and politically constructed. The nation-state remains the most central and enduring feature of the international landscape. It is so prevalent, however, not because it is integral to human nature, but because it has proved to be so effective in providing security, economic welfare, and a sense of belonging to its members. Precisely because nationalism is not primordial or essentialist, it is malleable and its trajectory is susceptible to influence through policy instruments. Not only do elites have considerable ability to shape the central symbols and images that constitute national identity, but underlying social and economic conditions affect the course of nationalism within a given polity.[4]

Second, contrary to conventional wisdom in the United States, nationalism has stabilizing as well as destabilizing effects on the international system. In the wake of so much bloodshed in the former Yugoslavia, the U.S. foreign policy community now tends to portray nationalism entirely as a pernicious force that breeds fragmentation and ethnic violence. To be sure, nationalism played a central role in the breakup of Yugoslavia and, earlier this century, was a principal cause of World Wars I and II. Yet nationalism also has been, and continues to be, a key ingredient of both domestic order and international cooperation. Nationhood legitimates the administrative and extractive powers of the state. Stable state structures and the transference of political loyalties from the local to the national level in turn provide fertile ground for mass political participation and the growth of liberal democracy.[5] In this sense, the cultivation of nationalist sentiment and loyalties will facilitate peaceful change in Europe's east. The absence of an intact national identity in Ukraine, for example, has made that country's postcommunist transition particularly difficult.[6] And in Central Asia, where clan ties and regionalism run strong, a healthy dose of nationalist sentiment should contribute to, and not impede, political and economic transformation.

The integrative function served by nationalism operates at the international as well as the domestic level. A domestic polity infused with nationalist ideology can, by instigating aggression or by fueling fears among its neighbors, be a source of interstate conflict. At the same time, polities with a strong sense of national identity can also serve as a source of interstate cooperation. A state that enjoys sovereignty and legitimacy can more comfortably devolve some aspects of its sovereignty to supranational institutions than one that is struggling to attain domestic cohesion and autonomy. Indeed, the EU has taken considerable strides toward political and economic union precisely because its members enjoy an intact sense of national identity and a high degree of administrative efficiency—features that enable them to enter safely into arrangements that impinge on the traditional realm of sovereignty.

Accordingly, the challenge for policymakers is not to dampen or suppress nationalism, but to cultivate its benign aspects and to channel the political momentum they engender into the enterprise of building stable state structures, tolerant civil societies, and robust international institutions.

A TYPOLOGY OF NATIONALISM: CONTENT AND INTENSITY

Although all nationalist ideologies share a commitment to the same enterprise—nation-building—they vary along two key dimensions: *content* and *intensity*. Content refers to the nature of the substantive symbols, images, and shared historical experiences that constitute national identity. Intensity refers to the level of emotional arousal that these national symbols evoke.

All forms of nationalism contain imagery that gives definition to a unique and distinctive national grouping. These symbols may be either ethnic or civic in character.[7]

Ethnic nationalism defines nationhood in terms of lineage. The attributes that members of an ethnically defined national grouping share include physical characteristics, culture, religion, language, and a common ancestry. Individuals of a different ethnicity, even if they reside in and are citizens of the nation-state in question, do not become part of the national grouping. Conversely, ethnic groups do not need states in order to become nations.[8]

Civic nationalism defines nationhood in terms of citizenship and political participation. Members of a national grouping that is defined in civic terms share participation in a circumscribed political community, common political values, a sense of belonging to the state in which they reside, and, usually, a common language. A citizen is a national, regardless of ethnicity and lineage. Civic nationalism can exist only within the context of a territorial state; it is the bonds forged through the enterprise of statehood, not the ties of ethnicity and a common ancestry, that serve as the basis for the formation of a national grouping.[9]

Conventional wisdom holds that civic nationalism, because it defines nationhood in terms of citizenship and political values rather than in terms of ethnicity, is more inclusive than ethnic nationalism; it erases, rather than reinforces, ethnic and racial dividing lines. As a consequence, civic nationalism is less likely to produce ethnic rivalries or the persecution of minority populations and is therefore more conducive to international stability. In theory—and to a large extent in practice—conventional wisdom is correct.

Civic nationalism does favor social cohesion and political equality in ethnically heterogeneous political communities. And it can reduce the likelihood of interstate conflict by removing ethnic rivalry as a source of tension. But civic nationalism is also a rather rare form of nationalism and one that is difficult to nurture; it depends on well-developed political and legal institutions to regulate relations and distribute political power across ethnic as well as other social boundaries. Accordingly, civic nationalism prospers only in relatively sophisticated political communities.

Ethnic nationalism is more prevalent and easier to nurture; it does not require robust institutions or political sophistication. In addition, it draws on the political infrastructure and cultural ties that often exist within an ethnic group even before it possesses a state.[10] There is nothing inherently destabilizing about ethnic nationalism. Indeed, nation-states formed around an ethnically homogeneous population often tend to be stable, cohesive political units. But in today's international environment—one characterized by a high degree of mobility among, and intermixing of, populations—ethnic nationalism can have profoundly destabilizing effects. As witnessed in numerous parts of the former communist bloc, it can lead to the persecution of minorities in states with a dominant ethnic group (Serbs in Croatia) and can fuel the nonviolent (Czechoslovakia) or violent (Bosnia) breakup of existing multiethnic states. Admittedly, the destabilizing effects of ethnic nationalism in Europe's east are particularly pronounced at this historical juncture because of the collapse of the Soviet empire. Nevertheless, in light of the hundreds of different cultural and linguistic groups that populate Europe, the unimpeded spread of ethnic nationalism threatens the viability of Europe's many multiethnic communities and bodes ill for Europe's stability.

WHETHER ethnic or civic in content, nationalistic ideologies vary widely in the degree of emotional arousal they evoke. Studying these various levels of intensity entails distinguishing between two phenomena: the intensification of ethnic nationalism among minority groups within an existing nation-state; and the intensification of either ethnic or civic nationalism among the dominant population within an existing nation-state. Although these two phenomena share significant ground—both entail increasing emotional attachment to the national grouping and its attributes—they are driven by different social processes and produce different international effects.[11]

As an ethnic grouping inside a multiethnic state becomes mobilized, it passes through three main stages of national identification and arousal. First, it claims *group distinctiveness* and sets itself apart from the political and cultural mainstream. During this stage, ethnicity may still be one of several competing identities and may coexist comfortably with civic notions of nationhood, but ethnic affiliation becomes an important determinant of political affiliation. The Catalans in Spain provide a good example. Second, the ethnic community plans *group autonomy* and seeks to separate itself from central political institutions. Ethnicity becomes a more exclusive determinant of identity, although distant affiliation with the state remains acceptable. Quebec's current status falls into this category. Third, the ethnic community claims *group secession* and seeks to establish its own nation-state. Ethnicity becomes the dominant determinant of political identity, precluding other loyalties. Slovenia and Croatia are examples.

As nationalism among the dominant population of an existing nation-state intensifies, it also passes through three principal stages. First, at the *state-claiming* level, nationalistic ideology transfers traditional loyalties and identities to the nation-state. Affiliation with the nation, be it defined in ethnic or civic terms, takes precedence over competing clan, religious, or regional identities. In Western Europe, this stage corresponds to the period of nation-state formation during the eighteenth and nineteenth centuries. Second, nationalism at the *state-building* level engenders rising devotion to and sacrifice on behalf of the nation-state. It contributes to the centralization and mobilization of the state. Nationalist sentiment in many of Europe's new democracies is currently at this level of intensity. Third, nationalism at the *state-expanding* level encourages hegemonic aspirations and fuels efforts to annex or control territory outside the homeland. It glorifies the power and superiority of the nation and justifies its domination over other nation-states. When civic in content, state-expanding nationalism produces classical imperialism; colonies are attached to the motherland and their inhabitants are given political status through an imperial governing structure. The British and French empires in the late nineteenth century are examples. When ethnic in content, state-expanding nationalism is characterized by racism and claims of ethnic superiority. It fuels predatory aggression and the conquest and subjugation of an imperial periphery.[12] Germany and Japan during the 1930s and Serbia in the 1990s are examples.

INTERNATIONAL EFFECTS

Depending on their content and intensity, different strains of nationalism have very different effects on the international environment. Nationalism in Western Europe, as long as it stays at moderate levels of intensity, is likely to remain a force for democracy and social harmony. Nationalism in most West European countries consists of both civic and ethnic elements. Civic elements continue to serve as an important source of legitimacy and cohesion in ethnically heterogeneous countries. Ethnic elements, because they provide only one of many sources of identity and have found expression through institutional and legal arrangements, do not threaten the viability of existing nation-states.[13]

In Europe's turbulent east, civic nationalism provides probably the most promising ideological foundation for the consolidation of stable, multiethnic states. Ethnic nationalism is playing a more ambiguous role. In much of East Central Europe, it is providing a sense of mission and cohesion for societies taking on the difficult task of building new state structures. In the Balkans, even though the mobilization of ethnic nationalism has already triggered the violent breakup of Yugoslavia, it may ultimately lead to the emergence of stable, ethnically homogeneous successor states. At the same time, Europe would be embroiled in chaos should all its ethnic groups seek statehood. And Serbian behavior in Bosnia has already demonstrated the potential for ethnic nationalism to escalate to destructive levels.

This book focuses on only two of the many international effects associated with nationalism: the breakup of existing states, and the incidence of predatory aggression carried out by nation-states imbued with nationalistic fervor. These effects constitute the most disruptive consequences of nationalism. They lead to three key questions which form the core of the research agenda pursued in this volume.

1. What causes ethnic groupings within larger multiethnic states to become state-claiming ethnic nationalities? What conditions erode civic and communal identities and fuel the mobilization of ethnic nationalism, thereby leading to group secession and efforts to create new states?
2. What conditions raise nationalistic ideologies to the state-expanding lével? Which domestic and international factors give rise to aggressive strains of nationalism?
3. Which policy instruments will most effectively influence the content and intensity of nationalism? What can the international community do to promote the viability of multiethnic states and dampen aggressive strains of nationalism?

UNDERSTANDING NATIONALISM

The following hypotheses are neither mutually exclusive nor exhaustive; they identify and refine a set of plausible explanations for what are admittedly very complex phenomena. The objective of this chapter, and of the book more generally, is not to provide definitive answers to these questions, but to advance efforts to think about nationalism and its international effects in a more systematic and rigorous fashion.

When Do Ethnic Groups Become State-Claiming Ethnic Nationalities?

Ethnic identity is a compelling, but elusive, basis for political community. At times, a given group of individuals may not even affiliate with an ethnic grouping and ethnicity may have little or no impact on political allegiances. At other times, those same individuals may have a very strong sense of attachment to an ethnic grouping and ethnic identity may be the dominant feature of the political landscape. What causes these dramatic changes in the intensity of ethnic identity? Why do communities that do not even identify themselves as an ethnic group later seek to establish ethnically based nation-states?

Loss of state capacity. States fulfill basic political, economic, and security-related functions for their members. The implicit social contract that underlies citizenship posits an exchange of loyalty for the provision of these public goods. When the state fails to provide the functions expected by its citizens, they may turn to other forms of political and social organization. The bonds of culture, language, kinship, and proximity make ethnicity a logical basis for the formation of a successor political community to the flagging state. From this perspective, ethnic groups become state-claiming ethnic nationalities when the state in which they reside founders; ethnic identity becomes the new focal point for organizing collective action and providing public goods.[14]

This explanation for the mobilization of ethnic nationalism portrays ongoing fragmentation in Europe's east as the product of the inability of the postcommunist successor states to provide basic services to their inhabitants. The proliferation of claims to nationhood stems from the search for new ways to organize collective action. This approach would similarly explain the mobilization of subnational ethnic identities in Western Europe in terms of the declining utility of the state. As the European Union assumes responsibilities previously fulfilled by the states, ethnic groups become less reliant on traditional state structures for public goods. Ethnic identity consequently becomes a more attractive and feasible focal point for political organization.

Treatment of minorities. An alternative explanation for the mobilization of state-claiming ethnic nationalities focuses on how minority groups are treated by a dominant population. The most intuitively compelling hypothesis is that groups that are persecuted or systematically mistreated seek protection by establishing their own states and acquiring the means of self-defense.[15] But ethnic mobilization also could occur through two other pathways. Efforts to encourage minority ethnic groups to assimilate into the dominant culture or to replace ethnic with civic identities could cause a backlash with renewed calls for a distancing from the state.[16] Invitations to participate in the political mainstream may be interpreted not as inclusive largess, but as a threat to group distinctiveness. From this perspective, efforts to facilitate assimilation, rather than explicit persecution or mistreatment, drive ethnic mobilization. Alternatively, it may be that accommodation of calls for increased autonomy, not efforts to encourage assimilation, triggers ethnic mobilization and separatist forces. Without deliberate and sustained efforts to integrate disparate ethnic groups into a civic political community, the centripetal forces associated with ethnic identification may eventually lead to the mobilization of state-claiming ethnic nationalities.

Consider how each of these discrete hypotheses would be applied to the case of the Kurds in Turkey. From one perspective, discrimination against the Kurds and efforts to use military force to suppress the militant Partiya Karkaren Kurdistan lie behind the separatist movement. From another, excessive efforts to assimilate the Kurds into a secular and civic Turkey fueled the mobilization of Kurd separatism. The third approach suggests that granting increased cultural and political autonomy to the Kurds, far from relieving separatist pressures, has only intensified Kurdish demands for formal secession and statehood.

Historical rivalries and hatreds. The mobilization of ethnic nationalism might be the product of historical ethnic identities or rivalries which rise to the surface when the forces that have held them in abeyance disappear.[17] In this sense, the breakup of many multiethnic states is "waiting to happen," and occurs as soon as the opportunity arises. The mobilization of state-claiming ethnic identities is less the product of the intensification of nationalistic sentiments than of the development of external conditions that allow preexisting sentiments to be acted upon. These conditions include the breakdown of traditional patterns of authority, a shift in the military balance, or other developments that empower an ethnic group that previously felt incapable of challenging the status quo.

From this perspective, the fragmentation of Yugoslavia, the war in Bosnia, and the split of Czechoslovakia were all the inevitable product of the collapse of communism. Without the presence of coercive regimes intent on preserving the integrity of the multiethnic state, long-suppressed ethnic tensions surfaced. In the Balkans, unlike in Czechoslovakia, freshly revived memories of past injustices ensured that violence accompanied the surfacing of these ethnic sentiments. This view provides cause for pessimism both about the viability of multiethnic states in Europe's east and about the ability of the international community to affect the course of nationalism in the former communist bloc.

Contagion and emulation. The mobilization of ethnic sentiments could be the product of contagion, the spread of state-claiming nationalism by example. One ethnic group's efforts to establish its own nation-state might encourage others to do the same.[18] Contagion can not only intensify ethnic identity, but also channel it toward a specific endpoint by making statehood the only true measure of nationhood. Mobilization could also occur through a more long-term process of emulation as opposed to through contagion. Ethnic groups in the former communist bloc or in the developing world may seek to emulate nation-states of the industrialized world, hoping to share in the stability, prosperity, and security those states have enjoyed. Claims of statehood are driven by the appeal of the Western model, not by the momentum provided by a sudden wave of new nationalist movements.

Proponents of the contagion model would view the ongoing fragmentation of Europe's east as a prime case of mobilization by example. For them, the unification of Germany, the successful secession of Croatia and Slovenia from Yugoslavia, and the peaceful split of Czechoslovakia fueled other attempts to transform nationhood into statehood. They would similarly view the mobilization of the Kurds in Turkey as a direct byproduct of the successful efforts of their kin in Iraq to carve out an autonomous region in the north of the country. Proponents of the emulation model would provide a slightly different explanation. From their perspective, the spread of nationalism eastward is primarily a function of efforts to imitate the West. Free from the ideological drag of communism, ethnic groups are seeking to replicate the mainstay of the industrialized world—the nation-state. While the contagion model should lead to punctuated bouts of claims to statehood as waves of nationalist activity spread, emulation should produce a smoother pattern of instances of ethnic mobilization provided by groups choosing, at their own pace, to pursue the benefits associated with the nation-state.

Social change and identity formation. When ethnicity is mobilized, it comes to dominate other forms of personal identity. This process can take place because ethnic affiliation, for any of the reasons discussed so far, is endowed with new importance. Or it can take place when other forms of identity erode, endowing ethnicity with pride of place through a process of elimination. The breakdown of traditional forms of identification could be triggered by any number of developments. Political centralization might undermine local patterns of authority. The emergence of markets and urbanization could encourage labor mobility and threaten familial ties nurtured through proximity. Secularization could threaten religious affiliation as a chief component of identity.[19] In all of these cases, ethnicity emerges as an anchor of identity in the midst of change. It provides a sense of belonging and self-definition when other guideposts and symbols of identity become unattractive or unavailable.

From this perspective, ethnicity is now a powerful force shaping Europe's strategic landscape because the overthrow of communism and the resultant social and economic dislocation undermined traditional forms of identity in the east. Indeed, Soviet rule explicitly sought to sweep away identities that could threaten communism, thereby leaving political communities unanchored and ill-defined when it collapsed. Ethnic affiliation became prime because other forms of identity were nonexistent or discredited. Yugoslavia, according to this argument, broke apart violently not because of historical hatreds unleashed by the collapse of the communist regime, but because that regime had failed to inculcate civic values and identities among the population—a step that would have made ethnicity only one of several competing identities among Yugoslavs. Political and economic transformation may as a matter of course induce the intensification of ethnic sentiment; such sentiment provides psychological bearings in the midst of change. Yet whether such intensification transforms ethnic groups into state-claiming ethnic nationalities depends on whether ethnicity emerges as *the* dominating source of political identification.

What Causes Aggressive, State-Expanding Nationalism?

The previous section examined alternative explanations for the emergence of strains of nationalism that lead to the breakup of existing multiethnic states. I now ask why nationalism at times intensifies to levels that cause the nation-state to engage in aggression against other states. Although both phenomena involve a process of emotional arousal, they are very different in character. State-claiming ethnic nationalism is predicated on the distinctiveness of an ethnic group and its right to autonomy. Aggressive, state-expanding nationalism is predicated on the superiority of an ethnic group and its right to domination. Aggressive nationalism contributes to the outbreak of interstate war by convincing elites of the strategic necessity of instigating conflict, by confronting decision-makers with powerful domestic forces that push them toward a decision for war, or by fueling escalating spirals of hostility with neighboring states.

State structure. The propensity for aggressive strains of nationalism to emerge within a polity could be a function of state structure. Nondemocratic nation-states may provide fertile ground for the development of state-expanding nationalism for two reasons. First, because leaders in authoritarian societies lack the legitimacy enjoyed by elected leaders, they may turn to claims of ethnic superiority and the right to dominate others to consolidate their domestic position. Under normal circumstances, democratic leaders do not need to resort to such ideological appeals to sustain legitimacy. Second, because of the closed nature of nondemocratic societies, extremist strains of nationalism are not exposed and discredited through open debate. Myths of ethnic superiority and calls for conquest may well emerge in democratic states, but it is more likely that exposure to open debate and public scrutiny will ensure their demise.[20]

This explanation for the emergence of war-causing strains of nationalism certainly resonates with the experiences of Germany and Japan during the interwar period. In both countries, authoritarian regimes whipped up virulent nationalism, which then burgeoned among the populace, unchecked by critical public discourse. The spread of racist, state-expanding nationalism helped fuel Germany's bid for hegemony in Europe as well as Japan's brutal advance through the Asian mainland and its futile attempt to establish the Greater East Asia Co-Prosperity Sphere. So too does Slobodan Milošević's Serbia conform to this model. Milošević used nationalist rhetoric for his own political gain. His monopoly of the media then ensured the unimpeded intensification of nationalist sentiment among the population at large, laying the ideological foundation for efforts to build greater Serbia at the expense of a multiethnic Bosnia.

Transitions in state structure. Rather than being the product of state structure, aggressive nationalism may emerge from breakdowns in state structure and capacity. When states lose their ability to sustain popular legitimacy and to deliver public goods and services, political chaos usually ensues. These periods of transition can trigger the ratcheting up of nationalism through several pathways.[21] Governing elites—or their opponents—may turn to nationalistic appeals to rally popular support and divert attention from domestic woes. The military, seeking to take advantage of the political vacuum to better its own fortunes, may generate nationalistic myths and inflate external threats. The public, in the absence of functioning political institutions capable of channeling mass activism and popular disaffection, may rally around strong and virulent currents of nationalism.

From this perspective, the painful transformations ongoing in Europe's east provide fertile ground for the emergence of aggressive nationalism. With widespread popular disaffection resulting from poor economic conditions and from unfulfilled expectations about the benefits of democracy, and with their independent and critical media still in formative stages, the public is susceptible to elites pandering illusory platforms for national renewal. In the midst of these difficult social conditions, irresponsible leaders—Milošević in Serbia, Istvan Csurka in Hungary, and Vladimir Zhirinovsky in Russia are cases in point—will seek to whip up nationalistic fervor to further their political ambitions. In so doing, however, they risk spawning the contorted, yet powerful, war-causing ideologies that took root in Germany in the 1930s and that have already infected today's Serbia.

Vulnerability and insecurity. Belligerent nationalism might be the product of international competition and the perceptions of vulnerability and insecurity that accompany it.[22] External threats, whether perceived or real, can accelerate nationalism by creating the need for a military buildup and, consequently, for the mobilization of domestic resources.[23] This mobilization may require elite appeals to nationalistic fervor. The perception of a threatening external environment also strengthens the hand of hard-line nationalists at home, increasing the likelihood of an intensification of nationalistic sentiments.[24]

This approach points to the collapse of a meaningful security structure in the east, the disrepair of national military establishments, and the operation of the security dilemma as the key causes of intensifying currents of nationalism in the former communist bloc.[25] Threat perceptions are by no means uniform across the region, but uncertainty and insecurity are pervasive. In East Central Europe, it is the perceived existence of a security vacuum between east and west that heightens a sense of vulnerability. In Ukraine and other former Soviet republics, the prospect of a resurgence of Russian imperialism fuels feelings of insecurity. In Russia, perceptions of vulnerability are heightened by the loss of empire, concern about the welfare of Russians outside the homeland, and the prospect of the fragmentation of the Russian Federation itself. In all of these cases, according to this line of argument, insecurity and the prospective steps needed to redress it serve to swell the currents of nationalism.

What Policies Can Shape Post–Cold War Nationalism?

Sobriety and realistic expectations should characterize all efforts to address how the international community can affect the content and intensity of nationalism in Europe. Policymakers and scholars alike are still struggling to understand nationalism and its causes, not to mention how to use policy instruments to influence it. Because nationalism occupies the realm of ideas and emotions, the task of formulating policies to deal with it is especially problematic. Nevertheless, its importance as an ideological and social force shaping the new Europe warrants efforts to address this problematic task.

The European Union. The EU promises to serve not only as an institution that will work against the renationalization of politics in Western Europe, but also as a vehicle for integrating the new democracies into Western structures and markets. How fast and how far should European integration proceed? Can integration move forward if the EU does not democratize further? Would such democratization produce a nationalist backlash in Western Europe? Should the expansion of the EU into Central and Eastern Europe take precedence over deepening integration in Western Europe?

Economic and technical assistance. The provision of technical and economic assistance is one of the international community's main sources of leverage in Europe's east. Can assistance be used to help sustain the viability of multiethnic communities or dampen virulent strains of nationalism? Should such assistance be contingent upon behavior consistent with the norms of civil society, or should aid be given without strict conditions on the assumption that civil society cannot emerge until minimum levels of economic welfare have been attained?

Treatment of minorities. The treatment of minority groups within multiethnic states will have significant impact on the long-term viability of those states. Is there an "equilibrium level" of autonomy that should be granted to these groups—a level that will encourage cultural distinctiveness without encouraging separatist movements? How can civic identities be nurtured in states dominated by a single ethnic group?

Education and social programs. Is it possible to affect the trajectory of nationalism through education and social programs? Would the content and intensity of nationalism be influenced by building local government and civic organizations, beaming radio and television broadcasts to a target country, sanctioning elites who disseminate inaccurate national histories and peddle war-causing ideologies, and helping education systems publish new, "ethnically neutral" textbooks?

Military measures. Under what conditions should outside forces be deployed in a preventative manner? Under what conditions should outside forces be deployed as peacemakers or peacekeepers? Where and under what conditions should international bodies consider extending some form of security guarantee to help moderate regional vulnerabilities? To what extent should concern about the West's credibility and "domino effects" shape thinking about when and how to intervene in conflicts emerging from ethnic and nationalist rivalry?

Recognizing new states. What standards should be established for the recognition of new states? Should the international community be predisposed against new claims of statehood, or will the dissolution of multiethnic states ultimately lead to a more stable Europe?

The chapters that follow provide a historical and analytic foundation for addressing this policy agenda. In the concluding chapter, I offer more explicit responses to these questions.

2

Reflections on the Idea
of the Nation-State

David P. Calleo

The nation-state remains the dominant political formula of our century, a reality regretted by many enlightened analysts of international affairs. Nation-states, they believe, are severe obstacles to a better world order or are generally too large and centralized to practice genuine democracy. Many also find them obsolescent, less and less able to perform their traditional functions. Nation-states cannot defend their security in the nuclear age, it is said, and are economic anachronisms in our interdependent global economy. And they sustain archaic cultural barriers and conflicts in our global village. Nevertheless, nation-states continue to be the principal repositories of political loyalty and legitimacy around the world, as well the leading international actors. Indeed, with the breakup of the Soviet empire, new nation-states are proliferating throughout Eurasia and "nationalism" is rising once again in the West.

Can a political formula so universal and tenacious as the nation-state be either as obsolescent or pernicious as so much current commentary suggests? Obviously nationalism, like any other ardent political loyalty, can grow pathological. But with the postwar international system now changing so rapidly in a nationalist direction, it might be more useful for theorists of the international system to understand and accept the enduring strength of the nation-state, in order to work more imaginatively and efficaciously to control the consequences. In short, perhaps our view of the nation-state needs fresh evaluation.

A good place to start is with the intellectual provenance of the nationalist formula for the state, the formula according to which a political state ought to coincide with a cultural nation. What are the political ideas that originally lay behind the linkage of states and nations? What gave such ideas their appeal? How did the great nationalist theorists themselves conceive of the relationships among nation-states, or the prospects for peace in a world of such states?

Such an inquiry obviously goes well beyond a single article. I make a modest start, however, by focusing on two major nationalist theorists of the state—Johann Gottfried von Herder (1744–1803) and Bernard Bosanquet (1848–1923)—one from the late eighteenth century and the other from the late nineteenth and early twentieth centuries. Their writings help elucidate the ideas behind the nation-state formula as it evolved up to World War I, as well as the limits and possibilities of an international system based upon nation-states.

After looking at Herder and Bosanquet, I add a brief sketch of four topics that follow logically and historically: how nationalist theories of international order related to more traditional hegemonic, pluralist, and liberal theories; why the nation-state formula gradually triumphed over its rivals; what broad "lessons" for theories of the nation-state system were derived from the disastrous first half of the twentieth century and how these lessons were applied in the second half. I close with a short discussion of a further major question: what are the lessons for the nation-state system from the Cold War era?

So brief a treatment of such large topics will have manifest inadequacies. It may nevertheless help open the way to a more constructive view of nationalism and its international implications.

THE NATIONALIST FORMULA FOR THE STATE

Historically, the nationalist state formula is the marriage of the ancient Idealist view of the state with the modern nationalist idea of a culture. Throughout a large part of Europe's medieval and modern history, such linkage between state and nation did not seem at all necessary. Two developments were required to make it seem natural. First, the ideal of what is required to make a political state legitimate had to evolve in a certain way. The state had to be seen not as a band of governors holding sway over a passive population of obedient individual subjects, but rather as a self-conscious community of consenting and cooperating citizens, joining together to create a good society. Second, those qualities that define a community—culture, history, and personal identity itself—had to be seen primarily in national rather than in universal, class, religious, racial, or tribal terms.

The first idea—that a state should be a moral community of participating citizens—sprang from classical Greece. Among political philosophers in the decades immediately preceding both the American and French revolutions, it was Jean-Jacques Rousseau in his most famous political writing, *The Social Contract,* who forcefully rejuvenated this Greek ideal of vigorous citizenship, animated by a "general will" to create a republic of virtue.[1] After Rousseau, the French Revolution acted as a catalyst for the spread of his Idealist political formula. A state's legitimacy, the revolution taught, could no longer base itself merely on past conquest, historical habit, or utilitarian convenience. It required free and vigorously consenting citizens.[2]

An Idealist theory of the state as a moral partnership of consenting citizens naturally called for a theory of community. The concept of the cultural nation, favored and developed by Romantic philosophers, provided a ready solution. As a practical matter, citizens of an Idealist political state had to be able to communicate and cooperate with each other. Hence they presumably required a common language and a shared universe of cultural symbols, monuments, and myths. Their sense of mutual political identity needed to be reinforced by a shared history—real and imagined. These are all qualities that characterize the Romantic concept of a nation. As that concept became widely accepted, it grew to seem natural that a state, to sustain the consentient community that made its sovereignty legitimate, had to be congruent with a cultural nation. Even in the early nineteenth century, as the French Revolution proceeded to the Napoleonic empire, the nationalist state formula had become a powerful ideal employed to rally opposition to French domination. Thus, the idea of the state soon grew deeply entwined with the idea of the nation.

THE ROMANTIC NATION: HERDER

The Romantic concept of the nation was developed above all by Herder, an eighteenth-century German Romantic philosopher and literary critic.[3] Since Herder was writing in the fragmented princely Germany of the old regime, he felt diffident about pressing the political corollaries of his nationalist view of culture and community. But even in his own circumspect writings, he could scarcely disguise his belief that political states, to be legitimate, needed to coincide with cultural nations, or that such nations, to flourish, needed a state of their own.

In any event, these corollaries were soon richly developed by numerous German writers in the early nineteenth century, including Fichte and Hegel. They were also taken up by British Romantic conservative writers such as Edmund Burke and Samuel Coleridge. Indeed, they soon spread everywhere and continued to be elaborated by new generations of theorists. Notable among those in the mid-nineteenth century, for example, were the German-American political economist Friedrich List and the Italian patriot Giuseppe Mazzini. Perhaps the fullest development of the Romantic-Idealist nation-state formula can be found in the writings of British neo-Hegelian philosophers in the years before World War I. As indicated earlier, I will turn to the writings of one of the major figures in this school, Bernard Bosanquet, for a definitive statement of the classic theory of the nation-state.

It seems appropriate, however, to begin with Herder himself, who, more than anyone else, launched the presumption that cultural nations are the natural communities of humankind. Behind Herder's cultural doctrines lay his resentment of French cultural hegemony over Germany. As a middle-class German Romantic intellectual, he found it unbearable that the culture of the French Enlightenment should dominate Germany's princely courts, where the fashions and manners of Versailles were the model and French often the spoken language. He was outraged at the demotion of German language and literature, and the way French critics set universal rules of taste and dismissed other cultures as uncouth. His writings strongly implied that German culture was being abused because Germans lacked a powerful state to defend their own nation.

In his reactions against French classicism, Herder reflected the *Sturm und Drang* phase of Romanticism, with which he was closely associated. Like other early Romantics, he found the eighteenth-century Enlightenment's views of art, personality, and freedom to be mechanical, monotonous, and sterile.[4] Romantics demanded freedom for individuality, in particular for the individuality of the artistic genius, which they were inclined to believe required expression in hot emotion rather than cold reason. As a critic and moralist, however, Herder grew frightened by the solipsistic and amoral tendencies in *Sturm und Drang*'s enthusiasm for unfettered individuality. Was every artist free to create his own private moral and aesthetic universe? It was, for Herder, a troubling prospect.

Herder's nationalist concepts of *Volk* and *Kultur* were his way of reconciling the free artist with collective social and cultural order. According to Herder, humanity divided itself into separate peoples and cultures, and therefore individualism had to be defined collectively as well as personally. In their basic genetic endowment, Herder believed, all men did share a common humanity (*Humanität*), but history had made them different. Each people (*Volk*) developed its distinctive culture (*Kultur*)—a bundle of linked ideas, memories, and sentiments that was its reaction over time to a particular environment and collective experience. Distinctive nations were the result. Such nations were the natural subdivisions of humankind, each the product of its own particular circumstances and innovations. Each nation developed its own special insight into human potential, and each had to be understood on its own terms. The nation also gave individual artists their "rule"—the aesthetic and moral framework within which they could work out their own individual visions.

Herder was himself a prodigiously learned and gifted scholar of the folklore of several nations. He was genuinely cosmopolitan, in the sense that he had deep insight, respect, and love for many cultures, past and present: "No nationality has been totally designated by God as the chosen people of the earth; above all we must seek the truth and cultivate the garden of the common good. Hence no nationality of Europe may separate itself sharply, and foolishly say, 'With us *alone*, with us dwells *all* wisdom!' "[5] Nevertheless, Herder's psychology of the self and its identity, and his views about the conditions required for an artist's creativity and integrity, limited his cosmopolitanism and complicated his views on nationalist coexistence.

Herder's limits on cosmopolitanism were psychological rather than biological. For him, even the greatest individual genius was always partly communal, the product of the culture that nurtured him. An individual, by absorbing the insights of other cultures, past and present, could greatly enrich his own personal and national vision. But one could not, at the same time, renounce one's national identity without destroying one's own cultural integrity and vitality. One would then become like eighteenth-century Germany's deracinated and sterile Francophone aristocrats. As Herder saw it, "The inundated heart of the idle cosmopolite is a home for no one."[6]

By making individualism collective, so to speak, Herder merely transferred the problem of order to a more general level. If history was the development of distinctive nations, and every culture had its own standards, what values applied to humanity as a whole? Were there no standards that applied across nations to provide the moral framework for their coexistence?

Herder's answer was a grand Romantic theory of history that prefigured Hegel. Throughout nature and throughout human history, Herder saw a divine energy, or *Kraft*, exploring and realizing through time humanity's potential. National cultures were the chapters of the human story, each to be understood and appreciated on its own terms. The diversity of cultures was the key to general human progress. History was a garden, and each national flower possessed its own particular beauty. It should not be crowded out by its neighbors or uprooted by imperial gardeners.

In summary, Herder's cultural, psychological, and historical views implied that states should be limited to nations, and he thereby mandated an international system of nation-states. His fatalistic but cheerful view of history, combined with his cosmopolitan sympathies, implied a peaceful coexistence of those nation-states, spoiled only by the arrogance of imperial regimes or cultures with hegemonic pretensions.

THE IDEALIST NATIONAL STATE: BOSANQUET

Throughout the nineteenth century, idealist political philosophers continued to develop the political implications of the nation-state. As suggested earlier, the British neo-Hegelian philosopher Bernard Bosanquet, who died shortly after World War I, provides a mature picture of the strengths and vulnerabilities of the nation-state formula.[7] He is particularly interesting for his elaboration of the moral and psychological bases for nationalism, for his critique of the liberal tradition of John Stuart Mill and the earlier economists like Jeremy Bentham and David Ricardo, and above all for his frank acceptance of the implications of his nation-state theory for international relations.

Like Herder, Hegel, and Idealist philosophers in general, Bosanquet rejected the definition of individual freedom typical of the liberal tradition stemming from the Enlightenment, a tradition that tended to see society as an aggregate of individuals—consumers in the case of the economists—whose freedom consisted of being left alone by the state to pursue their own self-interest. For such liberals, typified by Bentham, Ricardo, and—in some writings at least—by John Stuart Mill, the state was merely a necessary nuisance. This view reflected what Bosanquet described as their "miser's hoard" theory of liberty, according to which, to safeguard anything of his liberty, the citizen was forced to part with some of it. To sustain his own security, the citizen made a basic deal: he gave the state some of his freedom in order to safeguard the rest. Bosanquet rejected this liberal theory of freedom, but found it incomplete rather than simply wrong.

Liberty from unjust coercion was essential to the individual's freedom, Bosanquet agreed, but not sufficient for it. The individual realized freedom, Bosanquet argued, only by developing his potential as a rational human being. This development could not be achieved in isolation. The error of liberals like John Stuart Mill was that they saw an individual's capabilities lying in "a sort of inner self, to be cherished by enclosing it" rather than "evolved by the varied play of relations and obligations in society."[8] The modern constitutional nation-state was not the enemy of individual self-development, in Bosanquet's view, but the necessary framework for achieving it. The state in its proper role was a mutual association of citizens to pursue their own best selves. The "general will" of such a state demanded the public conditions and policies that would best foster that pursuit of individual development.

Bosanquet reinforced these familiar Idealist arguments with a theory of identity or "psychology of the moral self." The individual's identity as a self or soul was not an inherited endowment that needed merely to be protected. Rather, individual identity was something created through the interaction of experiences and mental processes. In Bosanquet's picture of the developing self, the mind organized its experiences into "appercipient masses," or systems of linked associations. These systems *were* the mind. They struggled among themselves to seize and integrate every new experience, and were themselves altered as they did so. Harmonizing diverse appercipient masses into some coherent rational identity was part of the individual's never-ending process of self-knowledge and self-realization.

Individuals were fully aware of themselves only in exceptional moments of self-consciousness. Normally, the mind was constantly passing from one aspect of consciousness to another and usually aware of only a small portion of itself. Most of the mind's appercipient masses were held unconsciously until aroused. "This subconscious mass changes very slowly and in every person probably has certain permanent and certain habitual elements," wrote Bosanquet.[9] The mind moved to its conscious level of self-awareness when it began distinguishing itself as an individual from the world around it, and reached its philosophical stage when it began to reflect upon itself. In so doing, the mind realized that the objects it perceived were not alien to its own self, but were constantly being absorbed into it.

Since members of the community had many common experiences, their appercipient masses were not only individual but also shared. Shared appercipient masses were, in turn, the basis of the "common mind and will" that characterized organizations of similar persons. They made possible a "wide self" for an individual—one that saw "a unity between itself and others, or even nature" as essential to its own personal identity: "Our connection with others is . . . in the Self, and not in the Not-Self."[10] The self, in other words, could not define its identity in a vacuum. It required a "medium of recognition." To achieve self-awareness required a role for the individual in a larger context. The individual self was part of that context, but that context was also part of the self.

For Bosanquet, a shared self also implied a shared will. Rational will arose from the mind's tendency to seek to resolve contradiction, and thus push beyond its own direct experience. The self thus became "a positive context to be realized." Our "moral self" arose from recognizing a shared identity and will with others in society, and thus tended toward a collective view of goals for the community. This "identity of mental organization . . . is the psychological justification of the doctrine of the General Will."[11] Collective action tended to follow when ideas demanding change were compatible with a large number or a particularly strong group of appercipient masses.

Beneath these ethical and psychological arguments about the individual's relationship to the state were the metaphysics of Herder, Hegel, and Romanticism in general. In this world-view, nature was not a cold, dangerous, and alien environment against which the self needed protection. Nature was filled with divine energy. The self was part of nature and shared that energy. Similarly, society and the political community were not, by definition, enemies of the self. Ideally, the state was a collective rational self through which individuals organized with others to achieve their individuality—personal and collective—generation after generation.

To the present-day reader the totalitarian potential in Bosanquet's psychology and state theory seems obvious. But Bosanquet had also inherited the Romantic's strong appreciation for the diversity of society. Every class and subgroup had a natural desire, indeed a duty, "to realize a life and culture of its own." Workers should not be expected to wear the second-hand clothing of the bourgeoisie. But in a good society, Bosanquet believed, these distinctive perspectives, loyalties, and identities of separate social groups and classes would share strong elements of common mind and identity. This sharing would make possible the mutual respect and toleration that allowed a plural society to live in enough harmony to permit a wide area of personal freedom. The delicate balance between diversity and unity was helped, Bosanquet believed, by enough economic and social opportunity for a reasonable circulation of elites. The balance also required sharp limitations on the active power of the government. According to Bosanquet, a state was justified in using its coercive powers only to "hinder hindrances," and only when it resulted in a greater "growth of mind and spirit" than would have been possible without state intervention.[12]

NATIONALISM AND INTERNATIONAL ORDER

Bosanquet's ethics and psychology were bound up with the nationalist formula for the state. The moral community essential to his ideal state was possible only for those whose "appercipient masses" contained sufficient common experiences and ideals to support the shared identity necessary for a legitimate general will. Bosanquet acknowledged a higher sphere where cosmopolitan ideals transcended national cultures. But relatively few people appreciated such ideals, he believed, and they could not support an international order that bypassed national states. A higher world culture and value system could not be achieved by rejecting national values, but only by absorbing and building upon them. Humanity's most sublime capacities, Bosanquet believed, were realized in art, literature, and religious beliefs. While genius in these spheres could transcend the national culture, it could not abandon the national culture. This, of course, was Herder's view as well.

In short, Bosanquet was leery of pretensions to universality, particularly in any political form. More often than not, he thought, those who asserted universal principles merely revealed their provincial insensitivity to the cultural norms of others. Too often, universal ideals were covers for intolerance and oppression.

> The best Churchmen will admit, I believe, that to a great extent at least the peoples of the world have already the religions that suit them best. And we all see that the gospel of Western science, valuable as it is, has no exclusive claim to be the doctrine even of civilized man. A number of great systems, profoundly differing in life, mind, and institutions, existing side by side in peace and cooperation, and each contributing to the world an individual best, irreducible to terms of the others— this might be, I do not say must be, a finer and higher thing than a single body with a homogeneous civilization and a single communal will.[13]

Applied to international politics, this nationalist doctrine meant that new forms of international organization had to *build* on nation-states rather than to reject them. From this perspective, proposing a universal sovereignty to supplant the nation-state was, like proposing a made-up universal language to supplant real national languages, a development that would result in a staggering loss of human achievement and potential. Encouraging everyone to master other national languages would, by contrast, greatly enlarge individual insight and potential. In short, higher human progress required accepting and relishing the diversity of nations. But maintaining that diversity meant a world of nation-states with all its innate potential for conflict.

Bosanquet lived long enough to see his ideals severely challenged in World War I. But he became, if anything, more vehement in defense of the national state: "The body which is to be in sole or supreme command of force for the common good must possess a true general will, and for that reason must be a genuine community sharing a common sentiment and animated by a common tradition." A nation-state's moral duty was to defend its own independence, Bosanquet believed. Morality *between* states was inevitably different from morality within them. The difference was not merely the absence of a reliable political order above states, it was still more "the absence of a recognized moral order to guide the conscience itself."[14] An international general will was difficult to imagine in the present state of humankind. And the phenomenon of war could not be properly considered "apart from the general problem of evil in the world," in his view. "Evil and suffering," he wrote,

> must be permanent in the world, because man is a self-contradictory being, in an environment to which he can never be adapted, seeing that at least his own activity is always transforming it. . . . While man

has a conscience, and things he values above life, and yet his conscience is liable to err, the root of war exists. Issues may arise between
group and group which cannot be compromised. Within the state
itself, which is cited as the convincing analogy for a universal reign of
law, both civil and individual rebellion remain possible.

With war, as with any other evil, man was bound "to do what he can for its
removal. And I do not doubt that its occasions may be immensely
diminished by the reform of states, and their reconstruction in certain cases,
and by what this will promote, a truer economic creed."[15]

Cooperative interstate organizations could help keep the peace, Bosanquet admitted, but only so long as they respected the sovereignty of their
members. But Bosanquet expected no miracles from such organizations.
More significant, he thought, would be the capacity of national states to
perfect themselves internally. With a better and more just internal equilibrium, he thought, states would be less driven to look to the international
arena to compensate for their internal inadequacies. In short, Bosanquet
offered no organizational solution, on the international level, to the problem of war among states. Instead, by emphasizing national consensus as the
basis for morality as well as political legitimacy, he deliberately restricted the
moral foundation for any transnational organizational solution for international order.

Bosanquet represents a high synthesis and summation of classic nationalist state theory. As he demonstrates, that theory left open a key issue: the
moral and practical relationship of nation-states to each other. To be sure,
Bosanquet's was not the only view about the normal climate of international
relations. Other nationalist theorists had quite different views. The variations often reflected the differing philosophies of history that proliferated in
the nineteenth century. The dependence of nationalist international relations theory on historical theory was, in effect, part of Herder's legacy. Many
nationalist theorists, moreover, continued to echo Herder's own cheerful
view of international relations—his cosmopolitan sympathies and expectations of more or less automatic harmony among peoples. His vision was
faithfully represented, for example, in Mazzini's writings to promote Italian
unification. Mazzini, like Herder, foresaw peaceful coexistence among free
nations, each adding its own riches to humankind.[16] This cosmopolitan
nationalism often had wide resonance in the arts. Italy's developing national
consciousness found rich sustenance in Verdi's operas. Verdi's nationalism,
like Mazzini's, was ardently humane and cosmopolitan in its sympathies.[17]

Other nationalists, however, had less generous expectations. English conservatives, like Burke and Coleridge, had embraced the nationalist formula,
among other things, to combat the universalist pretensions of the French

Revolution.[18] Though Romantic in much of their general outlook, they were also sufficiently Christian, in an orthodox sense, so that, unlike Herder, they did not see the benevolent hand of God in every historical outcome. In a fallen world, they regarded tragic conflicts among nations as normal. Nations could be bad as well as good; conflict among them was always possible and citizens had a duty to fight to preserve their nations. Statesmen should work to resolve international differences reasonably and peacefully, but could not always succeed. Hegel, whose ideas were very close to Herder's in many respects, but were formed through the years of the French Revolution and its Napoleonic aftermath, also had a harsher view of nationalist coexistence. However much he felt Herder's vital force coursing through history, he could not imagine that its progress would be without great struggle, injustice, and tragedy. Indeed, for Hegel history was "a butcher's block" and its succession of cultures often a tragic and bloody business. One people with its values and ideals was frequently sacrificed to the rise of another.

Some later nationalist theorists not only expected a struggle among competing national systems, but celebrated it as the Darwinian mechanism for human progress.[19] Biological racism also grew more prominent in some later nineteenth-century theory. It presupposed a people bonded by blood rather than culture, as in the historical theories of the comte de Gobineau or Houston Stewart Chamberlain. Both were close to Richard Wagner, whose bewitching, incandescent operas aroused and powerfully influenced German national consciousness in a racist and combative direction.[20] In short, among nationalist theorists some thought harmony was natural; others thought conflicts were inevitable but might be managed; still others believed war inevitable; and some rejoiced in it.

NATIONALISM AND TRADITIONAL THEORIES
OF INTERSTATE RELATIONS

Nationalist theorists were not, of course, developing their ideas about international coexistence in a theoretical or historical vacuum. The seventeenth and eighteenth centuries had already produced a rich panoply of models to describe and regulate relations among traditional states. These fell into three broad and familiar schools: hegemonic, balance of power, and liberal. For our purposes, it is worth noting briefly the basic ideas behind each view, and how each ultimately accommodated to the nation-state formula.

The hegemonic approach grew out of the Hobbesian view of human society—a "war of all against all" unless a sovereign imposed order. Translated into interstate relations, this Hobbesian view might prescribe a universal empire with an imperial sovereign or at least a hegemonic state—one that could dominate the others sufficiently to maintain order. Hegemony might be organized through a federation that gave all member states a sense of participation, so long as a single sovereign power was the practical result.

The balance of power or "pluralist" approach sought to maintain the liberty of each state and limit warfare by a calculated policy of shifting alliances to prevent any one state from achieving hegemony. Rational self-interest among states might encourage codes of international law to limit the damage that states might do to each other, or to private citizens during wartime. Confederal structures could encourage independent states to focus upon and cultivate their common interests and thus limit their antagonisms.

The liberal school argued that if only all nations were democratic in their politics and liberal in their economics they would be inclined to live in peace with each other. Thus Thomas Paine, the pamphleteer of the American Revolution, thought that there would be no more wars as soon as there were no more kings. Adam Smith thought that free trade, an end to monopolies, and a strict limit on government indebtedness would lead to a harmonious world. Economic competition would sublimate war, as well as bring greater prosperity to all.

These traditional theories of interstate relations were formed, for the most part, in the intellectual and cultural climate of the Enlightenment. Early nationalist theorists, profoundly influenced by Romanticism, had a more organic view of communities, a more complex psychology of individual and group identity, and a more developmental view of history. Nevertheless, when nationalist theorists thought about international order, their views often fell, superficially at least, into the categories created a century or two earlier. Thus, Social Darwinists and racists could sometimes keep company with Thomas Hobbes and develop an affinity for hegemonic theories of world order. Christian conservatives and neo-Hegelians could entertain confederal schemes to sustain a balance of power more efficiently and encourage more cooperative behavior. Herder's or Mazzini's vision of harmonious coexistence among free nation-states could find sympathetic support from the powerful current of economic liberalism that had emerged from the eighteenth century. The reverse was also true. Liberals borrowed nationalism. Richard Cobden, the great nineteenth-century publicist for Adam Smith's free trade, was a strong advocate of national self-determination.[21] For him, this meant free trade among independent democratic nation-states, living together in peace and growing prosperity.

Romantic nationalism and economic liberalism were, however, uneasy bedfellows. Unlike liberals, Romantic Idealists were unwilling to leave the determination of the public interest strictly to the market. Coleridge, even while agreeing that free enterprise and social "progression" were essential to liberty, emphasized that a balancing "Spirit of the State" should counteract and enlighten the narrow "Spirit of Commerce."[22] Mazzini was concerned with the dangers of laissez-faire and "egoism" for national solidarity.[23] The German-American nationalist political economist Friedrich List thought that nation-states should be protectionist in order to ensure that their societies reaped the social, cultural, and political as well as economic development that came with industrialization. He transformed free trade, in other words, into a pluralist doctrine of fair play and mutual benefit among independent and equally developed nation-states.[24] List also dreamed of a European confederation to balance the giant American national political economy developing in the New World.

List's preoccupation with international dimensions of nation-states was exceptional among nationalist theorists of the nineteenth century. Most were concerned with building a national community and thought little about the problems of interstate order. When they did, they remained bound by their belief that a political community based on active consent could not be sustained beyond the natural community of a cultural nation.

SUCCESSES AND FAILURES OF THE NATIONALIST IDEAL

However underdeveloped its international dimension, the nationalist formula nevertheless grew more and more compelling as the nineteenth century continued. The reasons can be found in the practical politics of the time. Europe's states, national or otherwise, were charged with the Western state's traditional functions. They were meant to preserve physical peace and security for citizens and their property, against external enemies and internal disorder. States were also traditionally charged with responsibility for economic security and material prosperity. And they were also expected to provide their subjects with a source of pride, awe, idealism, and emotional and psychological satisfaction. States that rested on a national community were, on the whole, more successful at these functions. They were better at mobilizing for war, or integrating and expanding their economies. And as traditional religious faith declined, political nationalism tended to provide a secular substitute.

The success of the nationalist formula arose from the domestic imperatives that largely determined politics within Western states. The profound social and cultural changes that accompanied economic modernization and urbanization brought mass politics and made achieving a consentient community all the more urgent. Managing a state's progress from absolutism, through aristocratic and bourgeois constitutionalism, and finally toward mass democracy required imagining and animating a corresponding national community. Some of the resulting nation-states were new creations, like Germany and Italy; some were old states transformed, like France and Britain. The principal holdout—Habsburg Austria—tried to sustain a multinational political community around its cosmopolitan dynastic ideal, and grew more beleaguered as time wore on. So, obviously, did the "Sick Man of Europe," the autocratic and heterogeneous Ottoman Empire. In effect, the nation-state provided a more successful domestic political formula than the alternatives.

By the beginning of the twentieth century, Western nation-states had succeeded in organizing orderly mass participation in politics and in reaching previously unimagined heights of material prosperity. In addition, with their radically increased capacity for political, economic, and military mobilization, they had built huge external empires and divided most of the globe among themselves. They thereby created new sources of international friction and introduced major contradictions within their own nation-state ideal. But whatever the tensions in the idea of nationalist coexistence, or nationalist imperialism, a Europe of nation-states did not seem any more quarrelsome than the old Europe of traditional states. The sixteenth and seventeenth centuries had seen titanic struggles to erect a hegemonic power. The eighteenth century, with its ideal of a rationally regulated balance of power, had nevertheless seen constant interstate warfare, often on a global scale. The nationalism that exploded in the French Revolution had, to be sure, unleashed another great European war, and continuing nationalist revolutions had kept autocratic Europe in turmoil through the mid-nineteenth century. But once Italy and Germany had achieved national unity, and Hungary autonomy within the Habsburg empire, a balanced alliance system appeared able to avoid major wars. Europe's principal states seemed to have found the mechanisms for orderly and peaceful relations, at least on their own continent.

But 1914 put an end to such complacency, as Europe's interstate system collapsed in cataclysmic disorder. The ensuing slaughter and prodigality mocked the nation-state's pretension to provide either military security or economic prosperity. Economic and military intervention from America was needed to decide the war's outcome, and the two "interwar" decades that followed produced no durable resolution. They did, however, provoke a good deal of philosophical and historical analysis of the weaknesses of the nation-state system. And many "lessons" from that analysis were eventually embodied in the state system that followed World War II.

LESSONS FROM THE NATIONALIST BREAKDOWN

For our purposes here, the interwar lessons fall into four broad categories: Wilsonian, Pan-European, Marxist-Leninist, and Keynesian. The first
two were primarily revisions and recombinations of traditional prenational-
ist approaches to international order. The last two could be considered as
elaborations on the nationalist theory of the state itself—attempts, as Bosanquet would have said, to eliminate its contradictions. All four lessons had
important implications for any broad theory of nationalist coexistence. Each
calls for a volume of explanation. I sketch them here, however inadequately,
in order to suggest how the nationalist formula evolved after World War II.

Wilsonianism began as a restatement of the liberal and relatively cosmopolitan nationalism of Herder and Mazzini. The elements of the old
liberal-nationalist fusion were all there: national self-determination for suppressed peoples, liberal democratic domestic regimes to replace autocracy,
free trade to bring prosperous interdependence, together with a confederal
League of Nations to organize collective sanctions against nations that deviated from liberal norms. For Wilson's later followers, the lesson of the Treaty
of Versailles was that the liberal nationalist formula had been applied too
imperfectly to succeed. As the interwar debacle unfolded, the apparent
inability to achieve the Wilsonian vision without strong American leadership
favored a blending of Wilsonian and hegemonic lessons—a tendency already manifest in Wilson's own statecraft.

The hegemonic school's basic historical lesson was clear and familiar: a
system of national states would be peaceful only if a leading state was willing
and able to keep order among the rest. The interwar experience also elaborated and reinforced the economic dimension to this hegemonic precept.
Since the world of economic blocs of the 1930s had been followed by war,
the lesson drawn was that blocs lead to war. Only a hegemon could keep the
world economy open and prosperous and therefore avoid blocs. To do so,
the hegemon had to perform certain basic international functions, like
providing ample credit and a distress market for goods during global economic crises.

Britain, it was said, had been able to perform these hegemonic political,
military, and economic functions from the Napoleonic wars until the later
nineteenth century. The rise of Russia, America, and Germany had gradually
deprived Britain of the necessary margin of superior resources. Without a
strong leader, the Pax Britannica and its structures of interstate economic
order, like the gold standard and free trade, could not be sustained. World
War I was followed by a profound and lengthy depression and a second
global war. To the hegemonic school the remedy seemed obvious: the

United States had to assume the role for which it alone was suited.[25] The onset of the Cold War forced these global precepts into a bipolar format. In the noncommunist world, a liberal global economy of nation-states did gradually materialize under American hegemony. Despite its inevitable shortcomings, this "Pax Americana" was a towering historical achievement and a great advance over the international system of the interwar years.

The hegemonic lesson, however, also contained a gloomy paradox. As Britain's experience seemed to show, exercising hegemony gradually weakened the hegemon to the benefit of its dependents.[26] Hegemony was thus naturally self-liquidating. A declining hegemon, to compensate for its growing weakness and unequal burdens, began itself exploiting and thereby destabilizing the international system, a putative lesson about hegemonic systems that grew more convincing as the postwar Pax Americana entered its "declinist" stage.[27] Thus, in theory as in practice, hegemony tended to give way to pluralism.

Whereas the hegemonic school emphasized the dangers of anarchy inherent in the relations of a group of roughly equal states, the pluralist school emphasized the instabilities that arose when too much power was concentrated in one state. That state was inevitably tempted to seek hegemony, which led to conflict with other states. Where hegemony was achieved, the hegemon was bound to overstretch its resources. As it grew increasingly insecure, it would become more inclined to exploit its position, as well as to stifle rising newcomers. Declining hegemony thus blocked peaceful accommodation to change.

This was the lesson of twentieth-century history developed by apologists for Germany in World War I. Britain was seen as a declining hegemon that refused to accommodate a rising Germany's global ambitions. When Germany began to compete seriously in global trade, Britain allied with France and Russia to encircle Germany on the continent. Britain used the obsolescent concept of a European balance of power to avoid acknowledging a genuine global balance.[28] In the end, rather than accept Germany as a global equal, the British sacrificed their empire and global economic position to a new hegemon, the United States. The British preferred to be Greeks to the American Romans. In their struggle to deny Germany, all Europe was ruined, Britain especially.

Pluralist arguments were also used to promote a confederation in order to restore Europe's global position and safeguard its internal peace without requiring an external hegemon. Without its own confederacy, it was said, Europe would be partitioned between Russia and America, which would bid against each other for global hegemony. At the heart of any European confederation would have to be a cooperative structure to reconcile France and Germany and to prevent either or both of them from dominating the rest. Ideas along these lines were popularized between the wars by the Pan-Europa movement and, of course, reborn in the European movement that flourished after World War II.[29]

The precepts of Karl Marx and John Maynard Keynes are, of course, well known. It is interesting, however, to consider them as "lessons" for the international system. As such, they are generically different from the hegemonic, pluralist, or even the liberal lessons. Both Marx and Keynes were primarily concerned with domestic social, economic, and political order. Both were touched strongly by the same Romantic Idealism that had nurtured the nation-state formula itself. And like nationalist theorists, their international views tended to follow from their domestic prescriptions.

Strictly speaking, Marx had no theory of international relations. As he had taught his followers in the nineteenth century, the whole ideal of the nation-state was an illusion, used to rationalize exploitation. The reality of modern political economies was capitalism, which dominated nation-states and mocked their democratic pretensions. Capitalism suffered from an incurable inner affliction: the inexorable tendency of capitalists to appropriate the lion's share of the economy's "surplus value." The result was an economy with too much capital and too little consumption, which led eventually to crisis and revolution.[30] As an ideal, Marxism was nationalism's deadly enemy, since it taught that consensus could not be built around a nation but only around a class.

Lenin's *Imperialism*, written during World War I, provided Marxism with a theory of international relations.[31] According to Lenin, the excess of capital in advanced states was transformed into "finance capital" that desperately sought external investments. This led to a scramble to control external territories, hence to imperialism. Conflict eventually followed between those states that had arrived at the imperial feast early, like Britain, and those that had come late, like Germany. That was how Lenin explained World War I. Lenin's solution was universal revolution followed by a world system of fraternal communist societies—no longer troubled by finance capital.

Unlike Marx and Lenin, Keynes was not implacably hostile to the liberal economic tradition. Rather like Coleridge, he merely believed that within the market economy the "spirit of the state" should systematically counterbalance "the spirit of commerce."[32] Keynes blamed the interwar depression on the tendency of mature capitalist economies to underconsume (or oversave) relative to real investment opportunities. But Keynes, unlike Marx and Lenin, believed the problem could be solved through the nation-state itself. His remedy, as everyone knows, lay in vigorous government countercyclical policy to promote the general welfare of the whole community.[33]

Keynes was flexible about the international implications of his remedies. In the Depression of the 1930s, to ensure that international competition would not prevent governments from pursuing the stimulatory policies he prescribed, Keynes wanted to protect national manufacturers, control capital flows, and permit floating exchange rates. As World War II ended the Depression and created the prospect of a liberal Pax Americana, Keynes tried to find a formula to reconcile his prescriptions for national economic management with an integrated global economy under American hegemony. The institutional result was the International Monetary Fund (IMF), born at the Bretton Woods Monetary Conference of 1944, where Keynes negotiated the future with the Americans.[34] An uneasy marriage between Keynesian demand management and American global hegemony, a union that seemed a stunning success, persevered until the 1970s.

These four lessons of interwar analysis—hegemonic, pluralist, Marxist-Leninist, and Keynesian—offered major insights into the weaknesses of the traditional nation-state system and inspired efficacious solutions during the postwar era. Wilsonianism and the hegemonic critique of American "isolationism" inspired the Pax Americana and NATO. The pluralist critique of hegemony inspired Pan-Europeanism in general and, after World War II, a Franco-German partnership to build a European Community. The Marxist critique of capitalism helped encourage the more enlightened responses of liberal capitalist nation-states. Among these, of course, were Keynesian economics with its welfare state, an international monetary system to reconcile rapid growth with monetary stability, as well as decolonization, free trade, and development assistance. After World War II, all these insights and remedies—domestic and international—constituted together a major advance in successfully managing the problems of nation-states.

By the 1990s, however, these familiar postwar remedies have begun to look ephemeral. The Keynesian balance between stimulated growth, monetary stability, and global integration is severely disturbed by inflation, unemployment, and a huge public and private debt burden. Meanwhile, the collapse of the Soviets has not led to a "unipolar" world hegemony. If anything, the parallel "decline" of the United States calls to mind the inner paradox of hegemonic theory: that exercising hegemony weakens the hegemon. In any event, the rapid spread of nationalism and capitalism to the non-Western world has made global hegemony increasingly unlikely, and probably undermined the prospects for global economic integration as well. In effect, most of the interwar lessons to improve nationalist coexistence seem to have exhausted their efficacy. At the same time the world seems fated to see a greater degree of nationalist pluralism than ever before.

LESSONS FROM THE COLD WAR ERA?

Given nationalist Europe's bloody history in the early twentieth century, a global system of nation-states in the twenty-first is not a reassuring prospect. It is still less so, given the apparent exhaustion of the Cold War remedies— hegemonic and Keynesian. Are there new remedies that have grown out of the experience of the Cold War era itself? The most obvious candidate is to be found in Europe—in the nascent confederacy that is the fruit of the pluralist lesson of the interwar era. In theory, a European confederacy could offer relief from the problems of nationalist coexistence at both regional and global levels. Regionally, it could provide a formula whereby nation-states preserve their independence while participating in a network of cooperation that makes wars among them much less likely. And globally, an effective European Union could make the problems of world order much more manageable.

How realistic are such prospects? Today's European Union is beset by problems. Yet, taken in all its dimensions, the EU is highly impressive—an elaborate structure of intergovernmental cooperation so entangling and resilient as to constitute a novel political form. As a model for governing on a continental scale, it can be seen to have certain advantages over more centralized federal or pseudo-federal models, which tend to grow overloaded in their centers. By preserving the vitality of the old nation-states, a confederal community may also preserve their advantages—their historical, cultural, and institutional capacity for achieving political consensus and administrative efficiency. At the same time, confederacy may reduce greatly the traditional weaknesses of nation-states. It provides a framework where interstate conflicts of interest are more likely to be resolved in a mutually productive fashion, and where war among the partners becomes close to unthinkable. In such a community, each nation-state reaches its own general will through its own national democratic processes, but these processes include a constant dialogue with its partners. Confederation, moreover, offers the partners collectively greater power to secure their national interests in the world than they could enjoy individually.

In its early years particularly, the European Community was often seen not as a confederation but as a nascent federation—an analogue to the early United States. Since Europe's states supposedly lacked the scale to fulfill their traditional functions, they were alleged to be caught in a process that would gradually rob them of their legitimacy and sovereignty. The shift in practical power from national states to federal institutions was supposed to bring about a shift in popular allegiance and identity. Europe's traditional nation-states would fade away. Some theorists thought they would be replaced by a single new "European" nation-state—an analogue to America's continental federal state. Others looked forward to a "neo-functionalist" order—a revived medieval system that would leave Europe a congeries of regional governments and technocratic functional authorities.[35]

As the years progressed, such federalist views, even if still widely held, were increasingly challenged by what might be called the confederal view. Articulated by General de Gaulle in the 1950s and 1960s, his ideal of a Europe of States saw the European Community as a novel form of interstate cooperation that did not so much diminish national sovereignty as create cooperative structures to enhance it. As de Gaulle was wont to observe, states joined alliances to preserve their independence, not to give it up. De Gaulle accepted that European states could not effectively exercise their sovereignty in isolation from each other, particularly not with two superpowers present in Europe. But this did not lead him to federalism. While as a diplomat, de Gaulle was an eighteenth-century pluralist who understood the uses of alliances and confederacies; as a political leader, he was a nineteenth-century nationalist. For him, the state was a moral community made possible because citizens shared a national culture, history, and identity. Such communities, forged over a long history of shared accomplishment and suffering, had, he believed, a collective spiritual grandeur that brought dignity and meaning to the lives of their citizens. Old nation-states therefore enjoyed a moral and psychological legitimacy that could not be transferred to some new construction put together by apolitical technocrats, lawyers, or bureaucratic politicians. Even if Europe's cosmopolitan elites wished to do so, the peoples of Europe would not stand for it. They would rise up in response to their own deeper intuition.

De Gaulle was often accused of being self-contradictory—of wanting to unite Europe without depriving its nation-states of their sovereignty. But his notions of national independence and sovereignty were more subtle than critics or admirers often realized. For de Gaulle, independence for the state was rather like free will for the individual, essentially a moral reality. Independence meant that a state was self-determining, that it could act as a subject choosing its own policies rather than be an object having policies imposed upon it. But practical independence did not require complete liberty to do anything that a state might wish. In the crowded European system, states had seldom if ever enjoyed absolute autonomy. They had always been "interdependent"—in the sense that the success of their policies depended heavily upon the reactions of their neighbors.[36] Practical independence could be secured only by having cooperative neighbors. Cooperation could be reliable only insofar as states made and kept serious engagements to each other. In effect, sovereignty could never be exercised successfully without being limited by mutual engagements. Above all, states could perform their vital functions—and thereby preserve their viability and independence—only by upholding certain basic rules of the game among themselves.[37]

Anyone familiar with nationalist theory in the nineteenth century would be unlikely to find anything surprising in de Gaulle's view of the nation-state. It had elements of Bosanquet's wide self, and indeed of Herder's cosmopolitan appreciation for other nations. But de Gaulle's approach to confederacy was a very significant addition to the theory of nationalist coexistence.

The continuing success of a Europe of States, however, depends on sustaining a basic working consensus among the still sovereign members. In the last years of the 1980s, that consensus did seem very strong.[38] It was built, however, within the geopolitically sheltered environment of the Cold War. Its efficacy had never really been challenged in military and geopolitical spheres. To meet today's suddenly urgent and heterogeneous needs, the European Union will probably expand and build a variety of new institutions with distinctive memberships, functions, and degrees of participation. But as membership grows more varied, the need for a compensating central core grows correspondingly. And Europe's new circumstances challenge the old Franco-German relationship that has traditionally formed that core.[39] While the basic geopolitical logic that initially bought the two leading continental states together should perhaps seem even more valid in today's world than during the Cold War, probably nothing should be taken for granted. The confederal formula, after all, can assist but does not supplant its member states. In the near future, it may be making very heavy demands on those members.

Perhaps if Europe's confederacy did fail, the ensuing crisis would finally provoke a genuine federalist mutation. A Europe of States might give way to a federal sovereign, perhaps in hopes of halting Europe's economic decline, putting an end to internal discord, or imposing peace on Europe's borders. But as de Gaulle expected, and certainly hoped, Europe's nations would be unlikely to put up with such a government. The failure of confederacy would probably mean not centralized federalism, but a return to a less structured form of nationalist coexistence. A new time of troubles might follow, which would perhaps be inspirational for theorists, but disagreeable for everyone else.

Whatever happens in Europe, the nation-state seems fated to remain the dominant political formula in the world at large. Its old strengths are still viable and, in essence, little altered since Bosanquet's day. In a world of rapid and bewildering change, with powerful, alien, and anonymous global forces, people seek shelter in a political community within which they can build their own psychological, cultural, and historical identity, a community with a workable consensus on what constitutes a good life and a tolerable society, and with a responsible government devoted to protecting that community's security and prosperity.

In short, the nationalist state will be the world's prevailing political formula for the foreseeable future. It is probably just as well. The modern democratic nation-state remains, after all, our best formula for curbing public and private power and nudging it toward the general welfare. Nationalism helps to remind us that economies exist to serve societies, and not the other way around. Nationalism's populist concern for community has its obvious perils, but so does today's elitist passion for globalism and technology. The power contained and mobilized inside nation-states no doubt can be dangerous, but the power that escapes nation-states is probably more dangerous still.

But so long as the old nation-state formula persists, so will the old problem of nationalist coexistence. For us, the problems are more intractable and more urgent than for the early theorists. We know better than to expect Herder's peaceful garden of blooming national cultures. And we should know better than to expect Cobden's global paradise of liberal free trade. We ought to share the skeptical pessimism of Coleridge and Bosanquet, but the risks in our world do not allow us to share their complacency.

If history has indeed been gestating a solution to nationalist coexistence, Europe's grand confederal experiment will probably prove the critical experience of our age. If Europe's old nation-states can perfect a formula to preserve their national strengths and surpass their collective weaknesses, perhaps it will help the new regional state systems emerging in other parts of the world to escape a reenactment of Europe's own bloody history. Certainly a stable and strong European confederation could be a major force for order in the rest of the world. In any event, if Europe can bring order to itself, it will have done a great deal to reconcile global nationalism with world order. If not, history provides ample suggestions for the possible consequences.

3

Nationalism and Ethnicity
in Europe, East and West

George Schöpflin

The 1990s have clearly seen a major shift in the functions, perception, and effects of nationalism in Europe.[1] In the immediate postwar years, nationalism was for all practical purposes a kind of political pariah, a phenomenon that was regarded with maximum disfavor, and the emphasis was all on integration, federalism, and the long vision of a United States of Europe. The last decade of the twentieth century, in contrast, has seen a seemingly sudden return of nationalism to the mainstream—a not altogether welcome change in the eyes of those who have never sought to understand the nature and functions of nationhood.

This chapter attempts to trace how and why nationalism has reemerged as a significant political force in the world system, with special reference to postcommunism in Central and Eastern Europe. It looks at some of the historical factors that have structured the political role of nationalism, at the implications of ethnicity as a primary ordering principle in relatively weakly grounded democratic systems, and at possible ways of creating political instruments that might stabilize the often negative energies mobilized by the use and abuse of ethnic nationalism. Reflecting on the role of nationalism in the legitimation of states and in the distribution of power between rulers and ruled, I consider the impact of modernity on the political systems of Central and Eastern Europe, not least the distorted modernization processes introduced under the aegis of communism. Finally, this chapter analyzes the relationship between ethnicity and civil society and the threat of new nationalist ideologization in the postcommunist era.

The Cold War acted as a discipline and a constraint on both the West and

Eastern Europe, locked as both were in a political, cultural, and ultimately a civilizational confrontation. The political mentalities, institutions, and the underlying epistemologies with which Europe emerged from World War II were frozen or altered only very slowly, certainly not at the same pace as economic and technological change. Because the devastation caused by Nazism was widely attributed to nationalism, the entire school of thought concerning nationhood, national identities, and nationalism was swept under the carpet and regarded as something that no longer concerned Europe—which had embarked on a different project, that of integration. Whenever political challenges were triggered by ethnonational demands, these were redefined as "protest" movements or "survivals from the past." The ethnic revival in Europe from the 1960s onward was largely assimilated into democratic politics, but persistent efforts were made to delimit it, to diminish its significance and to interpret it as something other than what it really was—the resurgence of ethnopolitics. Understandably, the end of the Cold War has left Europe, the front line in the confrontation, unprepared intellectually or politically for what followed.

Yet the sudden reemergence of nationalism is an optical illusion. In reality, under the surface of events and indeed not merely under the surface, ethnicity and nationhood not only remained in being, but they contributed significantly to the pattern of politics, though it was seldom understood in this way.[2] The argument that will be developed in this chapter is, in simple terms, that nationhood became an inescapable fact of political life in Europe in the nineteenth century. Far from disappearing or even weakening, it retained its key functions in the twentieth century and for the foreseeable future it will have a considerable saliency, whether it is conceived of in these terms or not. Hence, as far as policymaking is concerned, it is important that the true nature of nationhood and the political doctrine built on it—nationalism—be understood rather than dismissed.

A number of assumptions will be made in what follows without any attempt to argue them in detail. Nationalism is a political ideology that claims that the world is divided into nations and only into nations; and that each individual belongs to a nation and only to one nation. Nations may be defined by various characteristics, but crucial among them is their relationship to a particular territory and their claim to exercise political control over that territory in the name of the nation. Furthermore, membership of the nation is the medium through which rights are exercised, although this goes hand in hand with citizenship—nevertheless, one of the crucial tensions in modern politics revolves about the relationship between the two. In other words, nationalism is inextricably involved with the political process and must be interpreted in the same way as other facets of politics are.

NATIONHOOD: THE ETHNIC FACTOR

The definition of nation used in this chapter is connected with, but conceptually separate from nationalism.[3] Nations are a modern development, dating by and large from the late eighteenth century, and their saliency can be located at the moment when loyalty to the nation became the primary cohesive force to cement the relationship between rulers and ruled. Prior to this, various ethnic phenomena with political consequences did, in fact, exist and influence political actors, but they were secondary to religion or dynasticism or late feudal bonds of loyalty.[4] It was only in the modern period that nationhood emerged as the most important legitimating principle.

The emphasis in this definition, therefore, is on the legitimating functions of nationhood. After the end of the eighteenth century in Europe, states could claim to be authentic states only if they were the expression of the aspirations of a particular nation. Previously, states were legitimated by reference to loyalty to a secular ruler or by religion. The rise of nationhood as the primary agent of legitimation was not confined to international politics, but was central to the newly reformulated relationship between monarchs and subjects. Under dynastic or religious legitimation, that relationship, while involving elements of reciprocity, was one-sided and nonsecular. Ultimately, dynastic legitimation was grounded in the divine right of kings to rule, and with religion the proposition is self-evident.

In the eighteenth century, however, a very different pattern emerged, derived from secular propositions. This was the notion of popular sovereignty; namely, that legitimacy was a two-way relationship, giving both rulers and the ruled rights and duties toward each other. The bond between the two, then, had also to be reformulated, because the nature of community was something qualitatively different. This switch from religious to secular legitimation was not as sudden as it might appear with hindsight; secular aspects in the definition of kingship had been intensifying steadily since the Middle Ages.

This was where nationhood came in. Nationhood became the tissue that was to connect the entire population of the state with its political institutions and claim to exercise power or control over it in the name of popular sovereignty. This process is the civic core of nationhood, its channel into politics. Nationhood, then, should be conceptualized as simultaneously having a political (civic) and a cultural (ethnic) dimension. Of course, the role of ethnicity in politics had been present and understood previously. Various premodern references to the idea of a single ethnic group existing in one territory and the significance of this can be found in history, but this misses the point, just as reference to the premodern nation as being the premodern equivalent of the nation-state does. Universal citizenship and ethnicity were at best only one and not the chief source of legitimacy, whereas with the reception of nationalism, the nation has become the single overarching basis of political community, one that has never been superseded.

NATIONHOOD: THE NEW LEGITIMATION OF STATES

In the construction of nationhood both the state and ethnicity played a role, although in Western Europe there has been a tendency to deny the significance of the latter. This is misleading. It is evident that modern nations benefit enormously from an ethnic base, but the ethnic base has not been sufficient on its own to constitute the political community. It is one argument to say that ethnicity is significant in the constitution of states; it is something radically new that ethnicity should be the single most important factor in the equation, yet it is this transformation that took place with the end of the eighteenth century—the French Revolution is a suitably symbolic marker. The explanation for the sea-change lay in the unintended consequences of various historical processes and their particular conjuncture in time. The growing perception of the insufficiency of the neo-feudal bonds of rule, with their particularisms and exceptions cutting across new commercial patterns; the rise of mass literacy through the invention of cheap printing and the resulting access to reading material in the vernacular by large sections of the population; the awareness that outdated principles of legitimacy could not satisfy the demands of the newly conscious strata, especially the emerging bourgeoisie with its demand for more access to power and the consequent quest for alternative links—all played their parts.

The role of the state in the construction of communities should not be neglected either. Shared patterns of governance, of military service, of policing, taxation, and administration all helped (and still help) to create a sense of identity, by which boundaries were established and the sense of "we-ness" against "otherness" was strengthened.[5] Furthermore, along with state-inspired rituals, the evolution of high cultural languages that replaced Latin and the use of a single administrative language (which may have been introduced for the sake of convenience rather than anything else) aided and abetted this process of welding disparate groups together and giving them a new consciousness. England was the exception in this case, because a centralized administration through the operation of the court of King's Bench was in place by the Middle Ages. Elsewhere, multiple jurisdictions in the same realm were the norm, and that included such a relatively centralized state as France, where a single legal system was established only with the promulgation of the Code Napoleon in 1803.

The core of the proposition is that these newly emerging social groups turned to the idea of the nation as their intended vehicle for access to political power because the medieval nation had always been the body politic, the medium through which political power was wielded, in European thought.[6] Perhaps the cry of the American colonists against George III, "no taxation without representation," illustrates this most vividly. It constituted a demand for the construction of polities on a new civic (i.e., "rational") basis. In effect, the new demands were cutting across old loyalties and eroding them rapidly.[7] The Napoleonic wars, which temporarily destroyed old-established verities and undermined their claim to traditional legitimation in the Weberian sense, that institutions could demand obedience because they had existed since time immemorial, carried this process throughout Europe.

In this situation, the states with a well-established centralized power, which had not undergone major territorial adjustments, profited most clearly. In these so-called core states (England, France, Holland, Sweden), territory, political power, and community had coincided for several centuries and there were no major ethnic discontinuities. Without sizeable ethnic minorities threatening to disrupt the territorial integrity of the state, these core states were best placed to benefit from the new dispensation.[8]

The crucial element in the process of the shift from dynastic to national legitimation was that political power was to be far more widely distributed than ever before. This meant that the rulers had to be reasonably secure in the belief that the devolution of power would not be abused by a disaffected minority to demand independence. The doctrine of popular sovereignty encoded precisely this arrangement in the civic sphere of politics, but it was understood that civic unity on its own might well prove too weak a basis on which to establish a political system involving the thoroughgoing redistribution of power. Contract on its own was not enough. The construction of British identity illustrates these processes clearly. The establishment of a British identity began well before the rise of modern nationhood and was grounded in Protestantism and loyalty to the ruler. Shared religion was enough to overcome the ethnic divisions of Englishness, Scottishness, and Welshness, but significantly it could not integrate the Roman Catholic Irish. Thus the evolution of a civic identity with strong ethnoreligious undertones provided Britain with a political cohesiveness that was more than sufficient to take the strains of the massive upheavals brought about by constant war, the Industrial Revolution, and far-reaching demographic change.[9]

For the last two centuries in Europe, polities have subsisted on a mixture of civic and ethnic elements, sometimes in competition, sometimes overlapping, as a continuous process, with the relationship between the two being constantly defined and redefined.[10] It is crucial to understand that both these factors have been present, for there is a strong tendency in Western Europe, where democracies have been established and functioning for a considerable period of time, to ignore if not decry the ethnic aspects of nationalism and deny them any function. Yet the argument that a central constitutive element of any political community is the set of affective bonds derived from a shared culture, the basis of ethnic nationhood, is difficult to refute. To make the implicit assumption explicit in this context, all communities share a set of cultural beliefs. Ethnicity is the consciousness of sharing, while nationhood implies political demands legitimated by the doctrine of nationalism which declares that cultural and political boundaries should be congruent.

Democracy, therefore, rests on the strongly cohesive identities provided by nationhood—there is no democratic state that is without this, Switzerland included (discussed later). On its own, democracy is not capable of sustaining the vision of past and future that holds communities together politically, because it does little or nothing to generate the affective, symbolic, and ritually reaffirmed ties upon which community rests. Such civic rituals as the celebration of a national day can help, but are not strong on their own. The collection of individuals, the supposed actors in the liberal theory of democracy, who share interests and are supposedly in a contractual relationship with each other and the state, is insufficient for this purpose.[11]

What has happened in Western Europe is, as suggested already, that nationhood was pushed out of sight and effectively ignored in the post-1945 period, in what should be regarded as an epic battle between liberalism and Marxism. Now that this conflict is over with the defeat of the latter, the constraints on nationalism have loosened. There are many signs that nationalism has not only reemerged into the daylight but may in fact be an ideology with a future.

NATIONHOOD: THE HISTORICAL ASPECTS IN WESTERN EUROPE

The reasons why this displacement from consciousness should have taken place lie in a particular coincidence of events. In the first place, the dominant problem in Western Europe, indeed in Europe as a whole, for well over a century after 1848, was popular participation. How could the newly urbanized middle and working classes be given access to political decision-making without destroying the existing edifice of power? This was key, since the existing regimes did provide for a degree of stability and predictability in politics. The French Revolution was a terrible warning of what would happen when this process was accelerated or when extremists gained control of politics. Indeed, the negative legacy of the French Revolution for the spread of democracy can hardly be exaggerated, not least because it legitimated revolution as a desirable agent of change, rather than seeing upheaval as a consequence of the failure of the political system.[12]

For much of the subsequent century and a half, the problem of integrating the working class into democratic politics was fought out along two broad axes—the liberal and the socialist. Both liberalism and socialism should be seen as answers to the challenge of modernity. Both involved the mass of the population in dynamic and continuous change, growing complexity, and widening choice, and both mandated the redistribution of political power. Conservatism failed to produce a coherent philosophy to tackle these issues head on; rather it tended to sweep the problem aside and, at best, concerned itself with the consolidation of the status quo ante or sought to ally itself with organic, at times nationalist, theories of community. The dominant innovative lines of thought were the liberal and socialist. What these share is a difficulty in the understanding of nationalism, because they both derive their first principles from economic rationality, rather than culture. Consequently as long as the discourse in Europe was dominated by these two currents, nationalism was marginalized and political conflicts tended to be seen primarily in the terms defined by these two. Of course, nationalism remained on stage and numerous conflicts had their nationalist aspects. This was predictable, given the influence of nationalism on legitimation, but in these contexts nationalism was embedded in other conflicts and was perceived as only the first level of explanation (e.g., the Franco-Prussian War).

The period after World War I saw a massive loss of faith in building on the existing European tradition, understandably so in the light of the terrible devastation that Europe had undergone. The problem of broadening popular participation remained, coupled with a weakening of the self-legitimation of the ruling elites. This weakness inevitably produced a gap in the fabric of thought and through this gap emerged two broad radical alternatives—fascism and communism. Both these radical currents denied the viability of incrementalism and meliorism and demanded instead sudden, radical transformation. Fascism failed first, with the defeat of 1945, but the conflict exacted a terrible price. It left the Continent more exhausted than ever before and placed Europe under the hegemony of the two extra-European superpowers, which had their own agendas for the future. At the same time, by having linked itself closely to the organic-nationalistic currents of the right, fascism did much to discredit nationhood as well as nationalism. For a period after 1945, reference to either was of little use in legitimating ideas. It was not until the success of Gaullism, in the 1960s rather than in the postwar decade, that any change could be discerned.

The division of Europe also had far-reaching implications for the new European identity that began to emerge under the transformed circumstances. Europe was now essentially redefined as Western Europe. As long as the countries of Central and Eastern Europe remained under Soviet overlordship, there was little point in considering the countries east of the Elbe as parts of Europe, and the construction of the new Europe went ahead without them. Besides, the onset of the Cold War constrained the West Europeans to redefine their identities in terms of integration rather than rivalries, a process that was enormously aided by the memories of the devastation of World War II. The Cold War, the fear of and rivalry with the Soviet Union, had far-reaching ramifications for the new European identity. It meant that Europe would be defined against communism and by the criteria of liberalism, Christian Democracy, and a degree of statism. But the commitment to pluralistic democracy and market economics was firm and grew firmer with success—with political stability and economic prosperity.

The process of West European integration, from the Schuman Plan, Messina, and the Rome Treaty to the effective functioning of the Common Market, must be regarded not only as a major success story in its own right, but also as a significant redefinition of the European identity. The identity and agendas of independent European states were inextricably intertwined with the EC; the later entry of six new (West European) members confirmed this. There was no Europe other than the one centered in Brussels. This turn of events, however, had a marked impact on nationhood and nationalism. Political integration was perceived primarily as an economic, administrative, and technological process, from which the national-cultural element could, possibly *should*, be omitted. It was assumed that once the new structures were in place, nationhood would simply lose its relevance or at any rate its political saliency. This attempt to divorce political community from its cultural-emotional elements had a certain political attractiveness in the immediate circumstances of the post-1945 period, when reconstruction and redefinition were the order of the day. But once that task was accomplished and the outlines of the civic elements of a new Europe were in place, the ethnic elements were bound to resurface. The most prominent spokesman for this antitechnocratic, antifunctionalist integration was, of course, Charles de Gaulle. But de Gaulle's insistence on the reestablishment of nationhood as the central focus of politics was paralleled by the demands from the ethnonational, ethnolinguistic, and ethnoregional groups that were fated to disappear under the grand design of European integration. Not that de Gaulle had much sympathy for ethnonational demands other than his own, but his was a stance very much in the mainstream of nationalist discourse.

The new European identity received support and nurturing from another source, from the international order as a whole. In part, this support was derived from the overriding need for stability under conditions of the superpower rivalry, which could not tolerate minor conflicts with their origins in nationalism. Memories of the futility of the League of Nations, and its endless debates on frontier questions and *irredenta,* also played a role here, given that the interwar period was the dominant experience of the ruling generation of politicians until the 1970s. The new order, as encapsulated in the United Nations, was deeply antagonistic to the emergence of new states by secession.[13] Indeed, until the recognition of the independence of the Baltic States in 1991, only Bangladesh was successful in gaining recognition of its independent status other than by formal decolonization. And even at that, great care was taken by the West in according recognition to the Baltic States to define them as a special case, because these countries had already enjoyed independence between the wars. The West also wanted to distinguish them from other republics of the Soviet Union, for which recognition would not be immediately forthcoming. Biafra was an earlier example of an attempted secession that was not recognized. The Helsinki process was as strict on this matter as the UN.

Decolonization was another matter; new states could and did come into being by this route, but this was hardly applicable to Europe, where only Malta and Cyprus were decolonized states. On the other hand, until the completion of decolonization it is also true that the West European colonial powers were deeply involved with ridding themselves of empire, a process that ended with the collapse of the Portuguese empire in the 1970s. The abandonment of territory is always a traumatic experience for a state. The loss of empire and the proliferation of new states in the Third World probably helped to strengthen the general presumption that as far as Western Europe was concerned, nationalism, *irredenta,* frontier revision, and the like were unacceptable.

Mention must be made here of the role of the United States and its values. The United States was consistently hostile to Europe's overseas empires (e.g., Suez) and was, equally, supportive of the West European integration process, seeing in it a kind of embryo United States of Europe. On the other hand, Washington has never been particularly sensitive to questions of ethnicity in international politics, tending to regard them as a tiresome distraction. As long as European agendas were heavily determined by U.S. influence, the role of nationhood in European politics would be strictly circumscribed. The West Europeans accepted this willingly and happily or reluctantly and with reservations, like General de Gaulle, who, in contrast to his contemporaries, fully understood the meaning of nationhood, at any rate as far as France was concerned.

Finally, mention must be made here of the ethnic revival of the 1960s and after. The causes of this resurgence can be located in a variety of factors—dissatisfaction with the increasing remoteness of the state, particularly in its technological-technocratic manifestation as in France and Britain; the renewed self-confidence of greater prosperity; and the narrowing of horizons with the end of empire and the demand for greater democratic control based on the cultural community rather than the state where these latter two did not coincide. It is worth adding that no European state is ethnically homogeneous except Iceland, so that there is no complete congruence between ethnic and civic elements anywhere in Western Europe. Solutions to the question of ethnic heterogeneity were, therefore, important.

Nevertheless, the new ethnic movements were characterized by one crucial difference from previous nationalist upsurges—they did not call the integrity of the state into question. This was true even when the political rhetoric of some neo-nationalist movements, like the Scottish National party, did demand independence. Even in the Basque Country, where the ethnonationalist ETA did demand independence, the majority of Basques accepted the Spanish state framework after the introduction of democracy.[14] In reality, these movements were looking primarily for access to power within the confines of the existing state frameworks. Accordingly, they tended to limit their demands to local, cultural, or regional issues, which could be solved through devolution or better provisions for minority languages and so on.

With one or two exceptions, the democratic systems were able to cope with these movements fairly successfully—Northern Ireland and the Basque Country represent the main failures.[15] Elsewhere a variety of techniques were employed to integrate these new demands for power—new in that they based their demands for power on existing cleavages but ones that had not previously been used to legitimate claims to political power. The new techniques absorbed any possible shock to stability that might have arisen. This is not to suggest that this process took place entirely without political conflict, but major upheavals were avoided. The process by which the South Tyrol was accorded a high degree of autonomy by the Italian state is a good case in point. Rome was reluctant to accept or even understand the demands of the South Tyroleans, but political persistence, coupled with occasional bouts of low-level violence, plus a measure of support from Austria, proved sufficient to produce the devolutionary package that has kept the area stable ever since.[16]

Crucially, Western political systems and societies had become highly complex and were becoming increasingly so. This meant that ethnic identities, while salient, were only seldom allowed to dominate agendas. Groups and individuals alike found themselves caught up in a network of competing interests and identities, which tended to downgrade the impact of ethnic mobilization and permitted the operation of compromise mechanisms. Above all, where remedies for ethnically based grievances are feasible within the existing political framework, reductionist mobilization does not take place.

Reductionist mobilization is the state of affairs where all questions, problems, arguments, demands, and so on are interpreted exclusively in ethnonational terms. Political articulation is reduced to this one channel. Evidently in a situation of this kind, the normal arrangements, compromises, and deals that democratic systems bring into being do not take place, for when deep-level cultural issues come to the foreground, they cannot be bargained away and material concessions or incentives will be useless. Northern Ireland illustrates a case where reductionism of this kind, along an ethnoreligious fault line, has taken place. The kind of policies that bring this about include the ethnicization of the state; the use of its resources for the majority, coupled with the perpetual exclusion of the minority from what it regards as its fair share of goods of collective consumption; and, equally important, exclusion of the minority from participation in the symbolic constitution of the state.

CONSOCIATIONALISM

The most significant of the techniques used to integrate multiethnic populations is consociationalism.[17] Consociationalism is a way of governing deeply segmented polities. In states where there are major and strongly persistent cleavages (whether ethnonational, religious, racial, or linguistic), majoritarian politics—the classic Anglo-Saxon system of winner take all—will clearly be a recipe for disruption, as each group looks to maximize its advantage to the disadvantage of others. Indeed, if relations between two ethnonational communities deteriorate and reductionist mobilization takes place, separation and possibly territorial realignment will be the only solution. But short of that, the techniques of consociationalism are worth discussing, especially as they have been fairly successful in several multinational states in sustaining a democratic order.

The key aspect of consociationalism is that it is antimajoritarian and thus completely alien to the Anglo-Saxon tradition of political organization. Notably, the concept recognizes the collective rights of groups, both as against other groups and in relation to their members.[18] This arrangement may well derogate from individual rights and may seem contrary to the principle of equality of all before the law, but is nevertheless desirable if the alternative is disruption or low-level civil war (consider Northern Ireland, where the consociational solution was attempted too late, after reductionist mobilization made its chances of success futile). In fact, of course, European political systems recognize that combinations—group rights—are a part of modern social and political life and extending these to ethnic or religious groups, subject to certain safeguards, can hardly be termed undemocratic.

The adoption of consociationalism, however, imposes a major burden on the majority. By and large nation-states are regulated by the moral-cultural codes of the majority and it is precisely this that makes the position of the minority so difficult—it has to compromise its own codes in too many respects. When this happens, the minority will look for alternative ways to put its aspirations into effect; conceivably it will consider separation. Consequently, the majority must accept that its own codes must be compromised for the sake of maintaining the state. This is very much what has been put into effect in Switzerland, the ultimate consociational success.

Consociational systems seek to draw all the different segments into the decision-making process through elite representation, a kind of grand coalition, although other institutional forms can also be envisaged, like regular consultation with all groups by the president. The basic elements of a consociational system include consultation with all groups in order to build support for constitutional change; a veto by all groups over major issues affecting them; a proportionate sharing of state expenditure and patronage; and substantial autonomy for each group to regulate and control its supporters. The bureaucracy should develop an ethos of ensuring that policies are implemented accordingly, the government should keep much of its negotiation behind closed doors in order to prevent popular mobilization around a particular issue that could be related to group identity, and a set of tacit rules of the game should be adopted.[19]

Consociationalism, however, requires two essential conditions in order for it to work. In the first place, all the groups concerned must be willing to work toward accommodation and be ready to bargain and that, in turn, means the creative use of both substantive and procedural solutions that will help all the parties. In other words, all groups must work to avoid zero-sum game situations, even at the risk of ambiguity. Above all, there must be no major winners or losers. Second, the leaders of a group must be able to secure the support of their followers; otherwise the consociational bargains will fall apart. Success depends on the confidence of the members of group in the system as a whole—they must believe that their interests will be taken into consideration in the bargaining and that they are being given the symbolic as well as the material benefits of the state. Thus the leadership of the group must be able to sell solutions to the membership. Society, as well as leaderships, must be politically sophisticated for consociational solutions to work well.

The success of consociationalism also depends on a readiness to delegate as much as possible to the groups themselves, that is, it must encourage extensive self-government. This goal is complicated in modern societies by the erosion of the territorial principle; on the whole, in dynamic societies, members of different segments will tend to be dispersed throughout the entire area of the state and it would be fatal to consociationalism to base devolution of power solely on territory. Next, the principle of proportionality should be observed rigorously, with, if anything, an overrepresentation of smaller groups. The minority veto is, of course, the ultimate resource for the protection of small segments. Overrepresentation, however, should not be confused with affirmative action strategies, which have the different objective of promoting the equality, not the stability, of minorities.

There are various helpful though not essential preconditions for the success of consociationalism. One is relative equality in the size of the segments and the absence of a group with a majority. Another is a relatively small total population, for this means a smallish elite, in which there is a strong chance that members of that elite will share values through similar or identical educational and other experiences. There should be an overarching loyalty to a legitimating ideology of the state and a corresponding moral-cultural outward boundary toward other states. In addition, a tradition of political accommodation can be very helpful indeed. It should be noted that these preconditions are neither necessary nor sufficient for the success of consociationalism, but they are useful.

THE CENTRAL AND EASTERN EUROPEAN PATTERN

In Central and Eastern Europe, the pattern was in many respects substantially different than in Western Europe, for both historical and contemporary reasons. Historically the single most important factor in this context was backwardness and its consequences.[20] Whereas, as argued, in Western Europe the state developed more or less coextensively with the cultural community and indeed was important in forming it, in the East the state and polity, together with the economy, were subordinated to external rule. The fact of foreign overlordship was crucial, in that it separated the civic and the ethnic elements from one another and precluded the continuous interrelationship between the two that proved to be so significant in the evolution of nations in the West.

The weakness of the civic elements of nationhood and the corresponding emphasis on ethnicity had a number of results with further consequences of their own. In the first place, at the threshold of the modern period the Central and Eastern European countries had singularly lopsided social-political structures when contrasted with Western Europe. The politically conscious sub-elites were small, certainly well under 10 percent of the population, and they were not masters of their own political fate, because of alien, imperial rule. By and large these sub-elites were divided in their attitude to empire. Some accepted the benefits, whether personal or communal, to be derived from service, others did not; loyalty to the dynasty was in some cases given willingly, in others only grudgingly or with resentment. What was shared throughout the area was some awareness that the community's previous political autonomy had survived and could be used as a reference point by those looking to greater freedom from the imperium. In some instances, the legacy of the past may have involved legal provisions (e.g., the rights of the Bohemian crown),[21] in others it might have been only a memory of past statehood (as in Serbia), or it could have been statehood combined with religious separateness. The Polish case was especially poignant, as Poland lost its independent statehood at the very moment of the coming modernity, with the last partition in 1795.

This was the background against which nationalism was received at the beginning of the nineteenth century. The new imperative of political legitimacy, that ethnic and civic elements of nationhood coincide, ran up against the obstacle of the ruling empires, which rejected any thought of redistributing power. The Holy Alliance was, in effect, devised specifically with the aim of preventing the reception of nationalism from being pursued to its logical conclusion; namely, the creation of new states legitimated by nationhood and not by dynasty. The system devised at the Congress of Vienna held together for a century, with only the Ottoman Empire crumbling in the Balkans and permitting the emergence of a series of new states. The decline of Ottoman power from within and the sense among Europeans that it was not appropriate for Muslim rulers to govern Christian subjects, which informed repeated Western interventions in favor of granting independence to new Balkan states, accelerated this process.

In Central Europe and Russia, on the other hand, the existing empires' control was broken only by defeat in war and the determination of the victors to redraw the political map along ethnonational lines—this was the essence of President Woodrow Wilson's Fourteen Points. The belt of new states that came into being, however, proved to be weak in both ethnic and civic terms. They were unable to integrate their deeply segmented polities and lacked the cultural and economic bases necessary to create effective civil societies. In fact, they were caught in a near classic vicious circle, because as they sought to use the instruments of the state to bring civil society into being, they ran into various impediments deriving from backwardness, and so intensified state control, which made it even more difficult for civil society to come into being.

The ethnonational cleavages were among the most intractable. These ethnocultural communities, different from the majority, responded with resentment and hostility to attempts to integrate them into what they perceived as an alien polity. The terms of integration were, inevitably, loaded against the minority, in that no distinction was made between loyalty to the state as citizen (and taxpayer) and loyalty to the cultural community. Ultimately this meant that members of ethnic minorities were inherently suspect and that the terms of loyalty demanded of them amounted to the complete abandonment of their own moral-cultural codes, something that communities as a whole would seldom do, though individuals might.

Interwar Rumania illustrates these processes well. The creation of Greater Rumania in 1918–1920 with the addition of Transylvania, Bukovina, and Bessarabia to the new state was a profound shock to the Rumanian majority which had identified itself with a state that was rigidly defined by the Rumanian language and Orthodox Christianity. Suddenly ruling a state that was inhabited by about 30 percent of people who were "alien" in the eyes of the majority posed a challenge to which the majority was unable to respond except by instituting a rigidly centralized system that was moderated only by incompetence and corruption. This merging of citizenship with ethnicity inevitably became the seedbed of conflict, suspicion, and antagonism which neither the majority nor the minorities possessed political or cognitive instruments to resolve.

The state of affairs in Central and Eastern Europe after World War II was felt to be deeply unsatisfactory by all participants. This disaffection was exacerbated by the introduction of the collective principle—the proposition that all members of an ethnic community should be subjected to identical discriminatory measures—in dealing with minority ethnic communities, in an attempt to bring about ethnic purification. This approach intensified anxieties and did little to contribute to the integration of the population (the Holocaust was only the most extreme instance). After the war, ethnic German minorities were expelled or subjected to disabilities. Hungarians were similarly repressed in Czechoslovakia and Yugoslavia. And during the war itself, interethnic conflict had produced terrible bloodletting, the memory of which did not easily disappear.

The backwardness of Central and Eastern Europe gave rise to a further feature that characterizes the area. In Western Europe, the protagonists of the new doctrine of nationalism, the intellectuals, defined and proclaimed their ideas in relatively complex societies, in which the contest for power took place among various social groups, such as the declining representatives of the old order, the rising entrepreneurs, and the emerging working class. As a result, power was diffused and the intellectuals could not establish a preeminent position for themselves. Indeed, much of the nineteenth century was characterized by an ever more desperate critique of the bourgeois order on the part of intellectuals.[22] In Central and Eastern Europe, however, the older order was stronger and societies were far weaker, so that intellectuals came to dominate the scene and acquired an authority which they deployed in the definition of nationhood.

At the same time, because the political challenge to intellectuals was weaker, their claims were not contested. Indeed, to some extent, they could define their terms independently of society, imposing a concept of nationhood on it. The drive for intellectual purity was thus added to the various nationalist ideologies that were formulated and, as a result, nationalism in Central and Eastern Europe acquired an exclusive, messianic quality that it did not have in the West.[23] This high-profile role of intellectuals and the particular expression of nationalism have proved to be an enduring feature of Central and East European politics. In this respect, the nations that came into being in that region can be termed "nations by design" and many of their characteristics differ from those of the West. In particular, there is a long tradition of using or rather abusing nationalism for political purposes not connected with the definition of nationhood, such as discrediting political opponents by calling them "alien" or resisting the redistribution of power on similar grounds.[24]

THE COMING OF COMMUNISM

The arrival of communism transformed the situation in many respects. Theoretically, communism and nationalism are incompatible. Communism insists that an individual's fundamental identity is derived from class positions; nationalism maintains that it derives from culture.[25] In practice, however, the relationship between the two doctrines, both of which, as argued in the foregoing, were partial responses to the challenge of modernity, was much more ambiguous. Initially, communist rulers sought to expunge existing national identities and to replace them with what was termed "socialist internationalism," a crude cover-name for Sovietization. Gradually, and especially after the second de-Stalinization of 1961, communist leaders were compelled to come to terms with the national identities of their subjects. They made a variety of compromises, even though this diluted and undermined the authenticity of their communist credentials. There are countless examples of communist parties using nationalism in this way. When Edward Gierek took over as the new leader of the Polish party in 1970, he offered Polish nationhood two important symbolic gestures. The portraits of his predecessor, Wladyslaw Gomulka, had adorned every official space; Gierek decreed that instead of his portrait, the Polish eagle, a powerful symbol of nationhood, should be displayed. Second, he gave the go-ahead for the reconstruction of the Royal Palace in Warsaw, which had been razed during the Uprising of 1944; again, this was intended to emphasize the national quality of his rule.

For societies, communist parties could never be authentic agents of the nation, given the parties' antinational ideology. But this did not preclude their taking advantage of the new post-1961 political dispensation and to express national aspirations in the space provided. Society never abandoned its national identity or aspirations, on the contrary it tended increasingly to see nationalism as a safeguard against the depredations of the communist state, so that when the communist leaderships made real or symbolic concessions to nationhood, these were readily accepted and interpreted as a possible move toward some dilution of communist power. It was this intersection of the two agendas, that of the rulers and ruled, that helped to explain the initial success of, say, the Ceausescu regime's mobilization in the 1960s and 1970s in Rumania, when there was a coincidence between the aims of communists and societies.

Where there was no direct overlap, nationalism could be the expression of social autonomy; in other words, it was a demand for strengthening the civic elements of nationhood and of the hope that society would gain greater access to power. This raised a problem, however, in that it confused the civic and ethnic aspects of nationhood. Nationalism may be an excellent way of determining identity, but it has little or nothing to say about political participation (the functions of nationalism are discussed later). In this sense, the demands for autonomy expressed through nationalism—"we should have the right to decide for ourselves because we are members of the Ruritanian nation"—were another illustration of the confusion of codes to which Central and Eastern Europe is subject. Theoretically the demand for, say, freedom of the press or assembly cannot be derived from the ethnic aspects of nationhood, although in practice this may not so clear. In this respect, nationalism came to be entrusted with a function that it could not really discharge and tended to point societies toward confusion and frustration, as well as expectations that could not be met.

The communist period had further grave implications. By sweeping away all other competing ideas, programs, and values, which allowed the communists to sustain their monopoly, they made it much easier for an undiluted nationalism referring solely to ethnicity to survive more or less intact, more or less in its original state. This meant that some, though not all, of the national disputes and problems of the precommunist era were simply pushed under the carpet. With the end of communism these problems have automatically reappeared, though sometimes in a new form. In addition, the reflexivity of modernity, that "social practices are constantly examined and reformed in the light of incoming information about those very practices, thus constitutively altering their character,"[26] was much impeded by communism, which claimed to be guided by absolute standards. Thus the kind of relativization that has made nationalism a manageable problem in Western Europe, where the demands for power on the basis of nationhood compete for demands based on other identities (class, economic interests, gender, religion, status, and so on), has not really taken place or is only now beginning to emerge. The propensity to see all matters as involving ethnic nationhood, whether properly related to nationhood or not, is one of the key characteristics of the contemporary Central and East European scene and will not change until ethnic nationalism is "desacralized" and subject to other influences, thereby reaching an equilibrium with the civic elements. In effect, what is essential is that postcommunist polities develop cross-cutting identities, rather than cumulative ones.[27] This will take time.

ONE-SIDED MODERNIZATION

Communist rule forced the Central and Eastern European countries through a one-sided modernizing revolution, which has had a considerable impact on two areas directly affecting nationalism. In the first place, the particular virulence of nationalism in the precommunist period can be attributed at least partly to the fact that large sections of a backward population were subjected to the initial impact of modernization, whether through the market or the state. This is always a traumatic process as traditional communities are swept away, and Central and Eastern Europe was no exception. The communist transformation effectively liquidated the traditional peasantry of the area, of the type bound by the village, illiterate and suspicious of the city and urban life. This applies with minor modifications to Poland and Yugoslavia, for despite the absence of collectivization, the agricultural population was as closely enmeshed in the control system of the state as elsewhere.

Inevitably, those who were forced to leave the land looked for answers to their new-found existential problems and generally discerned these in ethnic nationalism, although for some sections of society the communist answers of utopia, hierarchy, and authoritarianism were quite acceptable. The failure of the communist system to integrate these societies meant that nationalism continued to provide answers, especially after communism was manifestly seen to have failed. However, this factor is not entirely negative. If the extremes of nationalism are to be associated with the trauma of modernization, the gradual assimilation of the Central and East European peasantry into urban ways should see the long-term abatement of the kind of nationalistic excesses that are so feared, but emphasis here is very much on "gradual." It may take decades.

Second, even though the communist revolution was a partial one, it did very effectively extend the power of the state over society and constructed a modern communications network that has allowed the state to reach virtually the whole of the population, in a way that was not true of the prewar era. The use of television to spread a message, whether communist or nationalist, is far more effective than what was available before electrification. In this respect, Central and Eastern Europe has been globalized: this makes the reception of the global message of consumption, leisure, new technology, and material aspirations easier to transmit, though its reception will be halting. The absolute claims of nationalism will be relativized only when the processes of reflexivity and globalization are advanced. No national community can be dogmatic in its nationalistic claims if these are constantly examined and redefined under the impact of ever more information.

THE FUNCTIONS OF NATIONALISM

At this point, it is useful to look at the functions of nationalism, both as a means of explaining its persistence and to offer perspectives on the future. The historical antecedents of nationalism in Central and Eastern Europe help to explain some of its more intractable features in the contemporary period, but what this sketch of the antecedent processes does not answer is the question why nationalism survives at all. Its Marxist and liberal opponents have written it off countless times, yet it lives on, despite having been dismissed as "irrational."[28] Its persistence implies that nationalism must have a function that no other body of ideas has been able to supplant and, contrary to the claims of its detractors, it remains a living and authentic experience, unlike, say, feudalism. Nationalism must operate by rules of its own, rules that are rational in its own context.

These functions must be sought in the cultural origins of nationalism, rather than in its political expression.[29] The proposition in this connection is that every community looks for its moral precepts—the definitions of right and wrong, pure and impure—in its storehouse of cultural values and seeks to defend these from challenges, whether real or perceived. In this way, communities construct the rules of a moral-cultural universe, which then defines them. If this system were to disintegrate, the community itself would be threatened. Crucially, it is by the moral-cultural universe that communities define the bonds of loyalty and cohesiveness that hold it together. These bonds, in turn, create the bases of identity which are at the center of a community. Reference is made to these whenever questions of communal existence and belonging are on the agenda.

Furthermore, communities also use this moral-cultural resource to articulate the affective dimension of politics. This is not in itself a pathology; all groups possess emotional as well as rational expression in their collective activities. The articulation of these affective bonds takes place through rituals and the loyalty given to symbols, which reaffirm and sustain the existence of the community in question.[30] Every political community has these rituals, and members who accept them are frequently barely conscious of their involvement. If Trafalgar Square in London is a celebration of Britishness as evoking the memory of the naval victory over France in the Napoleonic war, the opening of the Brandenburg Gate in Berlin in 1989 was undoubtedly the most potent symbol of the demise of communism. The reinterment of Imre Nagy, the leader of the unsuccessful revolution of 1956 in Hungary on the anniversary of his execution, on June, 16 1989, in Heroes' Square in Budapest, the pantheon of the country's national heroes, was a similar ritualized act of recovering 1956 for the historical memory of the Hungarian nation.

Finally, it is through these cultural traits that the psychological boundaries of a community are constructed, whether these are external boundaries or internal ones. External boundaries define the community in question against other communities. Internal boundaries refer to the acceptability or unacceptability of certain patterns of action or thought.[31] Boundaries can take many forms. They can include language and religion and even dress code and food.

Although in politics, nationalism has universalistic claims, in reality these are not true. In broad terms, nationalism is excellent in defining the identities of members against nonmembers of collectivities, but it says nothing about the distribution of power within a community or the allocation of resources.[32] But because nationhood taps into the emotions underlying collective existence, it is easy enough to confuse the codes relating to political power and those governing political identity, something that has happened repeatedly in the last two hundred years.

In this sense, nationalism can be used as an instrument to legitimate political demands that are entirely unconnected with, say, the distribution of power, but this lack of a logical and causal nexus is muddied by the reference to the affective dimension that nationhood conjures up. Thus in concrete terms, Slobodan Milošević has (for the time being) successfully convinced the Serbs that the reason for their economic plight is not that the Serbian economy is run badly, but because various aliens (the Kosovo Albanians, the Croats, the West through the embargo, etc.) are threatening the integrity of the Serbian nation, although in fact these factors have nothing to do with the economy. Indeed, what Milošević did was to mobilize one particular strand of the Serbian tradition, that of being the victims of a worldwide anti-Serbian campaign. That, in turn, has resonated with the much older traditions of Orthodoxy and the sense of being elect, of heroic resistance against the world, of *inat,* a word meaning that all possible action must be taken to defend the honor of the nation, regardless of any other considerations, including, or perhaps especially, material ones.

PERSPECTIVES ON THE FUTURE

There is every indication that nationhood and nationalism will play a growing role in the internal and international politics of Europe, though with different implications for the different halves of the continent. In Western Europe, the strength of the civic elements of nationhood, as expressed in the multiple and cross-cutting identities and interests of individuals and groups, loyalty to the state, coupled with the attractiveness of the integration process, are likely to be substantial enough to offset occasional upsurges of ethnic or even ethnonational mobilization. This does not mean that the resolution of ethnic disputes will be easy, but the traditions of compromise and bargaining over resource allocation, the commitment to democracy and the perception by these societies that they have a direct interest—political as well as economic—in the maintenance of democracy, should be sufficient to ensure that nationalist conflicts do not seriously destabilize any state.

The particular trouble spots of Northern Ireland and the Basque Country are likely to fester on for a while, but in both these instances, the status quo is, in effect, a kind of solution, inasmuch as any change in the equation would—at this stage—be likely to intensify difficulties rather than alleviate them. All the political actors see concessions as disastrous, given the intensity of polarization. In this sense, the status quo, however painful, is regarded as preferable to an alteration in the uneasy equilibrium that exists. Elsewhere regular adjustments in the distribution of power should be sufficient to absorb ethnonational demands. This will, however, place heavy burdens on majorities to accept and understand the needs of ethnonational minorities.

Crucially, majorities must be ready to see that the days of the supercentralized state are over, that ethnic identifications are here to stay and that early concessions are likely to be far more effective in defusing ethnic demands than having to make them later under duress, after ethnic mobilization has already begun. The painful and at times absurd demarcation that has taken place in Belgium since the late 1950s illustrates this process well. Although extremists among both Walloons and Flemings dream of complete separation, the ability to compromise has produced a process of continuous adjustment and readjustment between the two communities; which has currently created federalism along ethnic lines.[33]

However, the end of communism in the Soviet Union as well as in Central and Eastern Europe has resulted in two major changes. In the first place, the (re)unification of Germany has legitimated the national principle in Europe for the first time since 1945. Essentially, there were no civic grounds for German unity, only ethnic ones. There was no particular reason for Germans to unite in one state other than the fact that they were Germans. In other words, it was the ethnic factor that fueled this move. A democratized East German state could, presumably, have continued in being, in much the same way as the democratized Hungarian and Polish states have done, if it had had the ethnic underpinnings, but despite the best efforts of the Honecker regime to construct a separate East German ethnicity, the idea never acquired much authenticity and the application of the ethnic principle has unequivocally pushed the East Germans toward demanding and accepting a single German state.

The broader significance of this has not escaped others. If Germans can claim to eliminate state boundaries by reference to nationhood there is no reason why this proposition should not be applicable elsewhere and, indeed, German unification has become an offstage reference point for those seeking independence in other parts of Europe. At the same time, there is more than a suggestion that the sympathy entertained by German opinion toward Croatian and Slovenian independence derives at least in part from Germany's own experience.

The precedent-setting effect of both German unification and the recognition of the Baltic States was felt elsewhere, obviously in Yugoslavia, but also in Spain, where the difference in status and powers between Catalonia and the Basque Country on the one hand and the other provinces on the other was posing a growing problem.[34] The Yugoslav question requires more detailed discussion than can be attempted here, but it is worth noting that the central reason why the state collapsed as a single entity is that, after 1945, it was reconstituted by Tito as a communist federation with an explicitly communist legitimation. The collapse of that communist legitimation has brought about the decay of the state as such and the corresponding reversion to the much stronger nationalist legitimations of Serbian and Croatian (Slovene, Macedonian, Albanian) nationhood. The end of communism is likely to have other fall-out in the area of identity. Since the 1950s, Europe has tacitly or sometimes expressly defined itself against communism, insisting that what is European is not communist and to some extent vice versa (only to some extent, because commitment to democracy involves offering some political house-room to antidemocrats such as communists). In this respect, the end of communism will require a reappraisal of what Europe stands for, what its identity is. A redefinition of the socialist agenda is also called for, seeing that the defeat of communism will have reverberations for democratic socialism as well.[35]

Postcommunism and Ethnonational Questions

In the postcommunist countries of Central and Eastern Europe, the construction of democracy inevitably means coming to terms with the resurgence of nationalism and, equally, finding the necessary instruments for integrating ethnic elements into the new systems. This poses a number of problems, some of which can only be touched on in this chapter. The states of Central and Eastern Europe are all to a greater or lesser extent ethnically heterogeneous and will, if they intend to maintain their commitment to democracy, have to make provision for the well-being of minorities. Centrally, this will oblige them to accept and practice democratic self-limitation, something that will require considerable restraint on the part of the new governments.[36] There is little evidence that many postcommunist governments are ready to do this.

Furthermore, self-limitation also involves an understanding of the proposition that in a democracy the state is not the instrument of the ruling majority for the implementation of certain ideals and utopias, but the agent of governance for the whole of society, regardless of ethnicity. Citizenship regardless of ethnicity must become the paramount criterion for membership of the political community. By the same token, the sacralizing of territory, the belief that the particular frontiers that have come into being are in some way above politics, is harmful, because it can lead the majority into the dubious perspective of regarding all minority claims as an infringement of the sacred territory. Attitudes of this kind apparently inform Rumanian and Serbian thinking, concerning Transylvania and the Kosovo, respectively. Any attempt to insist that civic rights should be denied to those who claim different ethnic rights leads directly to major violations of human rights.

In addition, there is the broad problem of integration. In order for democracy to operate effectively, the great majority of the population must feel committed to it and must have an active interest in sustaining it. Without this, democracy will become the affair of the elites and thus be vulnerable to popular upsurges of an antidemocratic nature. Various scenarios illustrating this can be written, notably the rise of an authoritarian leader using nationalist slogans to divert the attention of the population from economic privation. The Milošević model or the model of "Latin-Americanization" comes very close to being a paradigmatic case, but the model is potentially applicable throughout the area, even with the relatively favorable international environment.

As the dynamics of postcommunism become clearer, the roles of nation-hood and nationalism are likewise emerging as central to the functioning of the new political systems. This phenomenon has far-reaching implications for the operation of democracy, which presupposes tolerance and com-promise as *conditiones sine qua non*. It is important to stress again the distinc-tion between the civic and ethnic dimensions of nationhood in this context and to understand that it is the weakness of the former that has allowed the latter an excessively influential role. The violence committed in the name of nationhood in, for example, former Yugoslavia is derived from the ethnic aspects of nationhood. Had the civic dimension been stronger, such vio-lence might have been avoided. Democratic stability, involving the distribu-tion of power and contest over the allocation of resources—normal stuff of everyday politics in liberal democracies—can only come into being in the absence of constant explicit or implicit reference to questions of identity and survival as a community. Civic nationhood has to be so rooted as to permit the institutional framework to operate in an authentic fashion.

Yugoslavia has been the extreme case, but numerous other ruptures jostle for attention. Hungary has serious ethnic minority problems with three of its neighbors—Rumania, Serbia, and Slovakia. At the same time, Hungary is the scene of the Gypsy (Roma) community's attempt to define itself as an ethnic group. The redefinition of Slovakia as an independent state has posed problems of identification for the Hungarian minority, but also for the Slovak majority, which found international independence wished on it and was completely unprepared for the experience. The rela-tionship between Bulgarians and Turks has been difficult, despite the readi-ness of the Turkish minority leadership to play a positive role in the running of the country.[37] In the Baltic States, there is major friction between Esto-nians and Russians and Latvians and Russians. In both cases, the majority fears losing its majority status, and argues that the Russians are present only because of their former colonial status as a part of the Soviet empire and that the minority should leave. In Lithuania, relations between the majority and the relatively small Polish minority have been difficult for many years. State independence has not changed this situation.

The Weakness of Civic Institutions

The tragedy of postcommunist Central and Eastern Europe is precisely that civic institutions and the identities derived from them are too weak to fill the public sphere, with the result that ethnic nationhood is called upon to decide issues of power, a process which is profoundly destructive of democratic principles and the institutions adopted after 1989. At the same time, it is essential to understand that the burgeoning of nationalism in the region is not something inherent in the makeup of the area, but can be explained by specific historical circumstances. The significance of this proposition is that it permits policymakers to focus on the appropriate solutions and avoid dismissing the events of the 1990s as evidence of irremediable flaws in the political fabric of the area.

The weakness of the civic dimension—the identification with institutions and the acceptance of institutions as authentic to create the conditions for the stable exercise of power—is in the first place attributable to communism, but the new postcommunist order has increasingly launched its own dynamic and its own imperatives, which do not look particularly encouraging from the perspectives of democracy. Thus precisely because institutions are weak, compensatory mechanisms have begun to emerge. These reactions are likely to make institutions weaker still. The key problem is that of personalization.[38]

Where institutions are not available to mediate the relationship between the individual and power, the codes of behavior appropriate to persons—patron-client networks; personal coteries and loyalties; exploiting state resources for personal gain; corruption; and nepotism and family networks—will be used to structure power. This has tended to lead to a highly fluid and unstable approach to politics, in which virtually all significant actions are understood in terms of personal gain or loss. The feebleness of the civic sphere means, at the same time, that reference to nationhood can be used to legitimate propositions or to delegitimate opponents—indeed, in this connection they become "enemies," "traitors to the nation," rather than political opponents who share the same basic commitment to the state as citizens.

The question that helps to clarify the new relationships is to ask what it is that the new governments actually seek to represent. If they are representing citizens, then they accept that they are involved in a two-way power relationship, that the ruled have some rights vis-à-vis the state. If, on the other hand, these governments regard themselves as the embodiment of the nation, then they will conceptualize themselves as being above politics, and will consider criticism, the cut and thrust of politics, as dangerous and irreverent.

Two examples illustrate these propositions. The Hungarian prime minister, the late Jozsef Antall, repeatedly described himself as "the prime minister of 15 million Hungarians in spirit," that is, including all the Hungarians of the successor states and in the West. This statement is manifest nonsense; in no sense, spiritual or otherwise, can the prime minister of Hungary be also the prime minister of people who have not voted for him or, for that matter, do not pay taxes in Hungary. At the same time, by having said this, Antall offered a fully grown hostage to fortune, in the sense of providing a pretext to the successor states for questioning the loyalty of their Hungarian minorities (that is, Slovakia, Rumania, and Serbia).

The new Slovak constitution refers to the state as being the state of the Slovak nation. This formulation evidently links citizenship with nationhood and seemingly makes the rights of one conditional on membership of the other. A political order based on this principle cannot strictly be called a democracy. Sections of the population will be excluded from both the civic and ethnic dimensions of nationhood, above all at the interface between the two, where the symbolic aspects of belonging to the community are reaffirmed. People in this category pay their taxes and perform the other obligations of citizenship, but are excluded in terms of what the state owes in return. In addition, their civic entitlements will generally be viewed with disfavor by the state. Objections will be found why minority schools should not be opened, why minority cultural events might be defined as threats to the public order, why bilingual signs will be treated as, say, undesirable from the standpoint of road safety (as a recent case from the Hungarian-inhabited areas of Slovakia showed), and so on. Given the power of the modern state and the extent of penetration by legislation into every area of life, reasons of this kind will not be hard to find. If a group finds itself to be the perpetual loser on the political swings and roundabouts, its loyalty will diminish and the majority will then turn around and say triumphantly, "You see, we always said so." Such scenarios, which are in no way far-fetched, constitute fine examples of self-fulfilling prophecies.

In exploring the political pathologies of nationalism in Central and Eastern Europe, it is worth noting the enormous importance of symbolic politics and the apparent downgrading of practical or empirical thinking. Major conflict can erupt over such seemingly trivial incidents as bilingual street signs precisely because these conflicts cannot be managed at the level of road safety in the absence of a meaningful civic dimension. From the perspective of the policymakers, these "trivial" issues should receive the closest scrutiny and not be dismissed as evidence of "tribalism."

The Threat of Neo-Ideologization

The permeation of public life by the ethnic dimension has other negative consequences, negative for majorities as well as for minorities. So far the argument has concentrated only on ethnic minorities, but social minorities can equally be disadvantaged by the excessive load placed on ethnicity. By and large, where the civic dimension is weak, ethnicity finds itself having to cope with various tasks concerning the distribution of power with which it deals badly. As unsolved problems accumulate—in Central and Eastern Europe the legacy of communism involves a quite extraordinarily tangled web of unsolved issues where each is interlocked with others—the temptation to rely ever more heavily on ethnicity can become irresistible.

The promise of ethnicity, precisely because it appeals to the emotions, appears all-encompassing and complete. If only, the discourse seems to suggest, we are all united in a just enterprise, all our current difficulties will be solved. Conversely, lack of success can be readily attributed to external or internal enemies. This is nonsense of course, but when faced with massive and apparently overwhelming problems, a politically unsophisticated population is vulnerable to such temptations. In these circumstances, the language of nationhood can create great illusions.

With the rules that are supposedly derived from the civic dimension being actually based on ethnic criteria, other consequences follow. The offices of state will largely be filled on grounds of ethnic loyalty, presumed or real, rather than competence. Members of minorities, whether ethnic or social or even political, will find themselves suspect. For example, the refusal of the Meciar government to appoint an ethnic Hungarian to one of the deputy chairmanships of the Slovak Parliament illustrates this tendency clearly. So does the way in which ruling parties seek to monopolize appointments for their supporters and to insist that the opposition is by its very existence "unpatriotic"—something seen in Hungary, in Rumania, in Bulgaria, and elsewhere.

Another point in this respect concerns language. Where the civic dimension is weak, the national language itself becomes a vehicle for a monistic view of the world. Words are overloaded with politicized meanings, particularly through the overemphasis on a pathos-laden perception of ontology. The treatment of history, one of the key pillars of ethnicity, becomes sentimental and the protagonists of this world-view will be prone to see the world only through its blinkers and to think in slogans, such as "we are the most resolute bastion of the West against barbarism" or "the West owes us recompense for all the injuries committed against us in the past," and so on. This mind-set not only clouds issues and impedes rational analysis, but it also leaves the population open to demagogic manipulation.

A different but related aspect is the penetration of this ideologically suffused language into the private sphere. Certain forms of expression can be understood only through the filter of nationalist-patriotic language and thought itself is distorted thereby. In a sense, the penetration of all spheres by Marxism-Leninism, which failed, may ironically be achieved by nationalism. Another aspect of this phenomenon may be called "ideological thinking." Naturally, this term applies to all ideologies, but is worth discussing it in the context of nationalism, because it is so seldom understood in this fashion. The greatest drawback of ideological thinking is that those who are in the grip of it are tempted to explain all events, all causes and effects, experiences and interactions in ideological terms and to look for solutions within the thought-system, regardless of the appropriateness of the procedure.

The difficulty with this approach is that ideologies provide a clear explanation of phenomena which are much more opaque in reality and consequently push their protagonists into homogenizing complexity and into seeing every effect as having a cause. If reality does not fit into this conceptual straitjacket, they will say, something is wrong with reality. Then they look for explanations that will support their own ideologically preconditioned world-view. Nationalists are as inclined to this as orthodox Stalinists were and there is more than enough evidence from the postcommunist world that many are tempted to think ideologically. In terms of European thought, this approach reverses the revolution in thinking initiated by Kepler and Newton: if the facts do not support the hypothesis, change the hypothesis. The contrary approach, which undermines scientific thought, is to try to change the facts until they do support the hypothesis.

Chauvino-Communism

A further development, at first sight somewhat unexpected, has been the emergence of the phenomenon of "chauvino-communism." Despite the theoretical incompatibility between Marxism and nationalism, by the period immediately preceding the collapse of communism many communists had effectively abandoned their belief in the legacy of Marx and Lenin. Sometimes explicitly, sometimes not, they allowed their thinking to be captured by nationalism. This became significant after the first phase of the collapse.

Once the initial pro-Western democratic euphoria of the immediate aftermath of the collapse of communism wore off, many highly placed functionaries discovered that they could salvage some of their political power by a rapid ideological conversion to nationalism. This strategy is the origin of "chauvino-communism." Its impact in the populations has been considerable, not surprisingly given their lack of political experience, and many politicians have had recourse to it. This is very marked in Slovakia, Bulgaria, and Rumania and, of course, in the country where it was effectively invented and practiced with the greatest success, Serbia. The postcommunist party in the Czech Republic, the Left Bloc, has been in the forefront of the campaign against making any concessions to those Sudeten Germans who are demanding that they be included in property restitution plans. The rise of chauvino-communism makes nonsense of the conventional left-right divide and requires a new ideological and political party classification.

In the emerging paradigm of postcommunism, the expansion of nationhood as the primary political category has had a number of other consequences with significant results for the exercise of power. In the first place, the ethnicization of governments has, as I have suggested, promoted a conspiracy-theory view of the world, in which there is little room for dissent. This suspicion places particular pressure on the media and the public sphere in general, which nationalist-minded governments will seek to control. The problem here is that this can give rise to a vicious circle, from which those affected cannot escape as long as they are caught in the thought-world. The vicious circle operates something like this. A government is confronted by some particular problem, say economic, for which it formulates a solution in the terms of its nationalist mind-set. Predictably, the solution does not work. Rather than going back to first principles and examining the situation from its economic perspective, the government then decides to redouble the nationalist input and exacerbates the problem, and so on.

The effect of this process can be felt in several areas of politics. In personnel policy, some features of the communist system have been revived— turned on their heads of course—by the renewed insistence on political criteria for making appointments, like "being a good son of the nation." Naturally this does little to help the growth of a professionalism that would actually be useful in the resolution of problems. Areas of social life which began to emancipate themselves from the communist-dominated political sphere are coming under renewed pressure from nationalism. This control can have dire results: the threat of the subordination of the non-political spheres (economic, social, aesthetic, religious, and so on) is again becoming a reality.[39] Political neutrality becomes virtually impossible in such circumstances, as all actions are assessed by the criteria of power. That in turn impedes the articulation of feedback and reciprocity. Ironically, one of the key long-term factors that undermined communism was its rejection of feedback in favor of an ideologically derived view of reality. The results were grave obstacles to the self-regulating and self-correcting mechanisms of society. The spread of ethnic nationalism threatens—so far only threatens— to reproduce this state of affairs.

All these trends that overemphasize the ethnic elements of nationhood against the civic ones are liable to result in growing instability and friction between ethnic groups, within states and internationally. They will contribute to undermining the best chance of building democracy that Central and Eastern Europe has ever had.

4

Is Democratic Supranationalism a Danger?

Ezra Suleiman

Conventional wisdom has it that post–Cold War Europe is somehow neatly divided between a part that is heading toward disintegration and a part that is moving toward consolidation and the creation of a supranational community. The collapse of communist regimes has set in motion the process of democratization and the release of ethnic and nationalistic forces in Eastern Europe, and it supposedly gave an impetus to the process of consolidation within the European Union.

Can we really proclaim with confidence that "a race is now on in Europe between the process of dissociation and disintegration, and that of integration"?[1] This is a view that is fraught with optimism for the West European countries. If ethnic conflict, nationalism, and independence characterize the Balkan and East European states, it does not follow that Western Europe is moving in the opposite direction.

A second critical aspect of what has become a generally accepted premise is that the democracy of the West European nation-state must be transferred to the supranational level. In order for a supranational European entity to be accepted by the masses as well as the elites, it cannot be a Europe characterized by unresponsive, unaccountable, bureaucratic institutions. Hence, the survival of the European Union, which itself depends on the willingness of the member states to cede greater parcels of sovereignty, requires the democratization of the Union. This point of view, today accepted as a self-evident truth, owes much to the difficulties that the Treaty of

The author wishes to thank Christianne Hardy and Matthias Kaelberer for their invaluable help and comments on this chapter.

Maastricht, signed in 1993, encountered on the road to ratification. As the former president of the European Commission, Jacques Delors, put it in the aftermath of the tepid French ratification of the treaty, "Either Europe will become more and more democratic, or Europe will be no more."[2] A Europe with accountable and responsible political institutions, along the lines of practices that exist within member states, will, it is argued, enhance the willingness of member states to devolve greater sovereignty and to preserve the democratic process within these states.

This chapter takes the postulate that a democratic European union both ensures the adherence of the member states to the Union and strengthens their national democratic institutions as a hypothesis that requires examination rather than as an incontestable truth. Indeed, it may well be that the democratization of the European Union could adversely affect democratic stability within individual member states.

My central argument is that, however attractive the idea of creating, or moving toward, genuine democratic supranationalism is, efforts to build supranationalism ought not to compete with or undermine democratic institutions within the member states. As I shall indicate, inherent tensions exist between the preservation of a democratic order in the nation-states and the creation of a democratic Europe. No one familiar with the collapse of democratic societies in the 1930s, with the attacks to which democratic institutions were subjected by extremist nationalistic forces and extremist leftist groups, and with the ultimate incapacity of democratic states to preserve their institutions and the social order, can be oblivious to the importance of creating conditions that safeguard democratic political institutions. Is there, then, a contradiction between the creation of democracy in Europe (or a democratic Europe) and the preservation of democracy in the individual European states? This is the question addressed in this chapter.

One implicit assumption of the premise that a democratic Europe would strengthen both the Union and national democratic processes is that the supranational process undermines the nationalistic impulse. The greater the degree of sovereignty that is ceded, the weaker the nationalistic tendencies. Similarly, the greater the centralization of the "common European House," as Mikhail Gorbachev referred to it, the greater the reduction in nationalistic sentiments and forces. Whether nationalism rises or declines with the extension of supranational, representative, and accountable institutions is, again, not a self-evident truth, but a hypothesis that needs to be examined.

In fact, substantial evidence indicates that the trend toward supranationality—whether in the guise of federalism, confederalism, pooled sovereignty, or some other variant—can nurture a backlash of nationalism. No democratic community can prosper without some form of identity. The same applies to Europe: a democratic Europe can only be based on a European identity. Without this identity, an attempt to create a democratic Europe may well result in awakening nationalist impulses. These, then, are the two hypotheses that will be analyzed in this chapter: (1) A democratic Europe not only consolidates the European Union but safeguards national democratic institutions. (2) Greater integration and association—that is, supranationality—leads to the decline of nationalism.

I will argue that both hypotheses ignore the tendencies toward fragmentation as well as the unanticipated consequences of the integration process within the European Union. The movement toward integration and supranationality, in whatever form, and the increasing fervor of nationalism are not mutually exclusive, even if intuitively or logically they may appear to be so. Indeed, one significant additional factor needs to be considered: the larger the European Union becomes as an *economic* unit, the greater are the chances that claims for smaller political units will be made.

Moreover, the construction of the European Union depends to a very considerable extent on underlying economic and social conditions in the individual member states. The optimism—at least among the elites— regarding economic and political union was a byproduct of prosperous economic conditions. The reaction to the Maastricht Treaty and the subsequent decline in enthusiasm among citizens and elites with respect to the acceleration of European integration are based on the economic and social insecurity that prevails within the countries of Western Europe.[3]

FROM ROME TO MAASTRICHT

European integration is not a manifestation of the strength of the nation-state, but rather reflects the advantages that can be derived from association. World War II had demonstrated that European states were unable to guarantee their own security. The outcome of the war was decided by non-European powers, who became the guarantors of the postwar security system. European integration was, then, a mechanism for collectively strengthening the security of the West. Its other important security objective was to integrate Germany into the collective system, rather than isolating it.

Moreover, European nation-states not only witnessed a decline in their ability to provide for their own security, but they were increasingly losing the capacity to sustain their welfare functions, which were regarded as crucial for the maintenance of social stability. It became clear in the postwar period that international economic interdependence was constraining the economic autonomy of the European states. European integration, starting with the signing of the Treaty of Rome in 1957, was a means of providing economic benefits to the nation-states which they could no longer provide individually. Not surprisingly, a number of contemporary EU policies are aimed at ensuring European competitiveness with the United States and Japan.

Throughout the period of the Cold War, the principle of Western European integration was not called into question. The East-West conflict allowed economic and security interests to move in the same direction. A system of intergovernmental cooperation ensured the democratic legitimacy of the European Community enterprise. The end of the Cold War has brought about an important change in the structural incentives toward integration.

The post-1989 conditions have necessitated different sources of legitimation for the European enterprise. Yet the Treaty on European Union (the Maastricht Treaty) was driven by the legacy of the Cold War, as well as by the momentum that the EU had built up before 1989. The Maastricht Treaty therefore has ambiguous origins, which may account for the difficulties it has encountered on the road to ratification. The conception of the treaty occurred before the collapse of communism, but its ratification had to take place after the Cold War had already passed into history.

What did the Maastricht Treaty seek to accomplish? According to Article A of its common provisions, the treaty establishes a "European Union" among the contracting parties.[4] Article B notes that the treaty is designed to lead to closer cooperation in economic and social policies, international politics, and domestic affairs.

The centerpiece of the treaty is the Economic and Monetary Union (EMU). With respect to the European Political Union, the treaty is more modest because it does not transform the European Union into a supranational entity, even if it does acknowledge this as an ultimate objective. But in the area of the EMU, the treaty creates a new supranational institution with the envisioned European Central Bank. According to the treaty, supranationality applies only to monetary policies, and it leaves a broad range of economic policies in the hands of the individual member states.[5] Thus, while other changes are conceived in the Maastricht Treaty, the one change that is significant and projected concerns monetary union.

Whereas the Maastricht Treaty does not alter much in terms of formal cooperation in the economic and political realms, the special treatment it gives to monetary policy has repercussions for cooperation in other areas and may lead to inconsistencies and further problems of accountability of the democratic political process within the EU as well as within the individual nation-states. The Maastricht Treaty succeeded in isolating monetary policy as the prime area of progress toward further integration because of a constellation of domestic interests as well as of international circumstances.[6]

In particular, integrating the newly unified Germany into a strong EU framework is a major objective of monetary union. This effort to achieve political goals by economic means creates potential tensions in European integration that are not addressed in the Maastricht Treaty.

Despite the relatively small degree of genuine and formal supranationality in the Maastricht Treaty, the treaty creates many areas in which the EU can acquire greater prominence. The goal of the EU is to provide the conditions for the free movement of people, capital, goods, and services (the "four freedoms"). The treaty seeks to separate the functions of the EU from those of its constituent members. Theoretically, all policy areas can affect these four freedoms. Consequently, the Maastricht Treaty relegates the function of coordinating domestic policies in such areas as education, vocational training, and youth (Articles 126–127); culture (Article 128); public health (Article 129); consumer protection (Article 129a); infrastructure and industrial policies (Articles 129b–130); economic and social cohesion (Article 130a–e); research and technological development (Article 130f–p); environment (Article 130r–t); and development cooperation (Article 130u–y). In many federally organized states, some of these areas are explicitly policy domains of subnational decision-making bodies. The exact differentiation of functions between the federal level and the regional or local level is determined in the constitution according to functional criteria. The Maastricht Treaty, however, does not explicitly recognize a functional differentiation in its task. This leaves open the possibility of an expansion of Union decision-making in many areas that are so far not formally regulated. This issue is problematic insofar as it creates greater problems of accountability if the EU does not democratize.

Another aspect of the Maastricht Treaty allows great leeway for EU interference with domestic decision making, namely the area of fiscal policies. The treaty acknowledges that there is a connection between monetary policy—which will be administered supranationally after 1999—and fiscal policies—which are formally still the domain of the individual nation-states. The Maastricht Treaty already limits the fiscal autonomy of the EU members. The treaty sets convergence criteria concerning government deficits as well as the overall public debt. In order to be able to join the EMU, EU members cannot run government deficits over 3 percent of their GNP, and their overall public debt cannot be higher than 60 percent of GNP.[7] Thus, if governments strive to reach the convergence criteria, their fiscal decision-making is severely restrained and will remain restricted once the EMU has become a reality. The schedule for convergence, coming during a recession, has already proved unrealistic and has had to be delayed.[8]

Thus, the Maastricht Treaty restricts individual states' policy autonomy in both monetary and fiscal policies. Nevertheless, monetary union could also require greater fiscal autonomy on the part of its constituent members, because the members of a monetary union would already forgo the possibility of monetary adjustments to regional economic disturbances. The question that arises from this construction, then, is, what adjustment mechanisms to regional and temporary economic imbalances do countries have left once they give up both fiscal and monetary autonomy? It is obvious that in this respect the economics of the Maastricht Treaty are based on three possible assumptions. First, regional economic imbalances are not likely to occur; in other words, all European countries will be faced with similar and simultaneous shocks. Second, labor mobility is sufficient to deal with temporary regional imbalances. The third assumption is that price and wage levels are flexible enough to adjust to any temporary economic imbalances. The validity of all three assumptions is open to question.[9]

If none of the three adjustment mechanisms works, the alternative would be even larger fiscal competence on the EU level. Within a single state, adjustment to regional disturbances is in part automatic due to the tax and insurance system. If unemployment rises within a particular area, federal taxes will decrease, but transfer payments in the form of unemployment benefits will increase. Thus, a central budget provides a mechanism that allows regions to adjust to economic shocks. The Maastricht Treaty has not explicitly provided for this solution but it implicitly acknowledges such a possibility, for the treaty does not establish an equal balance between these policy areas.

The solution that the writers of the Maastricht Treaty have chosen in this respect is contradictory: on the one hand, the treaty sets fiscal limits for the member states and, on the other hand, it allows the issue linkage between the treaty and the structural funds that are designed to help the convergence process in the poorer member states. Over the long run, monetary union will also require some pooling of fiscal policy. Especially because monetary policy can no longer be used to adjust to regional imbalances, federal transfer payments, in this case through the EU, will have to take its place. This situation will most likely give Brussels more and, if the EU does not democratize, unaccountable fiscal powers. Thus, more extensive fiscal mechanisms on the EU level may indeed be only a question of time. As Martin Feldstein has asked, "Although the EU has little revenue of its own, is there anything in the treaty to stop a flow of fiscal power and resources to the centre if a European majority wants to do so?"[10]

DIFFICULTIES IN THE RATIFICATION PROCESS

At the time of the signing of the treaty, the ratification process was not expected to be long and difficult. Except for monetary policy there was little substantive change in the formal procedures of the EU. The political elite in each country, including the leaders of the major opposition parties, supported the main lines of the treaty. Nevertheless, the treaty has met with significant resistance among citizens. The Danish electorate voted against the treaty in June 1992. France voted, with only a very slim margin of 51.05 percent, in favor of the treaty.[11] In addition, in December 1992 Switzerland voted against joining the European Economic Area—a common market that joins European Free Trade Area (EFTA) and EU countries, which was supposed to be a precursor for a full membership of the EFTA countries in the EU. In other countries, in particular Germany and Great Britain, sentiments against the treaty have increased.[12] In Germany this did not prevent ratification of the treaty because this decision was left to the national parliament despite strong support for a national referendum.[13] Great Britain's Parliament ratified the treaty only after the prime minister put his government's life on the line.

Many common elements appear in all the national debates about the EU. The political, economic, and social elites of the various countries—including all major parties, local governments, business groups, and unions—favor the treaty. Opponents to the treaty have generally been those groups left behind in the economy (farmers, industrial workers) and supported by the parties of the extreme left and right (for example, the National Front and the Communist party in France). Some environmentalist and Green parties have also opposed the treaty, as have a small number of dissidents from the mainstream parties. In all the major European countries these groups derived support by stressing the impact of the recession and of immigration, the loss of democratic accountability, and the loss of control over national policies. In addition, appeals to nationalism have played their part, with opponents emphasizing a future in which national citizens would live in a world directed by unaccountable foreign bureaucrats. Many other issues have been linked to the treaty: the Common Agricultural Policy, the immigration issue, and, particularly in Ireland, the abortion question.

Despite this mixed bag of issues, however, there is a common root for these concerns: the "democratic deficit" of the EU. The fear being expressed in the high degree of opposition to the treaty is that the European Union creates an unaccountable leadership. Citizens fear that they cannot influence decisions made in Brussels. It is this common fear of a dilution of influence that made it possible for groups and individuals that are on opposing ends of the political spectrum to join forces against the treaty. Abortion-rights and anti-abortion activists in Ireland, the Communist party, and the National Front, as well as the Socialist Jean-Pierre Chevenement and the Gaullist Charles Pasqua in France, have all opposed the treaty.[14] Thus, the root of the problem is the so-called democratic deficit of the EU. In order for the Maastricht Treaty to work, the Union must democratize; indeed this was the general conclusion drawn from the results of the Danish and French referendums.

A DEMOCRATIC EUROPE

The lessons drawn by European leaders and political movements in the wake of the difficulties encountered by the Maastricht Treaty are that (1) Europe has been heretofore constructed and the future is being developed by elites, whether national or European; and (2) the newly created European institutions that establish regulations, set standards, and change national practices are unaccountable to the citizens of member states. Hence, it is generally concluded that national political leaders need to explain the European project to their citizens and to associate them in the project. Consequently, the political leadership in EU countries is also calling for a more democratic Europe, one in which the authoritative institutions are held accountable for their actions.

The European Commission and the Council of the European Union are the authoritative institutions, and their authority comes from the member states, though commissioners are not supposed to be representatives of their governments. The European Parliament, the sole institution to possess legitimacy because it is elected, is also the weakest. "The 'democratic deficit,'" writes Shirley Williams, "is the gap between the powers transferred to the Community level and the control of the elected Parliament over them, a gap filled by national civil servants and operating as European experts or as members of regulation and management committees, and to some extent by organized lobbies, mainly representing business."[15] Accountability—the kind that would bridge the democratic gap—requires the transfer of powers from the member states to a genuine supranational authority. As of 1994 the European Community is organized "as a network that involves the pooling and sharing of sovereignty rather than the transfer of sovereignty to a higher level."[16] But, as most analysts recognize that "the European Community as a whole has gained some share of states' sovereignty."[17]

European Union "law" is made either in so-called intergovernmental conferences (in the case of major treaties such as the Single European Act or the Treaty on European Union), as decisions of the Council, or as directives of the Commission. Negotiations are secret. The general public never learns of the arguments for and against particular policies. Since these policy decisions are often fragile compromises, they are never subsequently presented to the people for discussion, either. What strikes many observers, as well as politicians who are opposed to the development of the EU in its present form, is that the members of these bodies lack democratic legitimacy because they have not been voted into a position of "lawmaker" by European citizens. There is no constituency that could hold these lawmakers accountable for the decisions that they issue.

Shirley Williams describes how insufficient the parliamentary control process is by using the example of the British Parliament: "Both Houses have committees to scrutinize Community legislation and can recommend that a proposal be debated by the House. Such debates are usually held outside prime parliamentary time and arouse only limited interest, as ministers rarely commit themselves before Council meetings and will therefore promise only to take parliamentary views into account. Ministers make a parliamentary statement after important Council meetings, and the Prime Minister invariably makes a statement (twice a year) after European Councils, but Parliament can only question and criticize after the event; the decisions cannot be reopened."[18]

The dilemma, however, is that strengthening the national parliamentary control process would make the EU unworkable, since the Council would have to respond to a fragmented and varied constituency. The alternative is, of course, to strengthen the European Parliament. The Maastricht Treaty, however, does not change the status of the European Parliament significantly. It still has no lawmaking function, no rights to raise revenues and control the budget, and no functions to elect or control the government.[19] Under these conditions the European Parliament becomes a lobbyist for its own rights rather than representative of its constituency.

In the wake of the Danish "No" and the difficulties of ratification in other countries, various political leaders in the European countries have started to realize that the current practices within the EU produce problems of legitimacy and that something needs to be done about the democratic deficit. The Brussels bureaucracy in particular became a favorite target of government officials of member nations who wanted to demonstrate that they were taking their citizens' concerns seriously. The president of the European Parliament promised a "crusade for democracy" headed by the Commission itself.[20] Moreover, the EU has begun to deemphasize the goal of deepening in favor of widening. The Lisbon Summit of 1992 agreed that it would not be necessary to pursue further institutional deepening in order to widen the EU to the EFTA countries.[21]

Despite this recognition of the democratic deficit, however, it is not democracy but rather the principle of "subsidiarity"—which states that all political decisions should be made on the lowest possible level of politics—that is the EU catchword today.[22] Although the term is relatively old in Euro-language, its current appeal lies in the fact that the term's obscurity allows all parties to avoid a precise commitment to a democratic or a federal

Europe. The principle of subsidiarity has little substance, and it is meaningful only in the context of the relative position of the user. For French or British government officials "subsidiarity" means that all relevant decisions should be taken in Paris or London. "Subsidiarity" almost certainly does not apply to their domestic order. However, in Germany local and regional authorities are particularly concerned about the degree to which the Maastricht Treaty removes decision-making power from the local level to the supranational level in Brussels—for example, in the areas of regional planning, culture, and education.[23]

Interestingly enough, the idea of subsidiarity (like the idea of democracy) does not apply to the core piece of the Maastricht Treaty: the Economic and Monetary Union (EMU). Characteristically, the Maastricht Treaty does not strengthen significantly the power of the European Parliament, and the only really powerful supranational institution that it did create is precisely an institution that is designed to be as independent as possible from democratic politics: the European Central Bank. The decision to delegate enormous economic powers to one particular supranational institution only worsens the democratic deficit of the EU. Even the comparison to the statute of the German central bank, the Bundesbank, is mistaken. The Bundesbank is embedded in a democratic framework. There is at least a sense of democratic accountability in Bundesbank decisions. The German Parliament can at any time change the Bundesbank statute. To change the statute of the European Central Bank, an entirely new treaty would be needed, which would have to be ratified by all member countries of the EU. The history of the Maastricht Treaty shows that under this construction it is extremely difficult to guarantee the accountability of the Central Bank.[24]

The restriction of fiscal policies again raises the issues of legitimacy and accountability. If elected national decision-makers have to make budgetary decisions based on restrictions that unelected EU officials set for them, the electorate is not in a position to hold anyone accountable for the decision being taken. The strict convergence criteria set in the Maastricht Treaty are certain to put severe strains on some of the poorer countries in the EU. The disinflationary policies required for Italy and other Mediterranean countries are almost impossible to achieve. The costs of disinflationary policies will be a rise in short-term unemployment. In this context the principle of subsidiarity becomes an almost cynical notion. In terms of the convergence criteria, the subsidiarity principle can be used by the wealthier countries as a justification to let the poorer countries pay the costs of their convergence. Massive pressure by the poorer countries, in particular Spain, has on various occasions been necessary to increase the resources for the structural funds designed to assist Spain in the convergence. Nevertheless, the amounts provided so far are well short of what is required. For large parts of the population in the poorer countries the costs associated with convergence may be intolerable. And the accountability problem arises again, because the final decision on the success of convergence will be a decision by the Council and not the parliament of the country in question.

Finally, a parliament in a democracy, particularly if it is to act as a legislature, and even if it is endowed with some shared powers and powers to amend decisions, will not, as J.-L. Quermonne has observed, "really be a separate legislative assembly unless it is structured along a majority-opposition basis."[25] The absence of European parties practically precludes such a structure. Hence, the national basis of representation is both an impediment to supranationality and an incentive to nationalistic representations. A democratic Europe can only come to exist when accompanied by, and dependent upon, a European identity. In the absence of such a transnational identity, the search for a democratic Europe can lead to a backlash resulting in separatist, nationalist, and subnational identities.

DEMOCRACY AND NATIONALISM

What, then, is the solution to the nagging problem of the lack of democracy on the European level? Assuming that the European Parliament obtains what national parliaments have long sought—greater control over the executive—what are the likely repercussions of this gain? Will it reduce nationalistic forces, or will it exacerbate them? In other words, will a democratic Europe, or what has come to be known as a "citizens' Europe," help consolidate democracy in the individual nation-states, or, on the contrary, will it constitute a threat to the democratic order?

Since the 1980s, the European Parliament has expressed its concern about the trend toward undemocratic decision-making processes within the European Community. It has asked for reforms that it views as necessary for rendering the EU a democratic entity. Among these are "joint decisionmaking with the Council over all areas where the Community has legislative competence; systematic majority voting in the Council; the Commission's right to exercise executive powers independently; the comitology of national civil servants, the confirmation of the European Commission and its President by the European Parliament; the right to initiate legislative proposals; the right of inquiry; and the requirement that the European Parliament ratify any constitutional decisions, international agreements, and conventions that require ratification by member states." [26]

That no legislature, with the exception of the U.S. Congress, comes close to possessing all of these powers in contemporary democracies does not imply that a supranational legislature should be denied all these powers. In fact, it can even be argued, as many political leaders have argued since the process of the ratification of the Maastricht Treaty began, that for Europeans to believe in the European Community, a far greater degree of democracy is needed on the European plane. Or, as Delors put it, there will be no Community without democracy. The general view, then, is that "if the Community is to be what it claims to be, the hub of Europe and the democratic model for Europeans, then its decisionmaking institutions must become truly accountable, not to Europe's governments or its bureaucrats, but to its people."[27]

What does democratization imply? The Maastricht Treaty, if anything, creates rather than resolves problems of legitimacy and accountability. At the very least, the treaty poses a dilemma: either the EU is organized democratically, or some of its provisions have to be renounced. Two problems are immediately discernible. One relates to the organization of institutions at the European level and representation to these institutions. The second problem concerns the allocation of the EU's resources and the costs that member states bear. The current political landscape of the European Parliament is organized along broad ideological lines. However, the membership within the European Parliament is determined by national representation. The national parties represented in the European Parliament cooperate with each other in the various European party networks. Nevertheless, selection of candidates for the European Parliament as well as decisions on programmatic issues have been national decisions. It is, of course, not inconceivable that the major political groupings might establish themselves on the supranational level. The major actors in the supporting social structure, like business groups, unions, and other relevant interest groups, may also be able to switch to a supranational arrangement.

The major political problem, however, is that again this would happen at the elite level. Parliaments and parties (as well as other interest groups) in a democracy are only tools for the expression of the electorate's will. Parliamentary forms do not necessarily establish democratic substance. It is difficult to envisage how parties and interest groups would be able to establish a truly supranational process of political expression. A Europeanization would occur on the elite level, but not at the level of individual party members or voters. Rather, it is likely that the process of political interest-building would still remain at the national level. Language barriers as well as the national character of the media will make it difficult for the public to engage in a European-wide political dialogue. The comparison with the United States does not fit, because the single states were settler colonies that never developed into nation-states with different languages, cultures, and political habits.

It is quite possible that the democratization of the European political process would lead to a renationalization of politics. Since the political process would still work mostly within national borders, the electorate would formulate national interests in its political expressions and would most likely vote for candidates that represent these particularistic interests most effectively. This is especially relevant given the recent rise in appeal of regional, separatist, and right-wing extremist parties in almost all European countries. The increase in regional egoisms even in such established nation-states as Italy, Belgium, and Germany does not bode well for the prospects of a democratization of the EU.[28] If nation-states cannot guarantee a fair process of redistribution among regions internally, how could the EU provide for such a process for even much more extensive problems? Nationalist sentiments are expressed and represented in all EU countries, and they constitute an impediment to the construction of the Union. As Delors noted in 1992 when asked what threats he saw looming in Europe's future, "Nationalism is resurgent. The positive aspect is that there is an identification between nationalism and the decline—the disappearance—of totalitarianism. But nationalism also has a negative aspect. It is like a contagious disease that is spreading everywhere in Europe. And that is another reason why there is so much reluctance when it comes to building Europe."[29]

Nationalist sentiments are not merely an impediment to building a European Community. A democratic European Community exacerbates nationalist sentiments and threatens both the community and the democratic institutions of the member states. This is because representation to the supranational level, if it is based on national expressions of interests, will lead to competition in nationalism. Hitherto, nationalistic sentiments in Europe have largely been expressed by the extreme right—the National Front in France, the Republicans in Germany, the Leagues in Italy. In some countries (France, in particular), a substantial part of the Gaullist party has begun providing an alternative to the National Front. This means that nationalistic forces, hitherto represented by the extreme Right, are likely to grow as European integration progresses and as the European Community distributes costs and resources among its members. (Table 4.1 shows the degree of representation achieved since 1981 by the nationalist parties.)

The European Union is not merely a community that is united to confront Japanese and American competition by creating the largest market in the world. It is a community of highly industrialized states that also compete with one another and that compete to attract foreign investments.[30] It is also a collection of countries with differing economic and geopolitical interests, a fact that is often ignored when straining to define so-called European positions in opposition to an American position on Yugoslavia or on trade issues. The efficiency gains resulting from the Common Market will actually

Table 4.1. Electoral results of extreme right wing, exclusionary, or separatist parties in selected European and national parliamentary elections (percentage of popular vote)

	1981	1982	1983	1984	1984E	1985	1986	1987	1988	1989	1989E	1990	1991	1992	1993
Austria															
FPÖ (Liberal party)			5.0				9.7					16.6	[a]		
Belgium															
VlB (Flemish Bloc)	1.1				1.3	1.4		1.9			4.1		6.6		
Denmark															
FRP (Progress party)	8.9			3.6	3.5			4.8	9.0		5.3	6.4			
France															
FN (National Front)	0.2				11.2		9.8		9.6		11.7	[b]	[c]	[f]	12.4
Germany															
REP (Republicans)										[d]	7.1	2.1	[e]		
Italy															
MSI (Social Movement)			6.8		6.5			5.9			5.5	[g]			
LL (Lombardy League)											1.8			8.7	
Netherlands															
CP86	0.1	0.8			2.5		0.4				0.8				
CD (Centre Democrats)							0.1			0.9					
Norway															
FRPn (Progress party)	4.5					3.7				13.0					
Sweden													6.0		
ND (New Democracy)													6.0		
Switzerland															
AN (National Action)			3.5					2.9					3.2		

Sources: Piero Ignazi, "The Silent Counter-Revolution: Hypotheses on the Emergence of Extreme Right-Wing Parties in Europe," *European Journal of Political Research* 22 (July 1992), 3–34; Christopher Husbands, "The Other Face of 1992: The Extreme-Right Explosion in Western Europe," *Parliamentary Affairs* 45 (July 1992), 267–284; and various issues of *Parliamentary Affairs, West European Politics, Electoral Studies,* and *Financial Times.*

Footnotes refer to notable regional electoral results:

[a] Vienna 1991 municipal elections: 22.7%, second largest party.

[b] 1988 presidential election: Jean-Marie Le Pen, 14.4%.

[c] 1992 regional elections: 13.9%.

[d] 1989 regional elections, Berlin: 7.5%.

[e] 1991 regional elections, Bremen: German Peoples Union: 6.2%.

[f] 1992 regional elections, Schleswig-Holstein: German Peoples Union: 7%; Baden-Württemberg: 11%.

[g] 4.8% in 1990 regional elections, 19% in Lombardy, 12 regional council seats.

lead to greater rivalries among countries and regions to attract investment.[31]

Another problem concerns subsidies accorded by national governments—which are subject to EU control. The Union distributes resources to backward regions in order to create greater equality among the member states. Almost a third of the EU's budget is devoted to aiding poor regions. As Table 4.2 shows, the EU receives nearly a third of its contributions from Germany and almost 20 percent from France.

Since every member state of the EU possesses its share of "poor regions," it becomes relevant for the member states to know which countries receive the largest share of this expenditure. Table 4.3 shows the funds allocated to countries, as well as the funds allocated for aid to poor regions. In both cases, it is clear that the wealthier countries are paying for the poorer ones. At the Edinburgh meeting in December 1992, the most intense discussions revolved around the EU budget for the next five years, what is known as the Delors II package. Delors had earlier proposed a budget of 1.37 percent of the European GNP. A hostile reaction from the member states forced Delors to reduce the figure to 1.27 percent. Britain demanded an even greater reduction in this figure.

The Maastricht Treaty calls for the wealthier countries to aid the more disadvantaged ones—Greece, Ireland, Portugal, and Spain—countries that the British refer to as "Club Med." In exchange for the aid they receive, these countries undertake to reduce their public expenditure, trade deficit, and inflation if they wish to join the Economic and Monetary Union in 1999. Since they cannot achieve these goals without the help of their wealthier partners, such help is indispensable. But the richer nations—France, Britain, Germany, the Netherlands—have all expressed reservations about their largesse toward the Club Med countries. The wealthier partners that have objected to the level of required aid have their own budgetary problems. One British official's reaction was strongly negative when informed of Germany's proposal that Britain's receipts ("restitutions") should, in light of the Maastricht accords, be reviewed: "Out of the question. We are the second largest contributor, even though we are the eighth wealthiest country. On this point, we will not hesitate to use the veto weapon."[32]

The issue of the allocation of resources and the costs incurred by individual members evokes the specter of nationalistic reactions. As Pierre Hassner notes, "peace and interdependence, far from excluding inequalities among states, risk creating new inequalities." They "do not abolish violence within societies, but can, on the contrary, provoke it," and "the opening of borders does not abolish the need for community, solidarity and exclusion (or at least the distinction between 'us' and 'them') but can, on the contrary,

Table 4.2. Budget of the European Union

Contributions (1993)		Expenditures (1993)	
Germany	28.6%	Agricultural policies	52%
France	19.3%	Regional aid	29%
Italy	14.9%	Reserves	5%
Great Britain	12.9%	Administration	5%
Spain	8.7%	Domestic policies	5%
Netherlands	5.9%	Foreign affairs	4%
Belgium	4.1%		
Five others	5.7%		

Table 4.3 European Union aid to members

Member	Total aid granted (in billions of francs)	Percentage of total granted to poor regions
Spain	12.6	9.7
Italy	9.8	7.4
Portugal	6.9	6.9
Greece	6.6	6.6
Great Britain	5.9	0.7
France	5.7	0.8
Ireland	3.6	3.6
Germany	2.9	0
Belgium	0.7	0
Netherlands	0.7	0
Denmark	0.3	0
Luxembourg	0.07	0

Source: Adapted from *Le Nouvel Economiste,* March 5, 1993, p. 37.

exacerbate it."[33] The point is that European integration raises the danger of a return to national sovereignty and nationalism, rather than leading to supranationality and to the decline of nationalism.

The anti-Maastricht electorate was largely a disaffected group, bypassed by the modern economy and disadvantaged by international competition. The antidemocratic forces have seen their ranks swell as a result of governments providing aid to poorer groups and regions. In Germany, it was the costs of reunification, in France the presence of a large population of immigrant workers, in Italy the aid provided to the south—in all these cases, the extreme right-wing movements have been the chief beneficiaries.

The issue of the distribution of resources among member states is bound to become more acute as the unemployment rate rises in Europe. Less and less, as polls show, are citizens of one country willing to foot the bill for those of another. Just as the welfare state has come under attack in all the countries of Western Europe, so its transfer to a supranational level is coming under increasing scrutiny. The Common Agricultural Policy, for example, which consumes half of the EU's budget "is spent on 5% of the EU's population."[34] This explains why elections to the European Parliament are fought on national issues, and rarely ever on strictly European issues.

These economic insecurities have sharpened the salience of the issue of immigration. The tendency to blame economic difficulties on newcomers concerns the large immigrant population that has lived and worked in EU countries (North Africans in France, Turks in Germany), as well as the new immigrants fleeing the East European countries. The Single Act, which went into effect in January 1993, and the Maastricht Treaty call for the free movement of goods, capital, and labor. Not surprisingly, the flow of labor did not become as free as the flow of goods and capital. The reason is that EU countries have recognized foreign labor as a potential problem, both economic and social. Indeed, xenophobic nationalism in West European countries is clearly fueled by immigration.[35] The more the issue is brought to the forefront—within the member states by the economic recession, and at the European level by the fears of supranational decisions—the more extremist parties can claim to have a monopoly on the defense of the nation. Consequently, the center-right is beginning to join the extreme right as a mouthpiece of antiforeigner nationalism. Nor should we forget that the left (as in France) is also endowed with a nationalistic faction.

In addition to the concern with cost-benefit analysis and immigration, a third dilemma fuels nationalistic sentiments. This is the growing problem of ethnic identities within sovereign states (Catalan, Basque, Corsican, and many others).

The development of the European Union—when it is "deepened" and "broadened"—creates conditions that, paradoxically, encourage the rise of subnational ethnic identities within sovereign states. The deepening of the community allows for the recognition of the inequalities among regions as well as the recognition of unique regional characteristics. The enlargement of the community as an economic unit facilitates the existence of smaller political units. Consequently, as the European Union is enlarged as an economic unit, whether by full integration of additional sovereign states, or whether through different forms of association, the likelihood increases that smaller (subnational) political units will make claims for recognition as states. The breakup of what was once Yugoslavia is only an extreme case of the consequences of subnational political demands. Most European states contain ethnic groups that may become state-claiming ethnic nationalities, threatening the cohesion of sovereign states and, by association, the integrity of the Union.

THAT the long road taken toward European unity has known its ups and downs and has steadily made progress in the decades since the 1950s is beyond dispute. Whether that progress, even at a slower pace, can be maintained is today highly questionable. As the *Economist* noted, "It is not that the aims are themselves unworthy: a politically united Europe would be a fine thing; the intellectual case for monetary union remains powerful. It is that the political will to make either of these happen does not exist; in truth, it has never yet existed. It may one day, but to think that it already did was an illusion."[36] There remain a significant number of threats to European construction and even to democracy in the European states. Visions of what the European Union ought to be and how it should be constituted vary today more than ever in the past. Forces opposed to European unity have gained within moderate political formations, so that anti–European Union sentiments have today a measure of respectability that they did not possess in the past.[37]

The Maastricht Treaty lends itself to different interpretations.[38] Its ultimate goals are far from self-evident. It has encountered unanticipated opposition across Europe. The remedy sought by European leaders and by political leaders supporting European construction—democratization—is likely to threaten both the European project and national democratic institutions.

The difficulties of achieving a democratic Europe are immense. Granting legislative and control powers, as well as the power to raise revenues and impose taxes, are often called for in support of the European parliament. It is argued that an accountable parliament is the only parliament that will be acceptable. Only a Citizens' Europe can be a genuine Europe, and only this will be acceptable to European citizens.[39]

Any democratic parliament must confront the issue of representation. Granting greater powers to a European parliament is certain to unleash forces within European societies that would compete with one another to take the lead in questioning the legitimacy of such an institution. A European parliament without a genuine European, as opposed to a national, representation is certain to pose perils both for the enterprise of union and for democracy in the individual countries.

Furthermore, successful supranational democracy depends on the creation of a European identity. Yet the very process of European integration in the political and economic sphere is creating a backlash that calls the success of this identity-building process into question. Without a European identity, the idea of a democratic Europe likely will not survive.

This scenario may, however, prove to be the most desirable outcome. Rather than pushing for greater integration and democratization—a process that could undermine the enterprise of European unity—the EU may well want to focus on broadening and put off deepening—perhaps permanently. The result will fall short of a federated Europe, but it will also reduce the likelihood that Western Europe will find itself faced with the least desirable outcome: its renationalization.

5

Fear Thy Neighbor: The Breakup of Yugoslavia

Aleksa Djilas

> Owing to frontiers being constantly changed in Eastern Europe, those
> being marked on the map must be accepted with reserve.
> —A *note bene* on a silk map of Eastern Europe given to British
> officers dropped behind enemy lines in World War II.

The creation of Yugoslavia in 1918 and its more than seven decades of existence reflected the many similarities among its national groups and their desire to form a single modern state. At the same time, the forging of this state did not expunge the unique historical myths and political loyalties of these different national groups. The communist regime established in 1945 did succeed in keeping national conflicts from surfacing. But it failed to erect the political institutions and to nurture the civic culture needed to overcome historic tensions. The collapse of the communist regime, therefore, led to the reawakening of old and the mobilization of new nationalist rivalries.

The nationalist ambitions, fears, and frustrations of Yugoslavia's constituent groups, which form the background of the civil war that began in 1991, were thus not the inventions of nationalist intellectuals or political elites. However, the Yugoslav civil war would not have happened if elites—and especially Serbia's president Slobodan Milošević and Croatia's president Franjo Tudjman—had not irresponsibly and deliberately manipulated nationalist sentiments with their propaganda and policies. The force of nationalist passions whipped up by these opportunistic leaders not only made conflict inevitable, but it also made the war exceptionally brutal. New borders were created not just by force, but by "ethnic cleansing" and the rape, persecution, and murder of civilians.

The goal of this chapter is to provide a historical interpretation of why Yugoslavia broke apart and why nationalist sentiments intensified to the point of triggering brutal conflict. My key concern is the interplay between longstanding national identities and the manipulation of these identities by opportunistic political leaders. I will show that the war, while it was fueled by the collapse of the communist regime, certainly occurred in an environment conducive to the rise of nationalist politics, especially in light of the weakness of the country's civic institutions. But it was the deliberate mobilization of nationalist sentiments and rivalries by political elites that ensured the outbreak of violence. I will also argue that Western involvement, although it did limit the destructiveness of the war, was inadequate and ineffectual. More decisive and intrusive action by the West, including the use of military force, would have stopped, if not prevented, this most recent round of conflict in the Balkans.

SOUTH SLAV IDENTITIES

Until the twentieth century, most of Central and Eastern Europe was divided into large empires—Russian, German, Austrian, and Ottoman Turkish—which encompassed different national groups.[1] As nationalist ideologies and movements spread throughout Europe during the nineteenth and twentieth centuries, these groups (usually on the basis of common languages) developed distinct political loyalties and set about building separate nation-states. In the case of Yugoslavia, significant similarities among its national groups in language, ethnic origin, and custom made it almost a homogeneous nation-state. Except for two large minority groups in Serbia—Albanians in Kosovo and Hungarians in Vojvodina—South Slavs represented an overwhelming majority of its population. In 1918, the sense of oneness among South Slavs was the main force behind the unification of Serbia, Montenegro, and the South Slav provinces of a disintegrating Austria-Hungary. The new state was first called the Kingdom of the Serbs, Croats, and Slovenes, but in 1929 it was renamed Yugoslavia, which means the "land of the South Slavs." (Sizeable German and Italian minorities had also lived in Yugoslavia, but they left—either out of fear or because they were forced to—following the collapse of fascist Italy and Nazi Germany.)

Differences in customs and traditions did exist, but these differences fell primarily along regional, not national lines. Differences between two regions inhabited by the same group (for example, between Croats from Dalmatia and Croats from Zagorje, the area around Zagreb and Varaždin) were often greater than those between two regions of different groups (for example, between Croats from Dalmatia and Serbs and Muslims from eastern Herzegovina).[2] National groups in Yugoslavia also differed less among themselves than from their neighbors, with the possible exception of the

Bulgarians who are also South Slavs. Many existing nation-states—Germany and Italy, for example—unite groups that are far more culturally heterogeneous than the South Slavs.

Yugoslavia's three languages—Serbo-Croatian (or Croato-Serbian), Macedonian, and Slovene—do not represent insurmountable barriers to communication and integration among the South Slavs. The large majority use Serbo-Croatian as their mother tongue, and most Macedonians and Slovenes easily learn it since the three languages are closely related.

As far as religion is concerned, Serbs, Montenegrins (most of whom feel closely related to Serbs), and Macedonians are Eastern Orthodox. Croats and Slovenes are Roman Catholics, and Bosnia-Herzegovina has a sizeable South Slav Muslim population. But it is misleading to claim that religious differences are the main cause of South Slav discord. Religion has played only an indirect role in inciting conflict among the South Slavs—by shaping culture and custom, which in turn influenced political loyalties.

The most important factor in the formation of competing loyalties among South Slavs has been historically based identities and affiliations. Mythical historical memories and a devotion to states inspired by those memories are the principal sources of cleavage and conflict. Because South Slav identities are rooted in sentiment, conviction, and imagination, they are often seen as arbitrary. For many Croatian nationalists, for example, the Serbian minority in Croatia had no real reason to declare itself Serbian; these people lived on Croatian territory, looked no different from Croats, and spoke the same language. Serbs in turn often had to be persuaded that Croats were not Catholic Serbs, but people with a different national identity. The refusal of most Muslims to regard themselves as either Croats or Serbs has often been met by angry disbelief from Croatian and Serbian nationalists.

The fluidity of national identities and religious affiliations is largely responsible for the elusive nature of national consciousness in Yugoslavia. Among the South Slavs, changes of religion were frequent, especially in the second half of the fifteenth century and in the sixteenth century when, after the Ottoman Turkish conquest, the Bosnian nobility and many peasants converted to Islam. Conversions continued into the second half of the nineteenth century. Religious conversions resulted more often from fear and self-interest than from religious conviction.[3]

In the nineteenth and twentieth centuries the borders among national groups, especially among Serbs, Croats, and Muslims, were often crossed without changing religion. Muslim Serbs and Muslim Croats, and Catholic Serbs and Orthodox Croats could be found, though mainly among the educated population. Croatian and Serbian identities were sufficiently secular to accept non-co-religionists as co-nationalists. Only the Bosnian Muslims became so infused with religious identities that anyone who wanted to be a part of that national group had to accept the Muslim faith.

National identities would sometimes change from one generation to another. A great grandfather could be Muslim, the grandfather a Muslim Serb, the father a Muslim Croat, and the son might return to the allegiances of the great grandfather. An individual could change his or her national identity more than once, and then return to the original one. The Bosnian saying, that one can be certain into which religion one was born, but one never knows what religion one will die in, is even truer of national identity.

THE TRAJECTORY OF SERBIAN AND CROATIAN NATIONALISM

Serbs and Croats predominated in Yugoslavia, making up more than half of the country's population and constituting the overwhelming majority in the three central and largest republics—Serbia, Croatia, and Bosnia-Herzegovina. Roughly 24 percent of the Serbian population lived outside Serbia (and its provinces Kosovo and Vojvodina), while 22 percent of the Croatian population lived outside Croatia. Because all South Slav Muslims lived intermixed with Serbs and Croats and because Montenegrins identified with Serbs, tensions between Serbs and Croats tended to spread across all of Yugoslavia. Only Slovenia in the north and Macedonia in the south (both of which have very small Serbian and Croatian communities) were at times able to isolate themselves from Serbian-Croatian rivalry.

The Serbian-Croatian conflict simmered throughout Yugoslavia's history. When Yugoslavia was created in 1918, many Serbs and Croats were already charged with strong nationalist sentiments hindering the development of loyalty to a common state. During the interwar period, ruling regimes claimed that they were pursuing enlightened policies which would overcome the centrifugal forces of nationalism. But both these regimes and opposition parties had nationalistic leanings. These tendencies were exacerbated by the agrarian problems of the period. Although agrarian reform in 1919 had abolished the vestiges of feudalism, it did not bring prosperity to the peasantry. Peasants were heavily taxed and very few resources were invested in improving agriculture. The political parties regularly distracted peasants with nationalist rhetoric or blamed the other side for the peasants' plight, and in the process exacerbated tensions among national groups.

In the late 1930s, the Communist party of Yugoslavia developed a new strategy toward the national question. This strategy aimed at ending Serbian "hegemony" and promoting the position of non-Serbs, while preserving Yugoslavia.[4] These policies and the Communist party's successes in suppressing internecine massacres during World War II increased the prestige of the party and helped it come to power at the end of the war. The party in fact kept many of its promises regarding national equality within a unified Yugoslavia. The problem, as I discuss later, was that none of these achievements became rooted in enduring political institutions. The party failed to establish a stable federal system that could have institutionalized and regulated relations among national groups.

Although the party was more open-minded than many of its East European kin, in its ideology, dogma always prevailed over analysis. All impulses for change had to come from the leadership, and when the party attempted any long-overdue reforms, it behaved like a trade union for the bureaucracy whose main task was to preserve communist power. Reform, therefore, yielded limited results. The party was strong enough to prevent open conflict among Yugoslavia's national groups, but its sterile doctrines and authoritarian methods could not overcome traditional loyalties. In the early 1960s, when the party's control over society began to weaken, old nationalist demands and animosities resurfaced. The party could not reach a consensus on how to respond. It was split between those favoring strong federation and those favoring more autonomy for the republics. This split became more pronounced in the late 1960s when new party leaders in Croatia escalated their nationalist rhetoric.[5] Although they encouraged liberal reforms and economic modernization and tried to distance themselves from the Croatian intellectuals who called for the separation of Croatia from Yugoslavia, these developments threatened Croatia's Serbian minority, representing between 12 and 14 percent of the republic's population.

Serbia's communists also had new leaders who were somewhat more energetic than their Croatian counterparts in the liberalization of cultural life and the economy and in suppressing nationalist tendencies within the party.[6] This tolerance, however, was exploited by influential Serbian intellectuals. They expressed their dissatisfaction with political developments in Croatia and opposed new amendments to the Yugoslav constitution that would increase the independence of the six republics and the two autonomous provinces. In their eyes, these changes would begin the dismantling of Yugoslavia and turn the Serbs in Croatia, Bosnia-Herzegovina, and in Serbia's autonomous province of Kosovo into persecuted minorities.

These intellectuals believed that developments in Yugoslavia were essentially the result of an anti-Serbian plot. Although they could not publicly attack Tito, they espoused the views that under the leadership of "this Croat" and "former corporal of the Austro-Hungarian army" the League of Communists of Yugoslavia, as the party was called after 1952, was continuing the policies of ancient Serbian enemies, in particular those of the Vatican, Austria-Hungary, and the Comintern.[7] To support this thesis, intellectuals concocted claims that Serbia's enemies were again seeking to divide, subjugate, or exterminate the Serbs. These claims were without foundation. The new Yugoslav Constitution adopted in 1974 did reopen the Serbian and Croatian national question by adjusting the relationship of the republics to federal structures, but it did not favor one national group at the expense of another.[8]

The paranoid ruminations of Serbian intellectuals would become the ideological foundation for Serbian policies two decades later. In this sense, these myths did contribute to the outbreak of the Yugoslav civil war. But at the time they attracted only moderate attention, since the Yugoslav public and the international community were distracted by "nationalist euphoria" in Croatia—in particular, the separatist efforts of Matica Hrvatska (Croatian Queen-Bee), the main Croatian cultural institution. Its membership and funds were increasing with great speed and it had become a rival of the Communist party. In November 1971, under the influence of Matica Hrvatska, students at the University of Zagreb went on strike. Among their demands was separate Croatian membership in the United Nations.

Tito concluded that events had escaped the control of the Croatian party leadership. In December, Croatia's leaders and many nationalist intellectuals were purged. Less than a year later, Serbia's leaders (who had avoided any involvement in the removal of the Croats) suffered the same fate. In Croatia, a few hundred people were arrested, many more than in Serbia. But the purge in Serbia was perhaps more thorough than in Croatia. About 6,000 people prominent in politics, business, the media, and education and culture were dismissed.

This repression succeeded in pushing nationalism—both Croatian and Serbian—underground. But events clearly showed that the communists were far from immune to nationalism, and that many of the country's intellectuals were passionately committed to it. While Croatian intellectuals dreamed of an independent Croatia (which would include at least a part of Bosnia-Herzegovina) and were not inclined to treat the Serbian minority in Croatia fairly, their Serbian counterparts were hoping that if Yugoslavia were to disintegrate, they could attach to Serbia the territories of Croatia and Bosnia where Serbs were in a majority, if not enlarge Serbia even further.

Although the Serbs were the main targets of Croatian nationalism, and the Croats were the main targets of Serbian nationalism, both ideologies were also hostile to other groups in Yugoslavia. Any talk of national or cultural pluralism was deemed a threat. Both groups made mention of the need to develop their respective economies and protect their cultures, yet their main concern was to augment Croatian and Serbian national power and make Croatia and Serbia homogeneous nation-states. They idealized such homogeneity, promoting the myth of spontaneous harmony among different social classes if it were to be achieved. Both Serbian and Croatian nationalists constructed romantic notions about a glorious national past. This rewriting of history fit comfortably with official Yugoslav Marxism, which discouraged analytic and objective historiography.

Tito judged that he could accommodate many nationalist demands because he believed that nationalist and communist authoritarianism were compatible. He was much more afraid of liberal reforms than of nationalism, since reforms directly challenged the communist monopoly of power and his personal rule. Indeed, nationalism, if supervised and channeled by the party, could even be an ally. Its mass appeal increased popular support for the party, and it enlarged the power of the communist bureaucracy by multiplying offices (each republic, for example, had its own foreign office). These incentives helped convince Tito to proceed after the purges of the early 1970s to strengthen the independence of the republics from the federal ministries and institutions in Belgrade. By promoting the republics as almost fully sovereign states under the 1974 constitution, he sacrificed the war-time communist goal of Yugoslav unity, but in doing so he strengthened his monopoly of power as the final aribiter of relations among the republics. In this opportunistic use of nationalism, Tito anticipated Serbia's Slobodan Milošević and other communist leaders in the republics of Yugoslavia, who would try in the late 1980s to reinvigorate their power by unleashing nationalist passions.

TOWARD THE CIVIL WAR

The Yugoslav version of the end of communism differed from that in other East European countries. As so many times before in the history of the South Slavs, the national question overshadowed all others. As elsewhere in Eastern Europe, opponents of the regime demanded the introduction of liberal democratic institutions. But the main conflict in Yugoslavia turned out to be among its different national groups, not between the communists and their opponents. The party split into national communist parties before the decision was made to hold free elections. The collapse of communist one-party rule in Yugoslavia was more a *result* than a cause of the disintegration of the country.

When, after numerous quarrels between Slovene and Croatian delegates on one side and Serbian on the other, the Slovene and Croatian delegations walked out of the fourteenth congress of the League of Communists of Yugoslavia, held on January 20–22, 1990, the Yugoslav Communist party was effectively no more. On February 6, the Slovene police unit in Kosovo, which had been struggling alongside the Serbian police against demonstrating and rioting Albanians, went back to Slovenia; the Croats followed suit on April 3.[9]

The conflict pitting Slovenia and Croatia against Serbia had been brewing for some time. During the mid-1980s, some political liberalization had begun to take place in Slovenia and Croatia. Slovene and Croatian elites encouraged moderate democratic reforms and began to seek greater independence. To many inside and outside Yugoslavia it seemed that their ultimate aim was complete separation. These separatist tendencies were exacerbated by Serbia's policies. Ruled by Slobodan Milošević since autumn 1987, Serbia opposed any attempts at liberalizing the communist system and demanded the recentralization of the Yugoslav Communist party.[10] The Slovenes and Croats feared that tolerating these efforts would ensure Serbia's and Milošević's domination. The Slovenes, because of their close cultural ties to Germany and Austria, were particularly keen on leaving the federation and heading toward eventual membership in the European Community.

In all Yugoslav republics, but especially in Serbia and Croatia, radio, television, and the press spread incessant and vitriolic nationalist propaganda, speeding the process of Yugoslavia's disintegration and fueling the subsequent civil war. The intellectuals, progenitors and foremost champions of nationalism, played a crucial role in this media war. And their efforts were effective. Broad sections of the population supported the nationalist policies of their political and intellectual leaders. A survey of 4,222 citizens from all Yugoslav republics taken toward the end of 1990 showed that most of the public shared in the nationalist sentiments of their leaders.[11] Among elites and masses alike, nationalist sentiments were gaining strength.

The Slovenes were the first to hold elections, on April 8, 1990. The DEMOS, an anticommunist six-party coalition, won 53 percent of the vote and took control of the Parliament, but the former communist leader Milan Kučan won the presidential race. As in all the republics, nationalism was the central issue of almost all the parties during the elections.[12] The Slovenes wanted to secede from Yugoslavia at all costs, and on July 2 the Slovene Parliament declared the Republic of Slovenia to be a fully sovereign state, although it refrained from proclaiming its separation from Yugoslavia. On December 23, a plebiscite for independence was held, with 86 percent voting in favor. On February 20, 1991, Slovenia announced that it would establish its own diplomatic relations with other states.

The Croats were the next to hold elections. On April 22, the Croatian Democratic Union, a right-wing separatist party, won the largest number of votes—41.5 percent—and, because of the nonproportional electoral system, as many as two-thirds of the parliamentary seats. The new parliament then elected the Democratic Union's leader, Franjo Tudjman, a former communist general and political prisoner, as president of Croatia. Like the Slovenes, the Croats aimed at complete independence. Unlike the Slovenes, the Croatian Democratic Union also had expansionist expectations and hoped to take at least a part of Bosnia-Herzegovina with them.

The new Croatian government mistreated Serbs living in Croatia. Serbs were discriminated against at work, frequently dismissed, and sometimes exposed to threats and arbitrary arrests.[13] Anti-Serbian propaganda filled the media, reviving the memory of Croatia's fascist regime during World War II. The regime had killed between 200,000 and 300,000 Serbian civilians, a number that Serbian nationalists characteristically inflate to a million or more.[14] Violent incidents between Croats, including the Croatian police and the Serbian minority, began soon after the Democratic Union's victory. These events intensified the Serbian minority's struggle for political and cultural rights, its demands for territorial autonomy, and its decision to withdraw from the Croatian Parliament. Although Milošević publicly condemned Croatia's policies toward its Serbs, he privately welcomed them because they allowed him to disguise his expansionist ambitions as aid for his persecuted brethren in Croatia.

Inside Croatia, both the Croatian government and the Serbian population were organizing armies. The Croats illegally imported weapons from abroad, while the Serbs obtained theirs from Serbia. The January 9, 1991, order of the presidency of Yugoslavia to dismantle all national military units, though backed by the federal army, was disregarded by all parties. Croatia declared on February 20 that only Croatian, not federal, laws were valid on its territory. Eight days later, the Serbian Parliament in Croatia's Krajina region announced that if Croatia were to secede, Krajina would remain inside Yugoslavia. As the violent clashes between armed Croatian and Serbian units continued, and Croatia moved closer to secession, Krajina declared itself a part of Serbia on April 1.

Separatist sentiments ruled in Macedonia as well. In the elections of November 11, 1990, Kiro Gligorov, a former leading communist, became the president. He wanted more independence for Macedonia, but within a Yugoslavia transformed into a confederation, and he made no irredentist claims vis-à-vis neighboring Greece. But the largest party in the new parliament consisted of extremists who advocated Greater Macedonia. On January 25, 1991, the Macedonian assembly approved a declaration of independence and soon demanded the withdrawal of the federal army from Macedonia.

On November 18, 1990, Bosnia-Herzegovina voted. Its national groups were the most intermixed of any republic. Bosnia's population of 4.4 million was 43 percent Muslim, 31 percent Serbian, and 17 percent Croatian. During World War II, brutal internecine massacres took place in Bosnia. Of a population of 2.8 million, the Serbs lost 209,000, the Croats 79,000, and the Muslims 75,000. The Serbs took the greatest number of casualties because Bosnia had been a part of fascist Croatia during the war and Croatian extremists, with some Muslim collaboration, attempted to exterminate or expel Serbs.[15]

Not surprisingly, most Bosnians voted in the November election for the parties representing their own national groups. The Muslim party won 86 seats in the Parliament, the Serbian 72, and the Croatian 44. The programs of the parties were fundamentally incompatible. The Muslim party wanted an independent Bosnia under Muslim domination, although it initially felt too weak to make such a demand openly.[16] The Serbian and the Croatian parties favored Greater Serbia and Greater Croatia; those parts of Bosnia with Serbian and Croatian majorities would be incorporated into their appropriate "homelands."

The three parties proceeded to form a coalition government, but disagreement rapidly led to stalemate. Muslims and Croats often cooperated against the Serbs, who then claimed that their presence in the government was meaningless. On April 26, 1991, the Serbs of Bosnian Krajina created a separate assembly, resisting the pleas of the Sarajevo government to keep Bosnia-Herzegovina united.

The Muslim leader Alija Izetbegović became president of Bosnia, since his party had won the largest number of votes. From the beginning, Izetbegović proved incapable as leader of a multinational country. His vision of Bosnia's future was too exclusive, too focused on the interests and welfare of only the Muslim population. In his widely distributed book *Islamic Declaration: A Program for the Islamization of [Bosnian] Muslims and Muslim Peoples,* published before the election, Izetbegović had argued for the "Islamization" of Bosnian Muslims and their supremacy in Bosnia; for the complete subjugation of Bosnian political, social, economic, and family life to Islamic law; and for political unity with Muslims throughout the world. Serbs and Croats living in Bosnia, as well as their brethren in Serbia and Croatia, found his views hardly comforting:

> First and foremost of these conclusions is certainly the incompatability of Islam with non-Islamic systems. There can be neither peace nor coexistence between the Islamic religion and non-Islamic social and political institutions. . . . By claiming the right to order its own world itself, Islam obviously excludes the right or possibility of action on the part of any foreign ideology on that terrain. There is, therefore, no lay

principle, and the state should be the expression of the moral concepts of religion, and their supporter.[17]

A volatile mixture resulted when Izetbegović's views mingled with the nationalist propaganda emanating from Belgrade and Zagreb.

THE CROATIAN-SERBIAN WAR

On December 9, 1990, elections were held in Montenegro and Serbia. The reformed Communist parties, which had accepted political pluralism and had become, at least by name, "socialist," won decisively. The leader of the Montenegrin socialists, Momir Bulatović, became the president of Montenegro, and the leader of the Serbian socialists, Slobodan Milošević, was reelected president of Serbia.

Milošević and his socialist colleagues, together with almost all the Serbian opposition parties and most of the intelligentsia, aimed at enlarging Serbia at the expense of Croatia. The Montenegrins supported these aims and became Serbia's only ally in the war that followed. Serbia's claim that it merely wanted to protect Croatia's Serbian minority simply lacked credibility. The secession of Croatian territories that contained a Serbian majority or a substantial Serbian minority would have only risked exposing to increased persecution and violence the two-thirds of Croatia's 600–700,000 Serbs who lived outside those territories.

Fighting finally broke three days out after Slovenia declared independence on June 24, 1991. The federal army and Slovene territorial defense forces fought for control of Slovenia's (and Yugoslavia's) border crossings to Italy, Austria, and Hungary. The conflict was short-lived. Through desertions of non-Serbian officers and indoctrination by Milošević's media, the federal army had been developing into primarily a Serbian army. The absence of a Serbian minority in Slovenia reduced the urgency of the war for the federal army, which quickly withdrew.

The federal army conducted itself very differently in the Croatian-Serbian war.[18] Armed conflicts with increasing casualties began in the spring of 1991 and multiplied after Croatia's proclamation of independence on June 25. During the spring and summer, the federal army avoided taking sides and tried to separate Croatian troops and the forces of Croatia's Serbs. By the beginning of autumn, the federal army had joined the fighting on the Serbian side.

The Croatian-Serbian war was brutal. According to official Croatian sources, 10,000 died, but other estimates indicate that two or three times that number were killed. Croatia's Serbs, the federal army, and volunteer units from Serbia and Montenegro bombarded Dubrovnik and completely destroyed Vukovar. Many other smaller towns and villages were bombed by both sides. The civilian population suffered greatly. Prisoners of war were tortured and murdered. Both sides engaged in "ethnic cleansing" and there were over half a million refugees. The Serbs carried out the worst bombardment of civilian centers, but the Croats also used force and intimidation against the Serbian population. As the British journalist and author Misha Glenny points out,

> Even before the war began, the government [of Croatia] was concerned to hush up nationalist-motivated crimes against its Serb population while when applying for [international] recognition, its police were involved in the slaughter of innocent Serbs in Gospić, Ogulin, Sisak, Karlovac, Daruvar, Virovitice, Zagreb and elsewhere. . . . These urban Serbs were among the greatest victims of the war, whose plight, however, is one of the least well known. Tens of thousands were hounded from their homes in the big cities either through direct intimidation, expulsion or through the pervasive climate of fear.[19]

And according to Ivan Zvonimir Čičak, the leading Croatian opposition activist and the president of the Croatian Helsinki Committee for Human Rights, about 10,000 Serbian homes were blown up.[20]

The troops of Croatia's Serbs, the federal army, and the volunteer units from Serbia and Montenegro captured over a quarter of Croatia's territory. In most of these regions, the Serbs had before the war been somewhat more numerous than the Croats, but soon came to represent close to 90 percent of the population. Some Croats left simply to escape the fighting, but most were forced to leave. The Croats themselves expelled at least half of the Serbian population from other parts of Croatia.

In January 1992, the Croatian-Serbian negotiations presided over by Cyrus Vance, the UN special envoy, led to a peace agreement. United Nations troops moved into the territories under Serbian control to keep the unstable peace. These territories remained formally part of Croatia, but all local administration was in Serbian hands.

THE WESTERN REACTION

During the Croatian-Serbian war, Western media, public opinion, and leadership showed much more sympathy for the Croats than the Serbs, but the governments did not intervene militarily in the conflict.[21] They were fearful of casualties and of being unable to withdraw their troops in a timely fashion. They also judged the causes of the war and the patterns in which it was fought to be too complex for military solutions. The West put intense diplomatic pressure on the Serbs to stop advancing, while the UN imposed a ban on the export of weapons to both belligerents. This embargo harmed the Croats more than the Serbs, since the Serbs had most of the reserves of the federal army to draw on. Nevertheless, Croatia was able to arm itself through illegal imports.

The United States and the European Community refused to recognize Croatia's independence as long as there was no proper peace treaty. The only dissonant voices were those of Austria and Germany. The Austrians encouraged Slovene independence beginning in 1990.

By the early summer of 1991, the German government, closely followed by Austria, began campaigning for the immediate and unconditional recognition of both Croatia and Slovenia. Gemany considered Croatia's president Franjo Tudjman a West European Christian Democrat, in spite of his obvious authoritarian tendencies.[22] Germany also decided to ignore Croatia's predatory designs on Bosnia-Herzegovina, although President Tudjman had in July 1991 publicly argued for its division between Croatia and Serbia.[23] The Bosnian government was naturally against recognition of Croatia and Slovenia, since it would leave Bosnia-Herzegovina to choose between domination by Serbia or secession and the risk of dismemberment by Serbia and Croatia.

The greatest weakness in Germany's position was its indifference to the predicament of Croatia's Serbs. For example, Hans-Dietrich Genscher, the German foreign minister, declared that Croatia "has achieved the highest imaginable standard of respect for minority rights," ignoring the very different findings of a five-member arbitration panel working in conjunction with an EC-sponsored Yugoslav peace conference and led by Robert Badinter, former French justice minister. In a report sent to European Community capitals on November 26, 1991, this panel concluded that Croatia's treatment of minorities did not conform to EC guidelines and that Croatia did not fulfill conditions for recognition.[24]

By insisting that it would recognize Croatia and Slovenia if the war continued, Germany also delayed a Croatian-Serbian armistice. Germany's position encouraged the Croats, whose principal goal was recognition, to continue fighting. In addition, the Germans did not withdraw their demand for the recognition of Slovenia once the fighting there had ceased. Germany pressed for recognition partly because it was well aware that historical ties and proximity would entitle it to considerable influence in an independent Croatia and Slovenia. The government was also pressured by the media, by public opinion, and by Germany's active Croatian community, all of which tended to portray the Croats as "Western" and "democratic," while the Serbs were "Eastern" and "communist."[25] There were even calls for Western military aid to Croatia and for military intervention on its behalf.[26]

The United States and all other member states of the European Community except Denmark opposed the German request for recognition and promoted a comprehensive solution. The French proposed organizing a Western European Union peace keeping force for Croatia. But the British and the French in particular did not want to confront Germany openly since it would endanger the Maastricht Agreement of December 1991, which was an important step in the further integration of the European Community and included provisions for a common foreign policy. The Germans also resorted to explicit economic and political arm-twisting. When in late 1991 Germany threatened to extend recognition on its own, other EC members acquiesced and in January 1992 recognized Croatia and Slovenia.[27] The Croats responded accordingly, and streets and squares were named for leading German and Austrian politicians. Milošević's propaganda machine was also triumphant, announcing that Serbia had been right all along in exposing the alliance between the "Fourth Reich" and "fascist" Croatia, which, according to Milošević's version of history, originated during World War II, when the Third Reich's puppet state in Croatia persecuted the Serbs.

The timing of recognition had limited effects on the Croatian-Serbian war. There would have been violent conflict even if Croatia had been recognized sooner. Earlier recognition would not have eliminated either of the two main causes of war: the harsh treatment by the Croatian government of its Serbian minority, and Serbia's policy of territorial aggrandizement. Nor was the war in Croatia halted by German recognition, as many Germans and Croats believed. It stopped because Cyrus Vance had negotiated a ceasefire after both sides had realized that they would only lose more through continued fighting. In Slovenia, fighting had ended many months before the recognition.

Germany did not save Croatia and Slovenia from more violence and deserves blame for pushing for their independence before appropriate mechanisms to avoid conflict were in place. But German behavior mainly aggravated, and did not create, the sources of conflict. To be sure, its recognition of Croatia and Slovenia did leave Bosnia-Herzegovina inside a truncated Yugoslavia dominated by Serbia, forcing the Bosnian government to seek independence. But the main causes of the Bosnian war were already in place: mounting tensions among Bosnia's Muslims, Serbs, and Croats, and the land-grabbing policies of Serbia and Croatia.

THE BOSNIAN CATASTROPHE

After World War II, Bosnia-Herzegovina made great progress in overcoming national and religious intolerance; friendships and marriages among its three groups were common. If Milošević's Serbia and Tudjman's Croatia had not been determined to carve up Bosnia-Herzegovina, the war need not have happened. And the war might even have been prevented in spite of the predatory policies of Serbia and Croatia had Bosnia enjoyed stable institutions that could have regulated relations among the republics' national groups and protected their political, cultural, and territorial rights. During the communist era, however, no such institutions developed. The Communist party ruled through coercion and repression, not through the development of robust political institutions and the inculcation of civic values. As a result, the defeat of the communists in the 1990 elections left only a political vacuum, not an institutional structure capable of withstanding the currents of nationalism whipped up by irresponsible leaders and the centrifugal forces they generated.

Since Bosnia's Parliament, courts, press, and police, had no authority as impartial institutions, affiliation with one's national group emerged as the only source of protection, whether of one's human rights or physical security. It is, therefore, no surprise that Bosnia's Muslims, Serbs, and Croats all began to behave and to vote as national-religious groups. On February 29 and March 1, 1992, a referendum on Bosnian independence was held. The Muslim-Croatian coalition, which dominated the Bosnian government, had for weeks openly argued in favor of independence, as had most of the media. Almost all Muslims and Croats voted for secession, while the Serbs simply boycotted the referendum. Bosnia-Herzegovina promptly proclaimed independence from the rump Yugoslavia. It was recognized several weeks later by the European Community and the United States, which also extended recognition to Slovenia and Croatia at that time. The recognition of Bosnia, although intended to offer the new state international legitimacy and the protection of sovereignty associated with it, had exactly the opposite effect: civil war immediately broke out.[28]

Before it extended recognition to Bosnia, the European Community did make some efforts to mediate. On March 18 an agreement was reached in Lisbon to divide Bosnia into three national territorial units. But because populations were intermixed, these units would not have been ethnically homogeneous. Nevertheless, their establishment would have helped moderate the unease of Serbs and Croats about living in a state dominated by Muslims. Izetbegović initially accepted this "federalization of Bosnia" against the objections of the more militant among the Muslim ministers. But he reneged when he realized that international recognition could be achieved even if he did not adopt the plan.[29]

Within a few months of the outbreak of fighting, the Bosnian Serbs, supported by the Serbian government and the Yugoslav army (which was now in all but name Serbian), had captured almost two-thirds of Bosnia and engaged in large-scale "ethnic cleansing" of Muslims and Croats.[30] Despite their shared suffering and common support for independence, the alliance between the Bosnian Muslims and Croats broke down. As Bosnia disintegrated as a viable political entity, an increasing number of Bosnian Croats came to shift their loyalties toward Croatia. The military of Bosnia's Croats, together with regular units from Croatia, soon captured almost a third of Bosnian territory, expelling most Muslims and Serbs. Both the Serbian and the Croatian offensives were brutal, although the Serbian advances were far more extensive. Murder and rape were common and religious and cultural monuments were systematically destroyed. These crimes were tolerated and perhaps even encouraged by the respective military authorities as part of an overall strategy of intimidation and expulsion.

THE EMBARGO AGAINST SERBIA AND MONTENEGRO

On May 30, 1992, the United Nations imposed on Serbia and Montenegro an international trade embargo.[31] This punishment for belligerent policies at first hurt only Serbian pride; it was some months before the embargo began to harm the Serbian economy. Milošević's political position was not weakened, both because of the limited economic effects of the embargo and because even non-nationalistic Serbs thought that it was unfair to punish Serbia and spare Croatia. So too did Muslim intransigence, at least in Serbian eyes, deserve some reproof. For the government-controlled media, the embargo confirmed that there was a worldwide conspiracy, supposedly led by Germany and the Vatican, against the Serbian people. This line of argument was nothing new; Milošević and his collaborators had presented the international community's policies as anti-Serbian long before the civil war had started.[32] Milošević was also able to manipulate the embargo to his advantage by using it as an explanation for Serbia's economic difficulties. In reality, the costs of the Croatian and Bosnian war and government mismanagement contributed at least as much as the embargo to sharp increases in unemployment, inflation, and the price of consumer goods.

War, Milošević, and the embargo all but destroyed the Serbian economy. By December 1993, for example, an average monthly wage was over 50 times smaller than in 1991. Inflation was greater than it had been in Germany in the early 1920s. Inflation was brought under control in 1994, but not before the middle class had virtually disappeared. Serbian society was being divided into a wealthy minority, consisting mostly of war profiteers, and a very poor majority.

Although the embargo took a serious toll on the civilian population, it did have positive effects. Combined with preventive deployments and threats of large air-strikes against Serbian forces, it made Milošević readier to make compromises.[33] In addition, by weakening the Serbian economy, it limited Serbia's ability to carry out large military offensives. With a stronger military, Milošević's policies in Kosovo and Macedonia might have been more predatory.

THE TRAGEDY OF THE BOSNIAN MUSLIMS

The West initially reacted to the fighting and to Serbian and Croatian gains by insisting that it would not accept any change in the borders of Bosnia-Herzegovina by force and that a unitary Bosnian state should be restored.[34] Even the earlier plan for a tripartite federation was abandoned. Despite these high-minded and principled pronouncements, however, nothing was done to stop the Serbs and Croats from conquering more and more territory and from expelling more and more Muslims. Restricting itself to the delivery of humanitarian aid, the West offered the Muslims its moral support but little else.

By the late summer of 1992, it was becoming increasingly clear that the West's protestations were insufficient to make the well-armed and well-supplied Bosnian Serbs and Bosnian Croats give the territories under their control back to the Bosnian government. And even if they had withdrawn, the hatred and mistrust left behind by the brutal fighting made it hard to imagine that, without massive foreign intervention, the three Bosnian groups could have reunited into one state.[35] Intervention by a United Nations force of several hundred thousand soldiers tasked with disarming the military forces of all three groups and restoring Bosnia's original frontiers would have been the best solution for the majority of ordinary Bosnian people—for the Serbs and Croats no less than for the Muslims. It offered the most promise of giving peace. The presence of foreign troops would also have guaranteed safety and allowed the reintegration of communities. But fear of casualties and unease about committing a large military contingent for an indefinite time prevented the West from intervening and from putting Bosnia-Herzegovina under a UN protectorate. Absent the willingness to make this sacrifice, the West should have thrown its support behind the only other option for bringing peace to Bosnia-Herzegovina: its permanent partition.

It would not have been easy for the West to concede that it was a mistake to support the maintenance of a unified Bosnia-Herzegovina. Yet if in the late summer of 1992 or soon thereafter Western leaders had reversed their policy and decided to partition Bosnia-Herzegovina, a great deal of killing and devastation would probably have been avoided. The Muslims would also have retained more territory and were in a better negotiating position. They were not yet exhausted, and the Bosnian Croats and Serbs had not yet consolidated their hold over conquered territories.

The West should have pressed the Bosnian Serbs and Croats to give back significant territories to the Muslims. In return, Bosnian Serbs and Croats should have been offered the right to join the Bosnian territory under their control with Serbia and Croatia, respectively. Such a partition would have required Western military involvement, in particular for the patrolling of newly created borders, but the troops needed for the task would have been far fewer than those that would be needed to reunite Bosnia-Herzegovina. Serbian and Croatian leaders might initially have resisted returning territories, but any risk of losing the offer of uniting with Serbia and Croatia— which was the principal goal of the struggle—would have met with enormous resistance from ordinary Bosnian Serbs and Croats, probably forcing their leaders to compromise.

Instead of pursing this path, the West continued to view Serbia as the principal aggressor and to insist that aggression would not be rewarded. Since the beginning of the war in Bosnia, Western governments, analysts, and the media tended to place primary responsibility for the fighting on Bosnia's Serbs and Serbia. In doing so, they underestimated the extent to which the Croats also attempted to carve up Bosnia and the extent to which Muslim intransigence contributed to the outbreak of hostilities. So too did Western attention focus almost entirely on the crimes committed by Serbian troops while ignoring similar crimes perpetrated by Croats and Muslims.

To be sure, Serbian troops committed more atrocities than their Croatian and Muslim counterparts and the Muslims suffered far more grievously than the Croats or Serbs. In addition, the Serbs pursued territorial aggrandizement far more aggressively than other parties. But if Western media and politicians had devoted at least some attention to the crimes committed against the Serbs, their influence on Serbian public opinion would have been much greater. In addition, by proclaiming the Muslims to be the victims of Serbian aggression and their struggle as unquestionably legitimate, the West actually did the Muslims a disservice. Expecting that Western troops would come to their aid, they felt little need to compromise and continued their losing battle, even though their Serbian and Croatian adversaries were obviously stronger.

Western reluctance to admit the failure of its policies led to the Vance-Owen Plan, first formulated in January of 1993.[36] Cyrus Vance, representing the United Nations, and Lord Owen, representing the European Community, tried to achieve the impossible—keep Bosnia united and satisfy the Serbs and Croats at the same time. To do this they suggested dividing Bosnia into ten semi-autonomous units, all with mixed populations, but with one group a majority in each. The plan assumed that all refugees would return home, but it provided no guarantees for their safety had they done so. Instead it seemed likely that in the ten semi-autonomous units ethnic cleansing would have continued—a large presence of UN troops was not planned and there was nothing to prevent the strongest group from expelling everyone else. Those units having the same majority population might also have tried to unite with each other and establish buffers against units in which other groups dominated.

The greatest weakness of the plan was that it called for a common Muslim-Serbian-Croatian government for the whole of Bosnia. A coalition government of this sort had existed in Bosnia for over a year before the civil war started. However, it could neither govern nor legislate. After all the killing and destruction, it was unrealistic to suggest that it should be restored without troops to support it. By the beginning of spring, the West began to appreciate that the plan was unworkable. The Bosnian Serbs remained intransigent despite NATO's tentative steps toward greater military involvement. Even a frightened Milošević urged them to sign the Vance-Owen Plan.[37] Equally significant in convincing the West to abandon the plan was the intensification of Muslim-Croatian fighting, which underscored the difficulties involved in pushing the parties toward peace and in avoiding partition without much deeper Western involvement.

TOWARD THE PARTITION OF BOSNIA

In June 1993, after more than a year of brutal fighting, the West finally recognized the need for the partition of Bosnia-Herzegovina into three republics, even if these republics were to belong to a loose confederation. By that time, Bosnia was effectively already partitioned. All three national groups had functioning political and administrative bodies and armed forces on their territories and each unit enjoyed the adherence and loyalty of the majority of its population. The three parties were not, however, inclined to negotiate an end to the fighting.

Encouraged by their military successes and Western passivity, Bosnian Serbs and Croats were less willing in the summer of 1993 to satisfy Muslim territorial demands than they would have been earlier. And the Muslims found the territory being offered them unacceptable. The Muslim leader Alija Izetbegović repeatedly stated in Geneva in late August 1993 that for the Muslims to accept the territories offered in the Serbian and Croatian peace proposal was "worse than war." The Serbian leader Radovan Karadžić responded by threatening that if the war continued, Bosnia-Herzegovina might be divided between Serbs and Croats, leaving the Muslims with no territory at all. Mate Boban, the leader of the Bosnian Croats, also mentioned the possibility of leaving Muslims without a homeland. If this had happened, the Muslims would have remained as minorities in Serbian and Croatian territories.[38]

When the peace negotiations for Bosnia-Herzegovina began in September 1992 in Geneva, journalists called the talks "a peace marathon." The journalists were prescient: negotiations dragged on during 1993 and 1994. By the end of 1993, the Serbs controlled nearly two-thirds of Bosnian territory, the Muslims about 10 percent, and the Croats had the rest. Under Western pressure, the Serbs and Croats agreed that Muslims were entitled to one-third of Bosnia. The leaders of the Bosnian Muslims accepted in principle one-third, but there were bitter disagreements over individual territories and opposition to an overall agreement from within the Muslim camp.

At the same time, many Serbs and Croats opposed a settlement. Their hopes for territorial enlargement, mostly at the expense of the Muslims, remained alive. Vuk Drašković, the chief opposition leader in Serbia, spoke for many Serbs when in December 1993 he advocated dividing Bosnia-Herzegovina between the Serbs and Croats.[39] And the Democratic party, while claiming to be a champion of moderation and democratic principles, often opposed Milošević for not being sufficiently energetic in his defense of Serbian interests in Bosnia. Unhappiness with the terms of a settlement and skepticism about whether a settlement would hold prevented agreement from emerging.

In the beginning of 1994, the West's attitude toward the Serbs hardened. On February 19, following President Clinton's initiative, NATO issued an ultimatum to the Bosnian Serbs. They were to remove or put under UN control their artillery besieging Sarajevo; otherwise, it would be destroyed by NATO air-attacks. The Muslim forces from Sarajevo were also to put their artillery under UN control. Both sides acquiesced. Russian troops under the UN flag played an important role in this partial disarmament and moved into positions between the combatants. Russian involvement helped reassure the Serbs that their interests would be defended. It also reduced Moscow's reluctance to allow force to be used in pressuring the parties to accept a territorial settlement.

In late February and March, U.S. pressure forced Croats and Muslims to stop fighting. Both parties then sent representatives to the White House in Washington, D.C., and signed an agreement for a Muslim-Croatian federation in Bosnia and subsequently joining it with Croatia to form a confederation. The federation, however, never became a functioning political entity. The Bosnian Muslim and Croatian armed forces remained separate (although they did coordinate efforts in the fall of 1994), and the mistrust between the two groups was so intense that it made the functioning of democratic institutions impossible.[40] Nor did the "ethnic cleansing" cease: Muslims continued to leave areas under Croatian control while Croats left areas under Muslim control.[41]

In the summer of 1994, a new international peace plan for Bosnia was advanced. It permitted the Bosnian Serbs a large degree of self-rule and a confederation with Serbia, but demanded that Bosnia still be preserved as a single state. The plan envisaged that the Serbs would get 49 percent of Bosnian territory, and Croats and Muslims 51 percent. This plan meant that the Serbs had to give back to the Muslims and Croats a number of important cities, river valleys, and mineral deposits. The Bosnian Croats and Muslims accepted the plan, but the Serbs rejected it.

Milošević, however, decided to support the plan, as did the leading Serbian opposition party. In order to put pressure on Bosnian Serbs, Serbia closed its borders with Bosnia to all shipments other than food and medical aid. In return for Serbia's cooperation, the UN partly lifted the embargo: international air traffic and cultural and sports exchanges were permitted. Although it is uncertain whether Serbia is fully complying with its commitment to close its border with Bosnia, Milošević's gambit promises to ease his country's isolation in the international community.

THE nationalist forces that underlay the breakup of Yugoslavia and the war in Bosnia had deep roots in the ethnic, religious, and cultural identities of the region. Decades of Yugoslavia's existence as a unitary state did not eradicate tensions among the country's national groups; coercive state rule succeeded only in keeping them in check. But despite these historically based tensions, the war need not have happened. It was precipitated by two predominant factors. First, the communist regime never built viable political institutions to codify and regulate relations among the country's national groups. When the regime collapsed, neither civic identities nor the institutions needed to support them persisted. Conditions were ripe for ethnicity to reemerge as a dominant source of social and political cleavage.

Second, irresponsible elites—Milošević and Tudjman led the way—capitalized on these conditions to manipulate public opinion to their own political gain. The nationalistic sentiments that Croatian and Serbian leaders were able to incite among their respective national groups in turn fueled the pursuit of policies of territorial aggrandizement and "ethnic cleansing." While Izetbegović was by no means blameless, the Muslims did not embark on a policy of territorial aggression as did the Croatian and Serbian leaders. However, his frequent references to Muslim hegemony in Bosnia played into the hands of both Croatian and Serbian nationalists and helped to provoke anti-Muslim sentiments.

Inconsistent and tentative Western involvement was insufficient to arrest the violence precipitated by these mounting nationalist sentiments. The war could have been moderated, if not prevented, had Western governments reacted differently. The West's key mistake was that, during the early stages of the war, it failed to match its resolve with a realistic plan for peace. If the West wanted to keep Bosnia united, it should have used force early on and stopped aggression by all parties. If the West was unwilling to back up its words with military intervention, then it was wrong to stand in the way of the obvious alternative: the partition of Bosnia into three separate states. Western rhetoric simply built hope among Muslims of impending military assistance and played into Serbian myths of encirclement and conspiracy.

The West's policies during the later stages of the war have been more in line with the end-game it was seeking to achieve. By trying to nudge parties toward settlement through a mix of punishment and reward, and by demonstrating a willingness to send in troops to enforce a settlement, the West came upon a more appropriate recipe for peace. But after years of unfulfilled promises, all sides are fearful that a peace agreement will not hold, and the Bosnian Serbs in particular have been too difficult to convince that their interests will be better served through peace than through war.

6

Nationalism in
Southeastern Europe

Ivo Banac

In this chapter I seek to formulate a typology of Balkan national ideologies, understanding the region as a peripheral area within Europe, and to analyze these ideologies in the context of the ideological currents prevailing in the European center(s). This exercise will establish the central role of nationalism in current Balkan conflicts, and demonstrate the dependence of all Balkan nationalisms on West European and Russian models. In the process we will reveal the bankruptcy of much Western commentary on Balkan nationalisms, which shares the kinds of assumptions made by Francis Fukuyama when he recently invoked "senseless nationalism of the Yugoslav variety."[1] There is, in reality, no such variety.

For this author, nationalism is always an ideology, not a sense of identity (national consciousness) or a political movement (national-liberation movement). Its shapers generally (but not always) belong to the intellectual elite of society. Nevertheless, the ideologizing (or "imagining") of this elite must always depend on the language of real life. As Marx and Engels had it in *The German Ideology*, "Consciousness can never be anything else than conscious existence, and the existence of men is their actual life-process. If in all ideology men and their circumstances appear upside-down as in a *camera obscura*, this phenomenon arises just as much from their historical life-process as the inversion of objects on the retina does from their physical life-process."[2]

This essay proceeds from the authentic history of Balkan national ideologies, but we shall not explore the channels whereby the real life-processes of the Balkan peoples shaped these national reflexes. The emphasis is on selected types and subtypes, and it varies from one historical period to another. Thus, we follow the East Central European type in both its Croat variant and its Slovene subtype. In addition, we examine the Eastern Balkan type in its Serbian variant, making some references to the case of Bulgaria, and treat its multicultural subtype in the Albanian variant. We chart the development of nationalist ideology in the succession of European historical periods, from protonational, to national revivalist, integral/national, fascist, communist, and, finally, postcommunist.

SINCE medieval times the East Central European lands, or more precisely the lands of the Hungaro-Croat and Polish-Lithuanian crowns, have lagged behind Western Europe in terms of economic and cultural development. The rustic and nonurban vastness of the East lent itself to concentrated grain production for export. This lucrative business brought on the phenomenon of "second serfdom," which reached maturity in the seventeenth century, just as the Western peasantry was loosening the bonds of agrarian serfdom. The economy of grain export retarded the process of urbanization, the growth of manufacture, and the development of the middling strata. Instead, it further enhanced the corporate spirit of the gentry, especially its magnate upper crust, precisely at the moment when absolutism became the measure of royal (usually foreign) governance.

The resulting seesaw between the absolutist state and its gentry opponents took on a new guise with the emergence of the nineteenth-century national movements. Not only were these movements inspired and frequently led by the gentry, but they in several ways perpetuated a now democratized version of upper-class corporatism. First, they represented a coalition of interests for which social harmony was held to be the measure of national survival. Second, they preserved the political culture of the gentry within a new elite—the specifically East European intelligentsia, which was increasingly seen as the modern embodiment of gentry legitimacy in political leadership. Third, since the programs of these national movements generally did not transgress the bounds of struggle for state independence, social reforms were diminished, including those that could have benefited the area's overwhelming peasant majorities. Fourth, class corporatism was transformed into national collectivism, which, in turn, frequently and unwittingly undermined precisely the democratic goals that the national movements themselves espoused. Thus, the most dramatic historical crises of the nineteenth and twentieth centuries posed a choice between alliance with equal neighbors and dominance (usually in partnership with some outside power) over subordinate tenants. Most East Central European leaders, certainly from Ferenc Deák and Gyula Andrássy in Hungary in 1866 to the shapers of "independent" Eastern Europe in 1918, opted for the latter. This choice became preponderant along the whole political diapason, no less among Béla Kun's Hungarian Communards than on the nationalist Right.

In the Orthodox Balkans, where between the fourteenth and sixteenth centuries the Ottomans had destroyed the Christian landed elite, native leadership was vested exclusively in the Orthodox churches. Orthodox prelates substituted for the gentry, performing its tasks in national culture and historical memory. As a result, the nineteenth-century anti-Turkish uprisings (in Serbia, Greece, and Bulgaria) were by definition both confessional and national, and this circumstance occasioned a lasting popular suspicion of religious and national diversity. But these uprisings were also social, and brought about an economy of peasant smallholders, intolerant of class differences. Small wonder that the golden age of national statehood in the Balkans (from the Congress of Berlin in 1878 to the First World War) was also a period of extreme national tensions and attempts to correct history not just by the pen, but through state policy. Expulsions and exoduses of whole populations, culminating in the Balkan wars of 1912–13, were the sad epitaph to the lifting of the Ottoman yoke.

The Balkan experience would belie its sanguinary reputation had the historical evolution of nationalism within the peninsula's broad geographic expanse conformed to the two types—East Central European and Eastern Balkan—sketched above. But historical reality is messy, and recurrent variations complicate our story. Croatia is probably closest to the pure East Central Europe type, although its twentieth-century history contains unique twists and turns. Slovenia, the name coined for the Slavic parts of Carniola, Styria, and Carinthia in 1848, represents an interesting subvariant of the East Central European type in its absence of state tradition and domestic (national) gentry elite, as well as in the strong political influence of Catholic clerical leadership. The experiences of Serbia, Greece, and Bulgaria are the essence of the Eastern Balkan type, but subvariants also exist. Romania, for example, retained a secular Orthodox elite in both its Phanariot and domestic *boer* nobility. Nor was it a country of peasant smallholders, even after Alexandru Ioan Cuza's Reform of 1864 abolished the corvée and tithe obligations but, in the Russian fashion, fell far short of a genuine land reform. Finally, one can speak of a multicultural subtype of historical development among the predominantly Muslim Balkan peoples—notably the Bosnians (in their nationally undifferentiated early nineteenth-century guise) and Albanians. These communities had no Western-style gentry, but substituted for them the very un-Ottoman hereditary *fis* (tribal) chiefs in northern Albania (some of them Catholic) and the dynastic *ayan* (chief) and *kapudan* (captain) notables in Bosnia and parts of Albania. Both had a tradition of Western medieval statehood (*regnum Bozne, regnum Albaniae*), and their

Catholic and Orthodox hierarchs exercised political leadership among the Bosnian and Albanian Christians.

The protonational period in Croatia (from the sixteenth to the end of eighteenth centuries) was the era of Baroque and Enlightenment Slavism. With their grand sense for emotional states and their search, first, for unitary systems and, then, for societal perfectibility within a discernible and rational cosmos, these cultural modes sounded the main intellectual themes of the European Baroque and Enlightenment. Equivalents could be found in all Catholic Slavic countries and among the Slavic Protestants.[3] Their common themes were the unity of all Slavic peoples "from the Dubrovnik province to the frozen Northern Sea,"[4] the need for mutual reliance among the Slavs despite religious differences, the leadership role of the independent Slavic states (Poland and Muscovy), language standardization as the means of Slavic integration, and the corporate preponderance of the nobility (with allowances for occasional deviations toward autocracy in the independent Slavic states).

It should be stressed that none of the Croat protonational ideologists, perhaps least of all the increasingly rationalist clerics, nurtured religious bigotry.[5] But the integrative zeal of the Croat Baroque and Enlightenment Slavists never lessened the importance that most of them, particularly those from the Habsburg Kingdom of Croatia, accorded to Croat statehood. This was especially the case for Pavao Ritter Vitezović (1652–1713), the real father of Pan-Croatianism, who claimed the whole of the Slavic Balkans for the Croat crown.[6] This Croat emphasis on statehood stands in striking contrast to the regional consciousness of the German-speaking elite of Carniola. Johann Weikhard von Valvasor's *Die Ehre des Hertzogthums Crain* (1689) is an example of Baroque erudition, but also an indication that modern Slovenia had virtually no prerevivalist national reflection, let alone ideology.

The situation among the Orthodox Serbs (and to a lesser extent the Bulgars) was considerably different. The Serbs had transferred their autocephalous church organization from the Ottoman Balkans (Peć in Metohia) to the Habsburg lands after the Great Migration (1690). At the moment when the Habsburg armies were contending with the Ottomans for control of the Balkans, Vienna was not inclined to accede to the calls for a Serbian state, perhaps under Habsburg protection, made by Count Đorđe Branković, a Transylvanian Serb who employed a vast array of historical proofs in order to demonstrate his descent from Serbia's medieval Nemanjić dynasty. However valuable Branković might have proved as a pawn, the Habsburg authorities seized him and kept him in detention until his death in 1711.[7] Instead of allowing the migrant Serbs a secular leadership, Vienna preferred to extend the responsibility for national representation to the Orthodox church heirarchs, thereby transferring the essentials of the Ottoman *millet* system (religious autonomy and self-governance reserved for the Christian and Jewish "nations") to Central Europe.

With their see in Srijemski Karlovci (Carlowitz), the Serbian Orthodox patriarchs and metropolitans were not slow to take advantage of Habsburg confidence. Arsenije IV Jovanović-Šakabenta devised a comprehensive ideological system which suggested that the patriarch was not only the heir of the Serbian kings, but the leader of all the other Orthodox Balkan peoples, notably the Bulgars and the Orthodox Albanians. Within this system, Serbdom was held to be equivalent to Orthodoxy. Hence, there was a strong likelihood that within this new Serbian ecclesiastical jurisdiction Orthodox non-Serbs would be Serbianized just as they had been under the Ottomans.[8] This was the point of Karlovci's ecclesiastical policies in Croatia proper and Dalmatia, as well as among the Romanians in the Banat. The secular version of Orthodox ecclesiastical Slavism could be found in the works of Zaharija Orfelin, whose glorification of a modernizing Peter the Great included a spirited defense of Orthodoxy against Western criticisms.

Among the Albanians, protonational ideological activity in the sixteenth and seventeenth centuries was the solitary work of northern Catholic clergy, all of whom advanced Albanian language and literature and promoted liberation projects against the Ottomans. In Albania, as in Bosnia, Catholic clergy preserved the memory of medieval statehood. Frano Bardhi, for example, wrote an apologia on the Albanian character of Gjergj Kastrioti Scanderbeg, who was also claimed by Croats and Serbs.[9] Muslim Albanian contemporaries of these seventeenth-century Catholic authors, though occasionally social critics, advanced no theories or reflections on Albanian nationhood. They still operated within the Ottoman system of religious identity.

The decisive period of national ideology in Southeastern Europe was the age of national revivals, which corresponds with the era of revolution and romanticism in Western Europe. Indeed, following the Napoleonic incorporation of most Slovenian and Croatian lands (mainly those south of the Sava River) into the Illyrian Provinces (1809–14), the Slovenes and the Croats joined Western Europe and, with it, the French system of theorizing. This left direct traces in their national revivals, especially that of the Slovenes, who were stirred to national awareness by explicit Francophiles like Valentin Vodnik. In general, however, the Slovene revivalist movement followed the German romanticist trend of equating nationhood with language. Some intellectuals from peripheral Slovene areas, such as the Styrian Stanko Vraz, did incline toward Croat Illyrianism, whereby Slovenes would have been subjoined to an "Illyrian" nationhood predicated on the štokavian dialect (common to most Croats and nearly all Serbs) and incorporated into Croat statehood. The Carniolan line of Jernej Kopitar and France Prešeren prevailed, however, and Slovene national integration was based on native

Slovenian idioms, transformed into a modern literary language by the creative genius of Prešeren.[10]

The case of historicist Croatia could not have been equivalent. The Croat national revival commenced after the death of Emperor Joseph II (1790) with a conflict over linguistic prerogatives. At that point the Magyar nobility opted for the Hungarian language as the surest defense against the potential revival of Josephine centralizing Germanization. In its Illyrianist phase from the 1830s and 1840s, under the leadership of Ljudevit Gaj and Count Janko Drašković, the Croat revival opted for a literary language based on the štokavian dialect, thereby ending the standardized literatures of the Croat kajkavians and čakavians (that is, the literary traditions of Gaj and Drašković's native kajkavian dialect region around Zagreb). Gaj's dictum "May God grant long life to the Hungarian constitution, the Kingdom of Croatia, and Illyrian nationhood" sums up the complex themes of the Croat revival.[11]

Gaj operated within the common Hungarian (not just Magyar) legal theory which, however undemocratic and based on gentry corporatism, nevertheless represented an obstacle to autocracy. Whereas Austria was autocratic, Hungary and Croatia had their diets. When contending with the Magyars, Gaj used the weapon of Croatia's ancient statehood, or Croat state right (never in the plural as is often mistranslated, because there was only one state right). Neither he nor any other Croat national ideologist could abandon this principle, because this rusty weapon was the only sure defense within the concentric circles of Habsburg legalism. It also constituted the Croats' one advantage vis-à-vis all the other Slavs of Hungary (and the Austrian Slovenes, too). In the Habsburg system, the Croats had a diet and a prorex (viceroy). Serbs and Slovenes (as well as Slovaks) had no such advantages, which is why the legal interests of all the Habsburg South Slavs could be advanced only within the bounds of Croat statehood. In 1918, when Austria-Hungary collapsed, only the act of the Croatian Sabor (diet) could effect the legal separation of the South Slavs from both Austria and Hungary. Finally, Gaj made Croat statehood coextensive with South Slavic linguistic (Illyrian) nationhood based on the štokavian dialect.

In all this, Gaj followed the heritage of Vitezović. Croat national integration preserved the delicate balance between political Croatism and cultural Illyrianism (South Slavism, ultimately Yugoslavism). This was a formula that reflected typical East Central European dilemmas between Hungarianism and Magyardom, Bohemianism and Czechdom. Religion played virtually no part in its construction. In essence, this form of national integration represented a peaceful transition to modernity in which gentry corporatism and a romantic insistence on authentic linguistic expression were coequal. The Serbian case is very different. Here the shaping of modern national ideology was premised upon a revolution against the conservative ecclesiastical leadership and against notions that Serbdom and Orthodoxy were equivalent. The separation between the two was performed by Vuk Karadžić (1787–1864), the standardizer of the modern Serbian language who overthrew the artificial, Church Slavonic–based, Slavo-Serbian language of the elite and replaced it with the robust štokavian of the politically emancipated masses.[12]

Karadžić's activities in large part coincided with the struggle for Serbian state emancipation, an anti-Ottoman revolution that started with Karađorđe Petrović's uprising in 1804 and ended with the acquisition of autonomy in 1830. In this context, Karadžić's lasting contribution was the secularization of Serbian nationhood, which he defined not by adherence to Orthodoxy, but by use of the štokavian dialect which, bowing to the tradition of German romanticism, he defined as purely Serbian. Karadžić's "linguistic" nationhood created new problems. Orthodox believers (Bulgars, Macedonians, Albanians, Vlachs) who previously were assimilated within the Serbian nation by virtue of their membership in the Serbian ecclesiastic organization were no longer the prime targets of assimilation. The new targets were the speakers of štokavian, meaning that, in Belgrade, most Croats and all Bosnian Muslims were increasingly regarded as Serbs. In short, the emergence of the Serbian state and the new "linguistic" definition of Serbdom created the grounds for permanent conflict between the Serbs and their Western neighbors.

Secularized national ideologies, not religion, now became the motor of contention. But whereas the Croats, and in some respects the Slovenes, protected themselves from the logic of contention by the predominantly integrationist strains of their national ideologies, the Serbs had no such safety net. The logic of Serbian national ideologies was best expressed in the program of Serbian state expansion promoted by Ilijia Garašanin, Serbia's minister of the interior. In his *Načertanije* (1844), Garašanin argued that the frontiers of the new Serbia had to be extended to all areas where Serbs lived and, after Karadžić, these frontiers were linguistic. As a result, the line between romanticism and the scientistic integral nationalism of the positivist period (last quarter of the nineteenth century) would be quite blurred among the Serbs.[13]

Nevertheless, religion did not disappear as a factor in Serbian nationalism. Instead it became secularized, or more exactly, modern nationalism entered into theological discourse, weakening the integrity of the Serbian and other Balkan Orthodox churches. The influence of N. Ia. Danilevskii, a father of Pan-Slavism and one who manipulated religious themes to serve Russian imperial projects, was important in this regard. Danilevskii rejected the universal values of the Slavophiles (true Christianity, Slavic principles) and instead promoted the notion of the Pan-Slavic "historico-cultural" type, characterized by an Orthodoxy that was the handmaiden of Russian great-power chauvinism. Danilevskii's "Benthamite principle of utilitarianism," so typical of predatory themes in late nineteenth century European national-isms,[14] had its followers in Serbia and Bulgaria. Nikola Pašić, the head of the Radical Party and Serbia's leading statesman during the first quarter of the twentieth century, assimilated Danilevskii's ideas and used them to justify his thesis that the Serbs (who were always on the side of the East), not the Croats, had the historical right to become the axis of the South Slavic state. That state itself would be part of a Pan-Slavic empire, headed by the Russian tsar in a restored Constantinople.[15]

Among the Croats, integral nationalism was the handiwork of disap-pointed Illyrianists like Ante Starčević, the leader of the Party of (Croat State) Right, whose Jacobin instincts were expressed in a theory of "political nationhood" that owed a great deal not only to liberal centralism but also to overall assimilationist concepts of citizenship, as practiced in Western Europe—and in Hungary. For Starčević the Croats were, quite simply, the inhabitants of Croatia—all of them—and Croat territory included, he in-sisted, the lands of all the South Slavs, except the Bulgars. This grandiose vision inevitably provoked a conflict with the Serbs, whose right to a separate identity (but never to a separate political territory within Croatia) was pro-tected by Bishop Josip Juraj Strossmayer and other opponents of Starčević's. In fact Starčević's defense of state right became the only obstacle in the path of Croat political Yugoslavists. When the Nationalist Youth of the ante-bellum period (1908–14) adopted Yugoslavist national unitarism—that is, the idea that the Serbs, Croats, and Slovenes were identical, but trinomial—they merely took Starčević's Croat "political nationhood" and filled it with "Yugoslav" content.[16]

Among the Slovenes the era of integral nationalism developed in the direction of a typically Central European split between the Catholics and liberals/socialists, which was never a significant issue in Croatia. This split presupposed a struggle over Yugoslavism, which, with exceptions (Ivan Cankar), had a more integral flavor on the left than on the right. Integral nationalism was not important among the Albanians, where the belated national revival, culminating in the League of Prizen (1878), performed the task of national integration, which was predicated on sidestepping the re-ligious differences between Muslims and Christians.[17] Nevertheless, integral nationalism continued as a dominant trend into the era of national state-hood. Serbia and Montenegro were recognized as independent in 1878, Bulgaria in 1908. Albania became nominally independent in 1912, and Yugoslavia was established in 1918.

We shall not pursue the path of the national ideologies that accompanied the unification of Yugoslavia, except to note that the integralist and assimilationist strains of Croat and Serb national ideologies respectively persisted unabated during the early years of the new state. Still, the crisis of European civilization that marked the end of the First World War inevitably created a revolution in ideology, bringing to the fore two modern totalitarianisms— communism and fascism.

Practically all accounts of Balkan nationalisms in the age of European fascism overlook the dictatorship of King Aleksandar in Yugoslavia, which represented a variant of fascism of the East Balkan type. During this period (1929–34), Yugoslavist unitarism graduated into a fascist ideology. It acquired several aspects of fascism, including anti-Marxism, anti-liberalism, anti-conservatism (specifically anti-Catholic and anti-traditional reactionary modernism), and anti-urbanism. The Serbian fascist party Zbor (Assembly) of Dimitrije Ljotić inherited many of the themes of Aleksandrine monarcho-fascism and (like Romania's Iron Guard) developed them in the direction of an Orthodox religious exclusivism.[18]

Influenced by the writings of Fyodor Dostoevsky, the Zborists and their ecclesiastical mentors (Nikolaj Velimirović, Justin Popović) grafted a religiously based nationalism onto Serbian Orthodox theology. Earlier, religious polemics between Orthodox and Catholics had been argued in the language of theology. With the emergence of the ideology of *svetosavlje* (Orthodoxy of Saint Sava), named after the first autocephalous archbishop of the Serbian church, *cultural* differences came to define these disputes. The East was seen as the realm of grace, the West as that of law and power-mongering. Defined in these terms the minor theological differences between the Orthodox and Catholics were transformed into insurmountable cultural precipices that obviated the need for polemic, let alone the possibility of conversion. Such an approach dulled the assimilationist tradition of the Serbian national ideologies and eased the way for Nazi racism, particularly in regard to the Jews.[19]

Nevertheless, as an organization of the Orthodox clerico-fascist type Zbor was generally devoid of the characteristically fascist anti-conservatism, and racism was relatively underdeveloped in its ranks. The Chetniks, the Serbian royalist guerrillas who collaborated with the Italians and Germans during the Axis occupation of Yugoslavia, were not fascist in ideology or inspiration. Although they carried out "ethnic cleansing" of Muslims and Croats, accompanied by large-scale massacres in Bosnia and Dalmatia, their ideology was not racist and represented a continuation of Serbian integral nationalism.[20] Much the same can be said for various collaborationist tendencies in Albania, which, however impregnated by Italian fascist imports, represented no more than the activist phase of an older integral nationalism. Racism and anti-conservatism were not present in its ranks even during the Nazi occupation (1943–45).

Within the East Central Europe type, the Croat and Slovene fascist organizations were fragmented movements displaying all the elements of hybrid models. The Ustašas (Insurgents) of Croatia emerged after the beginning of King Aleksandar's dictatorship as a typical integral nationalist organization with characteristics that had long marked the Balkan insurgent tradition. As a result, the "fourth period" communists (1928–35) concluded that the Ustašas were bent on "limited parliamentary cretinism"[21] and, thus, could not be relied upon as allies in the struggle against the dictatorship. By the end of the 1930s, however, the Ustašas had become a typical fascist organization, bearing all the earmarks of Mediterranean fascism. But on their fringes, as later in Slovenia, one could detect examples of Catholic clerico-fascism of the Spanish Francoist type. As a result, despite the Ustašas' strong rhetorical anti-Semitism and their persecution of Jews during the Second World War, racist elements were relatively underdeveloped among both the Ustašas and the Slovene fascists. Their anti-conservatism was equally underdeveloped, as is plain from their petit-bourgeois infatuation with the gentry tradition. In fact, the most salient traits of the Ustašas were their cult of the Croat state and their virulent anti-Serbianism. Despite their deserved ill fame for death camps and massacres, the Ustašas left the door open to Serb assimilationism via Catholicism, thereby reaffirming that they were basically an integral nationalist organization committed to a statist, "political nationhood."[22]

IF Balkan fascist nationalisms were on the whole less extreme ideologically than the Nazi racist model, the nationalist themes of Balkan communism generally conformed to those that characterized the Soviet model. (The liberal period in Yugoslavia [1962–1971] is the obvious exception to this general rule.) In order to understand the nature of Balkan nationalisms under communism, it is important to bear in mind that communism (rather than fascism) represented the realization, however distorted, of nativist anti-capitalist themes. This was the case whether the seizure of power was accomplished by domestic armed struggle and revolutionary seizure of power (Yugoslavia, Albania) or by Soviet military intervention (Bulgaria, Romania). Under fascism the Balkans were a periphery of a West European–based *Festung Europa*. Under communism, for the first time since the Ottoman period (never present in Slovenia, but real in Albania until 1912), the Balkans found themselves a periphery of a non-Western center. Even at the height of the "socialist camp" in the 1950s, when Eastern Europe, the USSR, and China commanded vast human and material resources, communism failed to overcome its peripheral status vis-à-vis the West, thereby signaling its ultimate demise. This failure was immense not just in the realm of economic processes, but also in the realm of ideology.

Notwithstanding the widespread notion that communism had a kind of "icebox effect," immobilizing Balkan nationalisms for four decades, any discussion of East European socialism must include an analysis of national ideology, which except in Yugoslavia (after 1948) and Albania (after 1961) remained an intense area of political conflict, now within the context of Soviet/Russian hegemony.

One of the basic contradictions of the Soviet system in Eastern Europe was that the official ideology held that the struggle against "bourgeois nationalism" could be directed only against those who opposed Russification, not against the Russifiers themselves. Small wonder, then, that for a long time in Eastern Europe resistance to the Soviet Union—both at the elite and grassroots levels—was essentially national. Yugoslavia led the way in 1948, followed by Poland and Hungary in 1956, Albania and Romania in the 1960s, and Czechoslovakia in 1968. Throughout Eastern Europe—and not just in the countries that confronted or broke with the Soviet Union— the elites were alert to the legitimizing potential of carefully crafted national programs. These programs were not always meant as a challenge to Moscow; a more "national" regime could after all be a more effective ally. Frequently, however, they were meant to substitute for or to forestall democratization. They were examples of what might be called bureaucratic nationalism.

From the mid-1950s on the crisis of East European socialism thus helped the national revivals in two ways. From the time that a country entered the Soviet bloc, its grassroots opposition (mainly outside but also inside the ruling parties) had made the restoration of national sovereignty part of its (not always articulated) platform. Defensive national programs of this sort were regularly directed against Soviet supremacy, but they always had various local targets, as well. In Yugoslavia the target was the dominant position of the Serbs, but in all the Balkan countries minorities sought to erode the privileges of majority nations.

Though these grassroots national movements usually stirred to life during periods of democratization, they had the potential to restore presocialist national ideologies with all their attendant features, including exclusivist integral nationalism. The national programs of the elites, in contrast, generally tended in the direction of "bureaucratic nationalism." Increasingly, as the crisis of official ideology deepened, bureaucratic nationalism, too, incorporated many features of the old national ideologies. The prewar national question was being reproduced under the conditions of crisis socialism, but with a twist: the party-state's ability to homogenize its territory surpassed that of the prewar bourgeois nationalists.

Bureaucratic nationalism was most evident in the least democratic states of the Eastern Balkan type—states that had a history of national homogenization. Thus the long-standing policies directed against the minorities in

Albania, Romania, and Bulgaria, the repression of the Hungarians in Romania, and the expulsion of the Turks from Bulgaria were not simply instances of the drastic social surgery in which communists frequently
delighted (and which Stalin had granted a kind of legitimacy through his
wholesale removal of nations). These policies represented the practical application of a new ideology—that of a disillusioned "real socialism" ready to
cohere with integral nationalism in direct resistance to democratization.
This was no longer vintage Stalinism, with its revolutionary voluntarism,
extremist zeal, and boundless optimism. This was an attempted synthesis of
national legitimacy and post-utopian state socialism in which collectivism
lost its class component and became nationalized.

Throughout the communist era, periods of democratization spawned the
growth of nationality rights, the development of federalist and autonomist
forms of governance, and the creative ferment of national cultures.
Yugoslavia's federal reform began in earnest in the mid-1960s, Czechoslovakia was federalized in 1968, and Hungary started paying serious attention
to its Slavic minorities in the 1980s. In a similar vein, repressions of mass
national movements and attacks on institutionalized diversity signaled the
repudiation of democratizing policies. Examples include Romania's aboli-
tion of the Mureş-Magyar Autonomous Region in 1968 and the denigration
of the autonomous status of Vojvodina and Kosovo within Serbia in 1989.

Outside the Soviet bloc since 1948, Yugoslavia was the Balkan country
least susceptible to the blandishments of bureaucratic nationalism. Or,
more correctly, Yugoslav bureaucratic nationalism could be predicated only
on Yugoslavist unitarism, which Tito actually favored as an ideological expression of his nationality policy from 1950 to 1962. Nevertheless, Tito's
policy of amalgamating the South Slavic nationalities into a single Yugoslav
supranation became one of the obstacles on the path to reform. Tito
changed this policy in 1962, sensing that unitarism undermined national
equality and helped the Serbian nationalist forces that were entrenched in
the Serbian organization of the League of Communists of Yugoslavia (SKJ).
There followed a series of moves that restricted centralism and legitimized
greater national liberties for the Croats, the Bosnian Muslims, and the Albanian minority in Kosovo. In fact, Tito's unstudied way of handling the national question led him in the 1960s and 1970s to espouse formal axiomatic
constructions (rotating party and state presidency, exact proportionality in
party and state organs by republic and province of origin, limited tenure in
office) that transformed the Yugoslav national question from the prewar
conflict of opposing national ideologies into the conflict over the structure
and composition of Yugoslav federation.[23]

The Titoist center was further split in 1971 with the purge of the Croatian
party leadership of Savka Dabčević-Kučar and Miko Tripalo, who argued for

what amounted to a liberal partiocratic confederation; and, in 1972, with the purge of the Serbian party leadership of Latinka Perović and Marko Nikezić, who called for Serbia's emancipation from the federal center, something that Tito saw as a direct attack on his personal rule.[24] The tragedy was that these leaderships represented the most enlightened elements on the postwar political scene. For Croatia, the forcible end of the "Croat Spring" was more than the resolution of an internal dispute in the party elite. It represented a national humiliation, which retrospectively spelled the real end of Croat Yugoslavism. For Serbia, the removal of Perović and Nikezić turned out to be the end of the high tide of Western influence. They were unquestionably the most Westernized Serbian leadership since the beginning of the Serbian revolution in 1804. After 1972 Serbia started down the path of reaction against Tito's policy of bureaucratic decentralization, which was caricatured as anti-Serbian ("Weak Serbia = Strong Yugoslavia"). In the process, the Serbian party leadership adopted a form of Serbian bureaucratic nationalism, turned against Yugoslavism in all but its Serbocentric variants, and became increasingly anti-Western and reactionary. That is why the transition to post-communism in 1990 was hardly noticed; socialism disappeared, but authoritarian collectivism remained.[25]

THE "post-communist" nationalism of Slobodan Milošević, which began to take shape in 1987, represents a new form of Serbian integral nationalism, with strains of fascist and communist influences. Though it maintains the appearance of support for parliamentary democracy, Milošević's ideology subjoins anti-democratic influences from both the left and the right. It is imbued with communist hostility to the "formalism" of democracy even as it maintains the rightist faith in the spontaneity of a homogenous people. Milošević's ideology is also anti-liberal and anti-Western. It has borrowed the restorationist communist thesis that the West is responsible for the destruction of socialism and Yugoslavia—as well as the USSR. It also expresses the reactionary Pan-Slavist thesis that the current war is the conflict waged by the Atlanticist civilization of quantity against the Eurasian civilization of quality, of vulgar materialism against the spirit of sacrifice and nobility.

Except for its few vestiges of Titoist suspicion for the Moscow center, the anti-communism of Milošević's ideology comes entirely from the right. In its more virulent contemporary forms (not necessarily Milošević's own), Serbian integral nationalism views communism as a Western ideology that sought to destroy Orthodox civilization. The Comintern in particular is portrayed as manipulative, Masonic, and alien. As for the Titoist past of Serbia's ruling Socialist party (SPS), its salient features are blamed on Tito and his "Croat-Slovene" group. The anti-conservative side of Milošević's ideology reconciles leftist and rightist themes. It is explicitly anti-Catholic, portraying the Vatican as a historical enemy of the Serbs and the principal obstacle to Serbian assimilation of the Catholic Croats. It is also explicitly anti-Islamic, thereby telescoping the traditional theme of the "Hagarite" Turkish yoke with current anti-Bosnian operations. Finally, the Milošević ideology is explicitly anti-traditionalist. It is voluntaristic. It wishes to change history. And "ethnic cleansing" is the expression of its counter-historical project. The aim is to create a nationally homogenous Great Serbia, even on the most remote territories of Serb settlement. Similar themes are present in the ideology of the formerly communist Bulgarian Socialist party. In fact, equivalent themes can be found in all the Orthodox countries of Eastern Europe, not least of all in Russia. Predominantly Muslim, but notably multicultural, Albania and Bosnia no longer fit into this pattern: their cultural subtype—represented either by Sali Berisha, Ibrahim Rugove, or Alija Izetbegović—increasingly tends in the direction of East Central Europe. The Orthodox Balkans are again aligned with a non-Western periphery. The only question is the location of its ideological epicenter.

In Croatia and Slovenia post-communist nationalisms have been less virulent. Slovene post-communist politicians, who are as varied as Milan Kučan (former Slovenian party leader) and Janez Janša (former dissident and prisoner), express the common East Central European ideology of national collectivity, but always as a subset of the dominant West European ideology of human rights. This is not a unique position and is typical of the current nationalist mean in Poland, the Czech Republic, Slovakia, and Hungary. In practice, however, Slovenia has been rough with its minorities of "southern provenance." Many of its resident Croats, Serbs, and Bosnian Muslims are being exposed to pressures over citizenship papers and tenants' rights.

The Croat situation has been somewhat different, with a fraction of Franjo Tudjman's governing Croat Democratic Union (HDZ) openly expressing integral nationalist positions. This was evident in Tudjman's leniency toward anti-Serb discrimination and vigilantism, but most especially in his anti-Bosnian war from November 1992 to March 1994, during which Croat national ideologies assumed openly anti-Muslim forms for the first time since the 1860s. In fact, Tudjman's ideology is interesting for its purely Croat national (ethnic) cast, a significant departure from the statist emphasis that is more typical of Croat national ideologies. It is evident that Tudjman, like Milošević, believes in the stability of nationally homogenous states and that he aims to gather Croats from the fringe areas of Croat settlement within a single state through "humane transfers" of people and exchanges of territory. His ideological world and political practice have isolated Croatia from Western Europe, but not to the extent that Milošević has isolated Serbia.

NATIONALISM is notoriously difficult to assess because it has myriad faces. We have demonstrated that Balkan nationalism developed in two historical types—East Central European and Eastern Balkan—that have been remarkably consistent over the last several centuries. National ideologies of both types were always rooted in the prevailing European intellectual currents, though those of the Eastern Balkan type deviated in the direction of Europe's non-Western periphery, centered primarily on Russia. The developments at the center represent horizontal and international currents; those in the Balkans vertical or historical trends. Since international currents have consistently been dominant, Balkan nationalism has never been unique or original; it has merely reflected European trends. The seemingly aberrant cases, exclusively within the Eastern Balkan typology, have been influenced ideologically by developments in Russia. Within this framework the Milošević ideology is something of a puzzle; for its history seems (so far as we can tell) to predate equivalent developments in Russia itself. All the same, our analysis would indicate that this ideology, too, expresses ongoing trends in the European center, and this is one reason why it is so alarming.

The horrors of Bosnia-Hercegovina can be read as a warning to Europe—to the whole industrial world—not to be too haughty in its assumption that internationalism has been secured. The utopia of "ethnic cleansing" is not necessarily a Balkan product. In its present version it is more often a consequence of liberal failure at integrating colored and culturally alien (mainly Islamic) immigrants. Its framework was etched by Enoch Powell in 1968 when he concluded that such immigrants cannot be assimilated and called for a policy of voluntary repatriation. Le Pen and Schönhuber have made such a policy operational. It has also gained the implicit support of portions of the left as a result of growing unemployment.

The problem of the cultural alien was evident in Europe from the moment (12 Safer 1711) when Montesquieu's Usbek and Rica reported from Livorno on the first leg of their voyage to the West.[26] Montesquieu's aliens are no longer the objects of murderous crusades, such as those waged by the Christian lords of northern Spain for more than five centuries until the fall of Granada in 1492, nor are they representatives of the terrifying Ottoman war machine that Busbecq so greatly admired in his letters to Michault in the middle of the sixteenth century. Nevertheless, Montesquieu saw them as aliens, aliens that could never be assimilated. Thus, Milošević's conviction that "the homogenization of nations and men in general . . . is the sense and aim toward which humanity has always tended" does not contradict one of the more essential marks of the Enlightenment. Hence the snare of European unity, which will not embrace the "Hagarites," or most Eastern European nations, either.

7

Three Faces of Nationalism in the Former Soviet Union

Paul A. Goble

The extraordinary diversity of nationalism among the peoples of the former Soviet Union has been compounded by the kaleidoscopic transformation in the political and social position of each group over the last five years. Not only do the more than 400 peoples provide exemplars of virtually every form of nationalism found elsewhere, but the rapidity and scope of change there has meant that many groups have passed through a variety of stages of national development.

Examining nationalism in the former Soviet Union entails three main tasks. First, we should put in context the various forms of nationalism of this region. Thus, we must explore the ways in which the Soviet system by its approach to ethnic communities both sowed the seeds of its own destruction and set in train the manifestations of nationalism we see today. Second, we need to develop a typology of nationalism for the region. We must avoid the trap of the blind men and the elephant—of inappropriately generalizing from very distinct particular cases—and we must bring to bear on each of the kinds of nationalism there the insights of Western expertise. Given the speed of developments in the region, this is no easy task; we are tracking a rapidly moving target.

Finally, we need to consider the likely trajectory of each particular kind of nationalism. This will help direct our research agendas and guide the formation of policies that might restrict the manifestation of nationalist feelings that violate the rights of other groups and allow the peoples of the region to move toward democracy and the protection of human rights.

A CRUCIBLE OF NATIONALISM

The current upsurge of nationalism throughout the territory of the former Soviet Union has its roots in what many call "ancient ethnic animosities" as well as in the policies of the successor states. But the taproot is the Soviet approach to ethnicity. Indeed, in redefining and structuring ethnic identity and its transformation into nationality, Moscow set the stage for many of the developments occurring today.

Before 1917, the tsarist authorities ruled over an enormously variegated multinational empire and did everything they could to keep ethnicity out of politics. They provided no support for any ethnic group as such—no nationality lines in passports or censuses, no ethnically based political territories, and no quotas or reserved places for any particular ethnic group. They did so because they recognized that assertions of ethnicity were ultimately about participation and therefore anathema to their premodern political system. They also saw that any support for ethnicity would lead to demands for secession, particularly in the western regions of the country. Moreover, the Russians themselves were a minority within the empire, meaning that the integrity of the state itself would be threatened by any assertions of ethnicity.

Between 1914 when World War I began and 1922 when the Soviet Union was formed, three developments transformed this situation. First, Poland, Finland, the Baltic States, and two provinces in the Caucasus successfully exited the empire. In combination with casualties incurred during World War I and the Russian Civil War, both of which were fought largely on non-Russian territories, the percentage of Russians in the population under the control of the central government rose from 43 percent to 68 percent virtually overnight. In short, the Russian Revolution was truly a *Russian* revolution. Next, the rest of the periphery tried to leave—from Belorussia and Ukraine in the west to Turkestan and Siberia in the east—and was reconquered by a largely Russian Red Army, thereby creating conditions on the ground for a classically arranged empire.

But the likely consequence of these two developments—the creation of forces which would mean that ultimately the costs of empire would become greater than its benefits—were obscured by the third development: the coming to power of Lenin and the Bolshevik party. These people, on the one hand, confidently believed that ethnicity was a "survival of the past" and thus doomed to pass away in the socialist future, but, on the other, they in fact provided the support for ethnicity that transformed it into nationality and ultimately led to the disintegration of the Soviet system.

In 1920, in his "Draft Theses on the Nationality and Colonial Question,"

Lenin laid out his understanding of the role of the state and nationality. Domestically—that is, within the confines of what had been the Russian empire—Lenin saw support for ethnicity in the form of officially sponsored ethnic identities and the creation of ethnically based statehood as both a useful tool against the Whites and the only way possible to reach people in their own language. Internationally, Lenin saw this policy as the kernel of a design for a world state, with union republics becoming the model for future socialist countries as the revolution spread.

In many respects, Lenin's views on nationality and on the desirability of large imperially ordered states were remarkably similar to contemporaneous Western liberal opinion. Western liberals also saw ethnicity as something to be overcome by "civilizing" European great powers. But one person at least did not view the Russian situation or ethnicity in the same way. Joseph Stalin's approach to the problem was to become the basis of Soviet nationality policy. In a telegram to Lenin Stalin set out his objections to Lenin's plan. No people that had been an independent country in the past, Stalin suggested, would ever be willing to accept the diminished status of being a union republic.[1] Such status would be an attack on their national self-esteem, especially since in the Soviet context union republics had no more status than the formally lower-status autonomous republics. Only nations that had been part of the Russian empire would or could accept this status, said Stalin. By doing so, he established the basis for relations among future socialist states.

But domestically, Stalin—who was both the People's Commissar for Nationality Affairs and Lenin's successor—saw that institutionalizing ethnicity could promote his vision of an authoritarian state. In that telegram and subsequently, he insisted that everyone should have to have an ethnic identity, that ethnicity must be both official and linked to territory, and that borders and other means be used in order to both institutionalize and channel ethnic hostility. Stalin strongly implied that such hostility would both justify and generate popular support for authoritarianism. His system, which sought to exploit ethnicity, ultimately if unintentionally provided the very supports for nationality—such as ethnic statehood and nationality lines in passports—that led to the end of the Soviet Union. And while his approach was modified by his successors, it remained the defining element in Soviet political life.

Soviet nationality policy and its consequences can be summed up in terms of seven propositions. In the first place, nationality was officialized and territorialized ethnicity and existed only by the permission of the state. Every individual must belong to one and only one national group. The decision was state-controlled in that options for both initial self-identification and any change in identification were limited.

Second, nationalities recognized by the state existed in a state-determined hierarchy, with larger and more favored groups given more opportunities and resources and smaller and less favored ones less of each. This hierarchy was expressed in Soviet times by the creation of a four-tiered state system extending from union republics down to autonomous districts.

Third, for all groups except the Russians, nationality was completely territorialized: one had language and other ethnic rights only within one's own ethnic territory. Russians, on the other hand, enjoyed extraterritorial status, that is, the right to use their own language and to have their own Russian-language institutions throughout the country. This practice reinforced traditional tensions such as those between Armenians and Turkic communities, but it also created new conflicts such as between Uzbeks and Turkmens. Stalin used these tensions to help him manage Soviet society.

Next, all ethnic environments were structured by the use of a limited number of carrots. Members of the titular nationalities received certain benefits in the form of quotas and reserved places in educational and other institutions. These rewards were accompanied by a large number of coercive resources—first and foremost were the familiar organs of the party, the army and the secret police. But also—and for our purposes, critical—among the latter were minority ethnic communities who were dependent for protection on the good will of the central authorities and thus could be counted on to do its bidding (and who could always be sacrificed to appease the local community when that was necessary). These minorities—including such groups as Jews and Armenians in Central Asia and Armenians in Azerbaijan and Azerbaijanis in Armenia—were sometimes created by the careful drawing of borders and at other times by state-sponsored migration programs. Such policies also had the effect of reinforcing the widespread notion that ethnicity, not citizenship, was the basis of rights.

The fifth proposition explains that all other identities—whether religious such as Islam or more broadly cultural such as Baltic—were discouraged within the political system lest they become the basis for a challenge to the central authorities. At the same time, nationality itself—Russian as well as non-Russian—was deracinated, that is, drained of its old content. Soviet leaders saw this as presaging the withering away of ethnic divisions and the fusion of identities; ethnic figures saw it as yet another charge against the Soviet system. Here too, just as in so many other areas, Soviet ethnic developments parallel ethnic developments elsewhere, with ethnicity increasing in political salience even as it loses its former specific content. Thus, for example, the first documents of the Belorussian national movement were written not in Belorussian but in Russian, the language of the power being attacked.

Sixth, because of Soviet social and economic policies, none of the nationalities—neither the Russians nor the non-Russians—developed a middle class. As a result, the repositories of national identity and tradition were the intelligentsias, who were forced to operate within the constraints of the well-known formula of "national in form, socialist in content." Without the constraints of a middle class and ultimately without the constraints of the Soviet state, nationalist spokespeople became ever more radical. Such radicalism was also fueled by Soviet insistence on identity shifts if one was to rise through the system. Thus, an Uzbek who hoped to become an academic or a Ukrainian who aspired to be a general would be forced to "act and speak Russian" to achieve such goals. In such a situation, coercion was the only way to control the ethnic tensions generated by the state itself.

Finally, in the absence of any other form of interest articulation within the political system that might have served as a cross-cutting cleavage, the ethnically based regional divisions of the country and the party meant—in the absence of coercion—that interests would be increasingly expressed along national lines. Consequently, as Moscow became less and less willing and able to impose its will throughout the country by force, regional elites and hence regional politics were rapidly ethnicized, something that has survived the breakup of the Soviet Union. Indeed, in a resource-scarce environment where the states had or have ever fewer material rewards to distribute, the use of ethnic symbolism becomes a useful political tool for mobilizing and controlling populations.

In sum, the Soviet system made ethnicity more important than other identities such as class and citizenship, and exacerbated existing ethnic differences by seeking simultaneously to treat the Russians as a special case and to impose on all the much-variegated non-Russian groups, thus setting the stage for the variety and intensity of ethnic assertiveness that we face today.

TOWARD A TYPOLOGY

Given this diversity, a typology of nationalism in the former Soviet Union would integrate the study of these various phenomena into Western scholarship and develop a policy framework that does not—as Soviet policies did— unintentionally make things worse.

One potentially useful suggestion for a typology of nationalism in the Soviet context is Albert Hirshmann's application of "exit, voice, and loyalty" to multinational states.[2] Hirschmann's categories can be applied to ethnicity as striving for independence, striving for autonomy, or striving for acceptance or even assimilation within a broader dominant community. And these three strategies of an ethnic group—all of which may be labeled a form of nationalism—are paralleled by the policies of the dominant state—

devolution (up to and including decolonization), multiculturalism, and integration and assimilation.

There are examples of each of these in the former Soviet Union. Some ethnic groups—such as the Balts—actively sought to leave and radicalized others. Other groups—such widely dispersed communities as the Armenians—simply sought greater voice in the political system while generally being willing to assimilate. And still others—such as the Russians—sought to impose a new kind of loyalty and self-definition on themselves and others.

But such a typology does not address a variety of problems. First, many groups are rapidly moving from one category to another, with some groups such as the Moldovans being radicalized and others such as the Belarussians deradicalized. Moreover, groups are often subjected to sudden shifts in their social position. Thus, Russians outside of Russia who had enjoyed a privileged position in the past now find themselves in the position of "new minorities." Not surprisingly, their complaints are exactly the same as those of older minorities who are now in a dominant position.[3]

Change has brought additional complexity. None of the successor states—with the exception of the Russian Federation—has the capacity to enforce its will in the same way that the Soviet state did. As a result, the way is open for greater popular activism. For example, new minorities appear and mobilize themselves to take advantage of the chaos, particularly in the more multiethnic states such as the Russian Federation. The chances of intervention from outside in the name of ethnic solidarity also increase—for example, Moscow's oft-repeated concerns for its co-ethnics abroad. Many of the successor states have adopted new positions with respect to ethnic assertiveness ranging from continued or even enhanced support for the ethnic rights of the titular nationality—the governments of Estonia and Latvia are very much in this position—to a variety of programs seeking to deethnicize politics, for example, Kazakhstan under Nursultan Nazarbaev and Ukraine under Leonid Kravchuk.

Naturally, no single typology can hope to embrace all these aspects—particularly given the dizzying shifts in social and political position of particular groups and the enormous range of national agendas—but the typology proposed here flows from the original meaning of nationalism as a doctrine about the proper relationship between the nation and the state and the irritants that exist when the two do not correspond.[4] Clearly, in some situations, the two correspond with a decline in the level of irritation; in others, the state is larger than the nation with the state having to play a special role in crafting identity; and in still others, the nation is larger than the state and thus poses a permanent challenge to the existing state and its borders.

Using this general template, we can classify virtually all examples of nationalism in the post-Soviet territory. The nationalisms fall into the following categories:

1. The state and the nation are more or less congruent, either as the result of a national movement achieving its aims or through some other accident of history. This is the classical model of nationalism in Western Europe.

2. The state emerges first, and as the more important actor it plays a key role in the formation of the nation as a means of legitimating itself. This is the form of nationalism often found in former Third World states.

3. The nation is far larger than the state, either because of the collapse of an imperial system or the secession of regions that the core nation believes should properly belong to it. Such a situation—one that engenders a profound injury in the core nation—can either drive an aggressive nationalism of expansionism or a retrenchment and redefinition of the limits of the nation. Examples of the first abound; examples of the second are rarer: Ataturk's revolution in Turkey after the collapse of the Ottoman Empire is perhaps the model case.

For convenience, we can label the first category classical nationalism, the second, state-sponsored nationalism, and the third, challenged nationalism. Each deserves more discussion.

Classical nationalism—the desire of a group to achieve greater autonomy and eventually independence—is probably the most familiar form. Examples in the former Soviet Union include the Estonians who now have an independent state, the Kazan Tatars in the Russian Federation who have greatly expanded their autonomy, and the Hungarian minority in Ukraine which has achieved recognition of its special needs.[5]

But within the Russian Federation there are also as yet unsuccessful or at least unrecognized cases of this kind of nationalism—the Chechens, the Volga Germans, and all nonrecognized minorities—that is, those without a defined state structure. And there is still a third group—failed movements where ethnic demobilization already has occurred, including part of the Armenian diaspora in Russia, for example. Such nationalism may also power demands for territorial adjustments—*irredenta* or transfer of territories—for extraterritorial rights, as is the case of some ethnic Russian communities outside of the Russian Federation, or for new federal arrangements in neighboring countries, such as the demand by some Russians that the Ukrainian and Kazakhstan governments create ethnofederal structures for the large Russian communities on their territories. Both of these kinds of classical but unfulfilled nationalism can be studied using the broad literature on European national movements.

State-driven nationalism, the second category, is less familiar, although it really shouldn't be given its existence throughout much of what used to be called the Third World. I refer to the national programs of groups who achieved independence or autonomy not primarily by their own efforts but rather as the result of the collapse of an imperial center. Elites in such states thus often seek in the propagation of nationalism a justification for their new position and use it as a relatively inexpensive means to mobilize their communities.

Because elites in such states are in an inherently unstable situation, they frequently have more flexibility in articulating national identities and national programs even as they have more difficulty in securing mass approbation of such identities and programs. The situation in the Central Asian countries is instructive. In some, such as Kazakhstan, the elite has sought to promote patriotism rather than nationalism; in others, such as Turkmenistan, the elite has drawn almost exclusively on Soviet models of national identity; and in still a third, Tajikistan, rival groups within the elite have been unable to define any generally accepted program or identity.[6] All of these examples of this kind of nationalism (sometimes referred to as "nomenklatura" nationalism) have their counterparts in many of the smaller autonomous regions and republics in the Russian Federation, most of which are in fact dominated by ethnic Russians who wish to exploit the privileges of autonomy inherited from the Soviet system.

The third kind of nationalism, challenged nationalism, is found primarily among Russians who now have to cope with a situation in which the size of their state has been reduced to less than the size of the nation, thus creating pressures and simultaneously vastly reducing their position in the world. There are typically two responses to such a situation. The first and perhaps more common is a popular drive toward nationalism of the classical kind, one that may even acquire an aggressive nature precisely because of the relative size of the groups involved and the pain felt by the larger one.

The other reaction, a move toward acceptance of a new and more circumscribed national existence, is typified by Ataturk's construction of Turkish nationalism after the collapse of the Ottoman Empire. (It is ironic that the many Western scholars who drew an "Ottoman" analogy to the Soviet Union at its end have not discussed this analogy with respect to the Russian successor state.) As one Russian put it, Russia is a great power everywhere except in Russia itself.[7] As polling data suggest, most Russians are very unsure of either who they are or what the proper borders of their country should be, with many seeing Russia as something bigger than the Russian Federation and others seeing it as something less.[8]

Because Russia is the dominant power in this region, the outcome of this debate will likely make Russian nationalism the most significant in the region. Especially because this unstable nationalism remains largely unrecognized as a distinct form, some additional comments are in order.[9] The very uncertainty of the Russian position has its roots in both the origins of the Russian state in the late medieval period and the practices of the Soviet state which reinforced rather than modified earlier tsarist forms of state-building. One can say that the tragedy of Russia today reflects the fact that the Russian state became an empire before the Russians became a nation. As a result, Russia was a premodern empire with a center and a periphery rather than a metropole and colonies; and Russians were never forced to define what the proper limits of their identity or their territory should be.[10] That pattern was maintained, even reinforced, by the Soviet system, for the reasons mentioned earlier. Accordingly, Russians today are having particular difficulty coping with the loss of empire.

Russian discomfort with the current situation is reflected in a variety of statements and actions. Some Russians, especially those on the extreme right, simply want to reverse the situation by restoring the union or the empire. Others, more moderate, want to make sure that Russia retains its dominance in the region and that its "legitimate" interests are protected either through the Commonwealth of Independent States or some other means. But virtually all agree that Moscow must look after the 25.4 million ethnic Russians "stranded" in the fourteen non-Russian countries that emerged after the collapse of the Soviet Union.[11] As a bridge issue, one that unites both the extreme right and everyone else, the question of the Russians in the "near abroad" has many aspects. Some who raise the issue do so to deal with their own sense of dispossession, others in order to defend legitimate human rights concerns, and for still others it has become the acceptable way of talking about the restoration of Russian power throughout the former Soviet space.

Because of this diversity of nationalist motives, it is dangerous to make any single conclusion about such Russian discussions. But three preliminary observations are justified. First, to the extent that Russia insists on a role for protecting its own co-ethnics abroad—and it is worth noting that fewer than 200,000 of the ethnic Russians living outside of the Russian Federation are in fact citizens of the Russian Federation—Moscow will destabilize these neighboring countries by ethnicizing politics both directly and by generating a response on the part of the governments of the neighboring states. Ethnic Russians will have less incentive to integrate into the new states, and the new states will inevitably look at the local Russians with increasing suspicion and even open hostility. One of the striking features of the end of the Soviet Union was that there was virtually no anti-Russian nationalism and there were no attacks on Russians. That may change, with all the tragic consequences such a shift would entail.

Second, to the extent that Moscow refuses to accept the Russian Federation in its current borders as legitimate, the Russian government will be putting off the necessary coming to terms with new realities. It will also face greater instability within its borders, something that will almost certainly make the transition to democracy that much more difficult. This apparently counterfactual conclusion may be drawn from three possible situations. First, a Russian failure to accept the borders of the Russian Federation as final and legitimate would raise questions in the minds of many non-Russians *within* the federation's borders, thus necessitating a more repressive approach to these groups. Second, a Russian thrust abroad to retake the empire would require a larger army and military-industrial complex than Russia could afford if it is to make the transitions to democracy and free markets. Finally, in its current weakened position, Russia is unlikely to be successful in its attempt to retake the empire; the effort to do so and the resulting failure would almost certainly entail the rise of a more authoritarian and less economically successful Russian state. Again, we should recall that Kemalist Turkey was able to make the transition to a nation-state only because the international situation precluded its retaking of its former possessions and, even then, Turkey remained for a long period a highly authoritarian, albeit plebiscitarian state.

The third preliminary observation concerns citizenship principles. By insisting on the importance of ethnicity over citizenship in the case of Russians abroad, even democratically minded Russians are in fact subverting an important tenet of the post–World War II international system: the superiority of citizenship to ethnic identity. Ethnic assertions not only undermine the integrity of countries in the former Soviet space but also call into question Russian policy toward East European regimes. Recent Russian statements about and actions in the former Yugoslavia are especially frightening in this regard.[12]

MULTIPLE OUTCOMES

Nationalism in its various forms will continue to dominate political life throughout this region, with different kinds of nationalism having different results and with different communities changing places in a kaleidoscopic way and hence changing how their national identities become manifest. As in the past, sometimes this national assertiveness will lead to more intense conflicts as in the Caucasus and Central Asia. But at other times it will lead to the resolution of conflicts by providing legitimation to state authority or by eliminating an unsupportable pattern of ethnic oppression as in the case of the Baltic countries.

Obviously, some of these issues will involve only the non-Russian states, some concern only the Russian Federation, and others the international community. But here I would like to focus on specific questions that are likely to involve all three entities. These issues are pivotal to the direction of the entire region and to my mind they have not yet received sufficient attention: (1) the linkages between social change and moderation or transformation of nationalism; (2) the linkages between stability of borders and the possibilities for democratic change; and (3) refederalization of particular states and alternative methods of coping with ethnic assertiveness in a multinational milieu.

As I suggested earlier, most of the varieties of nationalism in this region are more radical than they would otherwise be if a middle class were involved. Another way to state this proposition is that, until economic reforms create a middle class, nationalist ideologies in this region will be dominated by the intelligentsias. They will resemble early modern nationalism in Western Europe, such as those described by Engels, or the nationalism of interwar Eastern Europe, rather than the more familiar nationalism of the post–World War II West. To the extent that this is true, continuing economic reform, by creating the preconditions for a more moderate nationalism, is certain to play a major role in determining the fate of different forms of nationalism and hence of democratization in the region.

Unfortunately, while this pattern is likely to hold if reforms continue for a generation or more, in the short term the dislocations of rapid economic change are likely to generate extremist nationalism, as the December 1993 elections in Russia showed. Consequently, in thinking about this region and designing our policies toward it, we need to reflect on the inevitable linkage of nationalism to other key political variables.

More immediately explosive is the question of borders and democratic change. Before the collapse of the Soviet Union, a group of Soviet geographers identified seventy-nine places where borders should be changed in order to bring them more into accord with ethnographic regions.[13] More recent assessments by Russian military writers have suggested that there are in fact considerably more places where borders should be changed if peace is to be maintained, democratization promoted, and stability reinforced. But to date, no border changes have taken place. The international community and the key players in this region are apparently afraid to open what is inevitably a Pandora's box. That reluctance may dissipate, however, as Russian pressure for the return of Crimea increases and Central Asian conflicts over scarce water resources intensify.

We need to begin to explore how such border changes might be accomplished in a peaceful rather than explosive way. So far, the consensus is that there can be no secession from secession, as Boris Yeltsin and virtually all the leaders of the former republics have put it. But in making these arguments, these leaders and many in the West have ignored the consequences for democratization and stability that such a view implies. If one makes the stability of borders the *summum bonum,* then the international community will inevitably be forced to countenance both increased pressure by states on their respective minorities with the authoritarianism that such pressure would engender and also demands by Russia and other states that they be allowed to intervene directly or indirectly on behalf of their co-ethnics in foreign countries. As should be obvious, both these developments undercut stability, democracy, and progress on human rights.

I am not arguing either for border changes in general or for any specific border change. Rather I am suggesting that in this situation, a decision to exclude the possibility of peaceful border changes a priori is virtually to guarantee that there will be violent border changes with all the sad consequences outlined here. Moreover, we should keep in mind that the often-cited Helsinki Final Act of 1975, which created the Organization for Security and Cooperation in Europe (OSCE), does not say that borders cannot be changed, only that they cannot be changed by force; moreover, the borders within the USSR just as those within Yugoslavia were in any case not covered at the time of the accord. In the absence of any real possibility, given past Soviet policy, for an immediate deescalation of ethnic mobilization in any of the states in the former Soviet Union, we need to face the fact that unalterable belief in the stability of borders *über alles* is likely to exacerbate rather than limit the expression of extreme nationalism and thus undermine the possibilities for democratic change.

Happily, this idea is coming to be understood by many Russians—and not just those inclined to the restoration of the Soviet empire. Vladimir V. Pustogarev, a senior scholar at the Moscow Institute of State and Law, for example, concludes that border changes may ultimately be the only way out of the current crisis around Russia. In May 1994, he wrote, "The application of the principle of territorial integrity in isolation from other principles, particularly the principles of non-aggression and the self-determination of nations, seems invalid and could have dangerous implications."[14] If these words mark the beginning of a serious discussion of this issue in Moscow, there may be movement in a positive direction.

Finally, we should recognize and even insist that these ethnic communities and their respective states need to explore non-Soviet solutions to ethnic assertiveness. For some, such as Russia, a new federalism may be the answer. Indeed, as more and more Russians understand, unless Russia refederalizes from above, it will face mounting pressures for refederalization from below, pressures that could simultaneously spark new demands for secession and consequently new demands for greater authoritarianism in Moscow. Indeed, it is precisely this combination that would be the most threatening, for Moscow's insistence on restoring its control of the regions—Russian as well as non-Russian—is already sparking resistance in the former republics and powering right-wing authoritarianism in the Russian Federation.

Federalization or refederalization, despite its superficial attractiveness to peoples schooled in territorial solutions to ethnic problems, seems inappropriate for most of the cases in which it is advocated. This is especially true in the Transdniester region of Moldova, northern Kazakhstan, and Abkhazia in Georgia, especially because much of the pressure for federal change comes from Russia. To concede in these cases could easily open the floodgates to other, less defensible demands and thus embroil Russia and its neighbors in a disaster. More attention should be given to nonterritorial methods of protecting the rights of ethnic minorities: Canadian-style multiculturalism may be one answer, extraterritorial national autonomy (the granting of rights to a community throughout a territory even if it is not geographically concentrated) such as advocated by Otto Bauer (an Austro-Marxist whose ideas on extraterritorial cultural autonomy were attacked by Stalin) and actually institutionalized in Estonia in the 1920s may be another. A greater role for OSCE and other international bodies in the development of domestic legislation—as Estonia and Latvia have already done and as other countries in the region have begun to consider—may be yet a third option.

One issue that cuts across all of these options is the chance that these various conflicts, if not contained, may turn violent. To a large extent, violence along ethnic lines has been confined to a tiny fraction of all the ethnic conflicts in the region: the wars over Karabagk and Chechnya, the Abkhaz and Ossetin struggles in Georgia, and Tajikistan. There are three reasons that these regions have been the most violent. First, the power of the states in these areas was significantly weaker than elsewhere. Next, all of these areas have a longstanding tradition of violence. Finally, in every case, arms were supplied by outside groups—typically the Russian army but by others as well. The only chance for peaceful resolution of these conflicts and others will be to restrict the inflow of weapons and other materiel. Unfortunately, that has not happened, even though it is obvious that it should be a priority for the international community and even the states themselves.

IN his seminal 1974 essay "The Russian Past and the Soviet Present," the great French sovietologist Alain Besançon argued that the Russian empire was difficult to understand and even more difficult to rule because it was not one empire but three: an empire like that of the United States in its expansion into Siberia, an empire like Great Britain's in its absorption of Central Asia, and an empire like Austro-Hungary's in its control of Ukraine and the Baltic States. Unfortunately, the rulers of the Russian empire, the rulers of the Soviet Union and the post-Soviet states, and most Western governments have tried to simplify things, to treat all of the periphery as the same. That is where most of our problems have come from.

I believe that we face a triad of immediate tasks with respect to nationalism in the former Soviet Union. First and foremost, we must recognize its very diversity. All nationalism is not the same either in form, intent, or moral standing. And thus there is no major lever other than repression—which entails its own costs—that can deal with them easily and quickly. We are going to have to learn to live with as well as to try to cope with these various kinds of nationalism. Second, we must recognize that the various forms of nationalism in this region are interlinked. Efforts to deal with them in isolation will be counterproductive: curing one problem may easily generate new, even more serious crises. For example, the United States has supported Russian efforts to protect ethnic Russians abroad without any discussion of the need to protect the even more numerous non-Russians who live outside their own ethnic territories or who do not have ethnic territories. Resentment and ethnic tensions have resulted.

Third, we must recognize that the forces which generate nationalism and which will ultimately overcome it are larger than nationalism itself. The current upsurge of nationalism is itself the product of specific social and political changes: it is not self-generating. But it can be self-sustaining unless we learn how to analyze and react to it.[15] None of this is going to be easy, but all of it is absolutely necessary.

8

Hypotheses on Nationalism and the Causes of War

Stephen Van Evera

Scholars have written widely on the causes of nationalism but they say little about its effects, especially its effects on international politics.[1] Most striking, the impact of nationalism on the risk of war has barely been explored. Most authors take the war-causing character of nationalism for granted, assuming it without proof or explanation.[2] Factors that govern the magnitude of the dangers posed by nationalism are generally unidentified. What types of nationalism are most likely to cause war? What background conditions catalyze or dampen this causal process? These questions are generally undiscussed, hence the causal nexus between nationalism and war presents an important unsolved riddle.

This chapter explores that nexus. I define nationalism as a political movement having two characteristics: (1) individual members give their primary loyalty to their own ethnic or national community;[3] this loyalty supersedes their loyalty to other groups, for example, those based on common kinship or political ideology; and (2) these ethnic or national communities desire their own independent state.[4] I leave the origins of nationalism unexplored, instead focusing on its effects on the risk of war. I address seven questions: Does nationalism cause war? If so, what types of nationalism are most likely to cause war? How and why do they cause war? What causes these war-causing nationalisms? Under what conditions are they most dangerous?

Thanks to Robert Art, Don Blackmer, David Laitin, John Mearsheimer, Barry Posen, Jack Snyder, Stephen Walt, and participants in the CFR book project review meetings for sharing their thoughts on nationalism and their comments on this chapter.

How, if at all, can the war-causing attributes of nationalism be suppressed or neutralized? How great are the risks to peace posed by nationalism in today's Europe, and how can these risks be minimized? In answer I offer unproven hypotheses that I leave untested for now. Our stock of hypotheses on the consequences of nationalism is meager; our first order of business should be to expand it, to set the stage for empirical inquiry by others.[5]

Causes of war or peace can be classified as proximate (causes that directly affect the odds on war) or remote (causes of these proximate causes, or background conditions required for their activation). I explore proximate causes first in the next section then turn to remote causes in the following one. Specifically, the first section identifies varieties of nationalism that are most likely to cause war (including both civil and interstate war). The second section identifies the causes of these dangerous varieties of nationalism and conditions that govern the extent of risk that they produce. Twenty-one hypotheses are proposed in all—nine main hypotheses and twelve sub-hypotheses. Some focus on the impact of the environment that surrounds nationalist movements; this environment can incline the movement toward peaceful or warlike behavior. Others focus on the impact of the movement's internal character, especially its ideology and vision of history; this, too, can incline the movement toward peace or war. These hypotheses are highlighted because they are deductively sound, they can survive plausibility probes, and in some cases they generate policy prescriptions. They are summarized in Table 8.1.[6] Viewed together, they suggest that nationalism is an important cause of war, but its effects are highly varied: some types of nationalism are far more dangerous than other types, all nationalisms are more dangerous under some conditions than others, and nationalism can even dampen the risk of war under some conditions.

If accepted, these hypotheses provide a checklist for assessing the perils posed by a given nationalist movement or by the spread of nationalism in a given region. To illustrate, I use them in the third section to assess the risks that nationalism now poses in Europe, since Europe is a region in flux whose future is much debated. This exercise suggests that nationalism poses very little risk of war in Western Europe, but poses a serious threat in the east, especially in the former Soviet Union. Current West European nationalisms are benign, and the conditions required for a return to the malignant nationalisms of 1870–1945 are almost wholly absent. In contrast, many East European nationalisms have many (though not all) of the attributes that I argue make nationalism dangerous, hence the risk of large-scale violence stemming from the rising tide of East European nationalism is substantial.

What prescriptions follow? The character and consequences of nationalism are not written in stone. The Western powers can influence the character and consequences of East European nationalisms, and should try to channel them in benign directions. Most important, the West should promote full respect for minority rights, democracy, and official respect for historical truth; if East European nationalisms adopt these programs the risks they pose will sharply diminish.

VARIETIES OF NATIONALISM: WHICH CAUSE WAR?

Four primary attributes of a nationalist movement determine whether it has a large or small potential to produce violence. (1) What is the movement's political status—is statehood attained or unattained? (2) What is the movement's stance toward its national diaspora (if it has one)? If the movement has a national state, but some members of the nation are dispersed or entrapped beyond the state's borders, does the nation accept continued separation from this diaspora, or does it seek to incorporate the diaspora in the national state? And if it seeks the diaspora's incorporation, will it accomplish this by immigration or by territorial expansion? (3) What is the movement's stance toward other nations: does it respect or deny other nationalities' right to national independence? (4) How does the movement treat its own minorities: are these minorities respected or abused?

Is National Statehood Attained or Unattained?

Nationalist movements without states raise greater risks of war because accommodation to them requires greater and more disruptive change. Their struggle for national freedom can produce wars of secession, which in turn can widen to become international wars. Their freedom struggle can also injure the interests of other groups, displacing populations whose new grievances sow the seeds of future conflict, as Zionism's displacement of the Palestinian Arabs in 1948 sowed the seeds of later Arab-Israeli wars. Finally, the appearance of new states creates a new, less mature regional international system that lacks "rules of the game" to define the rights and obligations of its members toward one another, and norms of international conduct. These rights, obligations, and norms can take years to define, raising the risk of crises and collisions in the meantime.

The international system tolerates change poorly, but the accommodation of new nationalisms requires it.[7] Thus the first measure of the risks to the peace of a region posed by nationalism is found in the proportion of its nationalisms that remain unfulfilled in statehood, a factor expressed in the nation-to-state ratio. Are the supply of and demand for states in equilibrium or disequilibrium? Peace in a region is more likely the more closely a supply/demand equilibrium is approached.[8] Modern nationalism disrupted peace over the past two centuries partly because many of the world's current nationalist movements were stateless at the outset, requiring vast change to accommodate their emergence. Nationalism still threatens peace because its full accommodation would require vast additional change: the number of states in the world has more than tripled since World War II (up from the 50 signers of the UN Charter in 1945 to 180-odd states today), but many nationalities remain stateless; the world has some 6,000 language groups, many of which have dormant or manifest aspirations for statehood.[9]

In Western Europe the transition of nations to statehood is largely behind us: that region's remaining stateless nationalities are relatively few and weak. In Eastern Europe and the former Soviet Union the problem is more serious because the transition to statehood, while largely fulfilled, is still incomplete. The bulk of these stateless nationalities are found in the former Soviet Union; 15 of the 104 nationalities in the former USSR have attained states, but the other 89 have not; these stateless nationalities total 25.6 million people, comprising 10 percent of the former USSR's total population.[10] Most of these nationalities are not potential candidates for statehood (e.g., the Jews) but some clearly are (the Chechen) and others might be (e.g., the Tatars, Ingush, and Ossetians). Their reach for statehood could sow future conflict, as in Chechnya.

Attitude toward the National Diaspora

Is partial or total national unity pursued? Are immigrationist or expansionist tactics used? Does the nationalist ideology posit that all or only a part of the national ethnic community must be incorporated in the national state? And if the whole nationality must be incorporated, would this be accomplished by immigration (bringing the diaspora to the state) or by territorial expansion (bringing the state to the diaspora)?

These questions suggest a distinction among three types of nationalism: "diaspora-accepting," "immigrationist," and "diaspora-annexing." Some nationalisms (the diaspora-accepting variety) are content with partial union (e.g., Chinese nationalism);[11] such nationalisms are less troublesome because they make fewer territorial demands on their neighbors. Some nationalisms (the immigrationist type) seek to incorporate their diasporas in the national state, but are content to pursue union by seeking immigration of the diaspora (current German nationalism and Zionist Jewish nationalism). Such immigrationist nationalisms are also easy to accommodate. Finally, some nationalisms seek to incorporate their diasporas by means of territorial expansion (pre-1914 Pan-Germanism and current Pan-Serbianism are examples). Such diaspora-annexing nationalisms are the most dangerous of the three, since their goals and tactics produce the greatest territorial conflict with others. Thus one scenario for war in the former Soviet Union lies in the possible appearance of a Pan-Russian nationalism that would seek to reincorporate by force the vast Russian diaspora now living in the non-Russian republics. This diaspora includes some 24 million Russians, or 17 percent of all Russians.[12] The future hinges heavily on whether Russian nationalism accepts separation from this diaspora (or seeks to ingather it by immigration), or forcibly seeks to annex it.[13]

Attitude toward Other Independent Nationalities

Does the ideology of the nationalism incorporate respect for the freedom of other nationalities, or does it assume a right or duty to rule them? In other words, is the national ideology symmetrical (all nationalities deserve states) or asymmetrical (only our nationality deserves statehood; others should be denied it)?

Hegemonistic, or asymmetrical, nationalism is both the rarest and the most dangerous variety of nationalism. Interwar Nazi nationalism in Germany, fascist nationalism in Mussolini's Italy, and militarist nationalism in imperial Japan illustrate such hegemonistic nationalism; the wars they caused illustrate its results.[14] No European nationalism today displays such hegemonism, but the vast trouble that it has caused in the past advises alertness to its possible reappearance in Europe or elsewhere.

The Degree of National Respect for Minority Rights

Does the nationalism respect minorities or oppress them? A minority-respecting nationalism grants equal rights to other nationalities living within the boundaries of its claimed state; it may even grant their right to secede and establish their own state. A minority-oppressing nationalism denies such rights to these other nationalities, subjugating them instead. Many of the nationalisms of immigrant nations (American, Anglo-Canadian) have been relative respecters of minorities (in the Canadian case this includes a tacit right to secession, which the Quebecois may soon exercise). Nonimmigrant nationalisms often display far less tolerance for their minorities: prominent current examples include Iraq's and Turkey's oppression of their Kurdish minorities, Bulgaria's oppression of its Turks, China's cruelties in Tibet, Croatia's intolerance toward its Serb minority, and Serbian oppression of its Slavic Muslim and Albanian minorities. Nazi German nationalism was an extreme case of a minority-oppressing nationalism.

The first three attributes—whether statehood is attained, attitude toward diaspora, and attitude toward other independent nationalities—define the scope of a nationalist movement's claims against others. Conversely, the fourth, policy toward minorities, helps determine the scope of others' claims against the movement. The more expansive these others' goals become, the more they will collide with the movement's goals, raising the risk of war. Minority-oppressing nationalism can bring war in two ways. It can provoke secessionist movements among its captive nations; or it can spur the homelands of these captive nations to move forcefully to free their oppressed co-nationals.[15] (Recall that Croatian threats against the Serb minority in Croatia helped spawn the Serb attack on Croatia in 1991.)[16] Nationalism that oppresses minorities is most dangerous if the oppressed minorities have nearby friends who have the capacity to protect the oppressed nation by force. (The Serbo-Croat war exploded partly because Croatia's Serbs had such a friend in Serbia.) The attitude of many nationalisms in Eastern Europe and the former Soviet Union toward their minorities remains undefined, and the future hinges on whether they evolve toward minority respect or oppression.

These four attributes can be used to create a nationalism danger-scale, expressing the level of risk posed by a given nationalism, or by the spread of nationalism in a given region. If all four attributes are benign, the nationalism poses little threat of war, and may even bolster peace. Specifically, a nationalism is benign if it has achieved statehood; has limited unity goals (i.e., accepts the existence of any unincorporated diaspora) or adopts an immigrationist strategy for ingathering its diaspora; posits no claim to rule other nationalities living beyond its national territory; and respects the rights of minorities found in this territory. Multiplied, such nationalisms may even dampen the risk of war, by making conquest more difficult: where these nationalisms are prevalent, conquest is harder because nation-states are among the most difficult type of state to conquer (since nationalism provides an inspirational liberation doctrine that can be used to mobilize strong popular resistance to conquest).[17] As a result, strong states will be deterred from reaching for regional or global hegemony and will also be less fearful that others might achieve it; hence all states will compete less fiercely with one another.[18] In contrast, a nationalistic entity is bound to collide with others if all four attributes are malign. If the nationalistic entity has no state, the risk of civil war arising from its struggle for national independence is increased; this also raises the risk of interstate war, since civil war can widen to engulf nearby states. If, after achieving statehood, the nationalistic state seeks to incorporate a diaspora by force, oppresses minorities found in its claimed national territory, and seeks hegemony over nationalities lying beyond that territory, violence between the nationalistic entity and its neighbors is inevitable.

CAUSES OF AND CONDITIONS FOR WAR-CAUSING NATIONALISM

What factors determine whether these four variables will have benign or malignant values? What conditions are required for malignant values to have malignant effects? In the following paragraphs the deciding factors and conditions are grouped into three broad families: structural (those arising from the geographic and demographic arrangement of a nation's people); political-environmental (those arising from the past or present conduct of a people's neighbors); and perceptual (those arising from the nationalist movement's self-image and its images of others, including its images of both sides' past and present conduct and character).

Structural Factors: Geographic, Demographic, and Military Settings

The size of the jeopardy posed by nationalism is influenced by the balance of power and of will between stateless nationalisms and the central states that hold them captive; by the degree and pattern of regional ethnic intermingling; by the defensibility and legitimacy of the borders of new national states; and by the correspondence of these borders with ethnic boundaries.

(1) *The domestic balance of power and will.* Unattained nationalisms are more troublesome under two conditions: (1) the movement has the strength to plausibly reach for statehood; and (2) the central state has the will to resist this attempt.

The balance of power. Stateless nationalisms whose statehood is unattainable will lie dormant, their emergence deterred by the power of the central state.[19] Nationalism becomes manifest and can produce war when the power balance between the central state and the captive nationalism shifts to allow the possibility of successful secession. Thus two safe conditions are possible: where national statehood is already attained; and where it is not attained, but clearly cannot be. The danger zone lies between, in cases where statehood has not been attained yet is attainable or appears to be.[20] In this zone we find wars of nationalist secession.[21] Such conflicts can, in turn, grow into international wars: examples include the 1912–14 Balkan secessionist struggles that triggered World War I, and the Serbo-Croatian conflict of the 1990s.

The Third World nationalisms of the twentieth century erupted partly because the spread of small arms and literacy shifted the balance of power in favor of these nationalisms, and against their imperial captors. Nationalism emerged because it could. Likewise, nationalism exploded in the former Soviet Union in the late 1980s partly because Soviet central power had waned.

The balance of will. War is inevitable if central states have the will to resist emerging nationalist/secessionist movements, but these movements can win freedom without violence if that will is missing. Many sub-Saharan African states gained freedom in the 1960s without violence because the European colonial powers lost their imperial will; likewise, the emergence of non-Russian nationalisms in the former Soviet Union was accompanied by (and encouraged by) the loss of imperial will in Moscow; this loss of will at the center allowed the non-Russians to escape the Soviet empire without waging wars of secession. French decolonization was far more violent, spawning large wars in Vietnam and Algeria, because the French metropole retained its will even after nationalism gained momentum in the French empire.

The will of the central state is largely governed by its domestic politics, but is also determined partly by demographic facts. Specifically, central governments can allow secession more easily if secession would leave a homogeneous rump central state, since permitting secession then sets a less damaging precedent. Thus the Czechs could accept Slovak independence without fear of setting a precedent that would trigger another secession, since there is no potential secessionist group in the rump Czech Republic. Likewise, the United States could grant independence to the Philippines fairly easily in 1946 because it had few other colonies, and none of these were large or valuable, hence Philippine independence set no dangerous precedents. Conversely, the Austro-Hungarian Empire strongly resisted secessions before 1914 because the empire contained many potential secessionists who might be encouraged if any secession were allowed.

(2) *The demographic arrangement of national populations.* Are nationality populations densely intermingled? If they are, does this create large or small national diasporas? Intermingling raises the risk of communal conflict during the struggle for national freedom, as groups that would be trapped as minorities in a new national state oppose its reach for freedom. Dispersion and intermingling will also trap some co-ethnics outside the boundaries of their nation-states, bringing the risk that new nation-states will pursue diaspora-recovering expansionism after they gain statehood, and raising the possibility that their abuse of minorities will trigger attack from outside.[22]

These perils are reduced if national populations are compact and homogeneous—diasporas and minorities then occur only if political boundaries fail to follow ethnic boundaries. The dangers are intensified if the nationality is dispersed abroad and intermingled with others at home. The Czechs can pursue nationalism with little risk to the peace of their neighborhood, because they have no diaspora abroad, and few minorities at home. They need not limit their goals or learn to accommodate minorities. The 1947 partition of India was a far bloodier process than the 1992 Czech-Slovak divorce partly because Hindus and Muslims were far more intermingled than Czechs and Slovaks. The partition of Yugoslavia has been especially violent partly because nationalities in former Yugoslavia are more densely intermingled than any others in Eastern or Western Europe outside the former Soviet Union.[23]

Overall, nationalism poses greater dangers in Eastern than Western Europe because the peoples of Eastern Europe are more densely intermingled. A survey of Eastern Europe reveals roughly a dozen minority group pockets that may seek independence or be claimed by other countries.[24] The ethnographic structure of the former Soviet Union is even more ominous; an ethnographic map of the former USSR reveals massively intermingled nationalities, scattered in scores of isolated pockets, a mosaic far more tangled and complex than any found elsewhere in Europe except the former Yugoslavia.[25]

Two aspects of intermingling determine the level of the dangers it poses: the scope of intermingling, and the pattern of intermingling. All intermingling causes trouble, but some patterns of intermingling cause more trouble than others.

Groups can be intermingled on a regional scale (regions are heterogeneous, small communities are homogeneous) or local scale (even small communities are heterogeneous, as in Sarajevo). Regional intermingling is more easily managed, because intergroup relations can be negotiated by elites. In contrast, elites can lose control of events when intermingling extends to the local level: conflict can flare against the wishes of elites when unofficial killers seize the agenda by sparking a spiral of private violence. Local intermingling can also produce conflict-dampening personal friendships and interethnic marriages, but the Bosnian conflict shows the limits of this tempering effect. Overall, local intermingling is more dangerous.

The most dangerous pattern of regional intermingling is one that leaves elements of one or both groups insecurely at the mercy of the other, but also allows for the possibility of forcible rescue—either self-rescue (secession) or external rescue (intervention by an already-free homeland.)

If rescue is impossible, then the goal of secession or reunion with a homeland will be abandoned. Israel cannot rescue Soviet Jewry, except by immigration, and Ukraine cannot rescue the Ukrainian diaspora in Russia; hence neither considers forceful rescue. This lowers the risk of war.

Even if rescue is easy, it may not be attempted, since the threat of rescue is enough to deter abuse of the diaspora. Russia could fairly easily rescue the Russian minority in the Baltics and perhaps elsewhere on the Russian periphery, because much of the Russian diaspora lies clustered near the Russian border, and Russia holds military superiority over its neighbors. These power realities may deter Russia's neighbors from abusing their Russian minorities, leaving Russia more room to take a relaxed attitude.[26]

It is the in-between situations—those where rescue is possible, but only under optimal conditions—that are most fraught with danger. This situation tempts potential rescuers to jump through any windows of opportunity that arise. Forceful rescue is then driven by both fear and opportunity—fear that later the abuse of diasporas cannot be deterred by threatening their rescue (since the difficulty of rescue robs that threat of credibility), and the opportunity to rescue the diaspora now by force.[27] Thus Serbia would have probably been unable to rescue the Serb diaspora in normal times: Serbia is too weak, and the Serbian diasporas in Croatia and Bosnia are too distant from Serbia. But rescue was feasible if Serbia made the attempt at a moment of peak Serbian military advantage. Such a moment emerged in 1990, after Serbia consolidated the weaponry of the Yugoslav army under its control, but before the Croatian and Bosnian states could organize strong militaries.[28] In contrast, such a moment may never emerge for Russia, because it can always rescue large parts of its diaspora should the need ever arise—leaving less need to seize an early opportunity.

These ambiguous situations are most troublesome when the diaspora is separated from the homeland by lands inhabited by others: wars of rescue then cause larger injury. Rescue requires cutting a secure corridor through these lands; this, in turn, requires the forcible expulsion of the resident population, with its attendant horrors and cruelties. In 1991 the Serbian diaspora in Croatia and Bosnia was cut off from the Serb homeland by walls of Muslim-inhabited territory,[29] and the vast Serbian cruelties against the Bosnian Muslims that began in 1992 grew mainly from Serbia's effort to punch corridors through these walls in order to attach these diasporas to Serbia proper. In contrast, more of Russia's diaspora is contiguous to Russia, hence a Russian war of rescue would do relatively less harm to others innocently in the way (though it would still do plenty of harm).

(3) *Borders: defensibility, legitimacy, and border/ethnic correspondence.* The risks to peace posed by a nationalism's emergence are governed partly by the defensibility and international legitimacy of the nation's borders, and by the

degree of correspondence between these political borders and ethnic boundaries.

Are borders defensible? The satisfaction of national demands for statehood extends international anarchy by creating more states: hence nationalism's effects are governed partly by the character of the extended anarchy that it creates. Some anarchies are relatively peaceful, others more violent. The acuteness of the security dilemma is a key factor. Anarchy is a precondition for international war, hence extending anarchy may expand the risk of war, but this is not always the case: the fragmentation of states can enhance peace if it leaves the world with states that are more difficult to conquer, hence are more secure, than the older states from which they were carved. The character of boundaries helps decide the issue: if the new borders are indefensible, the net impact of the creation of new national states will be warlike; if borders are highly defensible, the net impact may be peaceful.[30]

Defensible boundaries reduce the risk of war because they leave new states less anxious to expand for security reasons, while also deterring others from attacking them. The nations of Western Europe can be more peaceful than those of the East because they are endowed with more defensible borders: the French, Spanish, British, Italian, and Scandinavian nations have natural defenses formed by the Alps and the Pyrenees, and by the waters of the English Channel, the Baltic, and the North Sea. Icelandic nationalism is especially untroublesome because geography makes Iceland unusually secure, and almost incapable of attack. In contrast, the nationalities living on the exposed plains of Eastern Europe and western Asia contend with a harsher geography: with few natural barriers to invasion, they are more vulnerable to attack, hence are more tempted to attack others in preemptive defense.[31] They are therefore more likely to disturb the status quo, or to be victims of other disturbers.

Are borders legitimate? The international legitimacy of a new nation's borders helps determine the level of jeopardy raised when it gains independence: if borders lack international legitimacy or are unsettled altogether, demands for border changes will arise, providing new occasions for conflict. The successor states of the former Soviet Union find themselves with borders drawn by Stalin or other Bolshevik rulers; these have correspondingly small legitimacy. Israel's post-1948 boundaries at first lacked international legitimacy because they had no historical basis, having arisen simply from truce lines expressing the military outcome of the 1948 war. In contrast, the borders of the recently freed states of Eastern Europe have greater legitimacy because they have greater grounding in history, and some were the product of earlier international negotiation and agreement.

Do borders unite or divide national populations? Borders may bisect nationalities, or may follow national demographic divides. Nation-bisecting borders are more troublesome, because they have the same effect as demographic intermingling: they entrap parts of nations within the boundaries of states dominated by other ethnic groups, giving rise to expansionism by the truncated nation. Thus Hungary's borders bisect (and truncate) the Hungarian nation, giving rise to a (now dormant but still surviving) Hungarian revanchism against Slovakia, Serbia, and Rumania.[32] The Russian-Ukrainian border bisects both nationalities, creating the potential for movements to adjust borders in both countries.

The borders of new states can arise in two main ways: from violent military struggle (e.g., Israel) or as a result of cession of sovereignty to existing administrative units whose boundaries were previously defined by the parent multiethnic state (e.g., former Soviet Union). War-born borders often have the advantage of following ethnic lines, because the cruelties of war often cause "ethnic cleansing," and offensives lose strength at ethnic boundaries. Inherited administrative borders (e.g., the boundaries of Azerbaijan, which entrap the Armenians of Nagorno-Karabakh) more often plant the charge of future conflict by dividing nations and creating diasporas. The peaceful dissolution of the former Soviet Union was thus a mixed blessing: its successor states emerged without violence, but with borders that captured unhappy diasporas behind them.

Political/Environmental Factors

How have neighbors behaved? How do they now behave? The conduct of nationalities and nation-states mirrors their neighbors' past and present conduct.

(1) *Past conduct.* The degree of harmony or conflict between intermingled nationalities depends partly on the magnitude of the crimes committed by each against the other in the past; the greater these past crimes, the greater the current conflict. Memories of its neighbors' cruelties will magnify an emerging nation's impulse to ingather its diaspora, converting the nation from a diaspora-accepting to a diaspora-annexing attitude. Thus the vast Croatian mass murders of Serbs during the 1940s were the taproot that fed violent Pan-Serbianism after 1990: Serbs vowed "never again" and argued that they must incorporate the Serbian diaspora in Croatia to save it from new pogroms.[33] Past suffering can also spur nations to oppress old tormentors who now live among them as minorities, sparking conflict with these minorities' home countries. Thus the past horrors inflicted on the Baltic peoples by Stalinism fuel their discrimination against their Russian minorities today.[34] This discrimination, in turn, feeds anti-Baltic feeling in Russia. In contrast, nonvictim nations are less aggressive toward both neighbors and

minorities. Czech nationalism is benign partly because the Czechs have escaped full victimhood; Quebec nationalism is mild for the same reason.

Mass murder, land theft, and population expulsions are the crimes that matter most. Past exterminations foster diaspora-recovering ideologies justified by self-protection logic. Past land theft fosters territorial definitions of nationhood (e.g., the Israeli Likud party's concept of "the Land of Israel," a place including "once-Jewish" lands that Likud argues were wrongfully taken by others) and land claims that exclude the rights of peoples now on that land (Likud rejects equal rights for the Palestinian inhabitants of these once-Jewish lands; Serbs likewise reject equal rights for Albanian Kosovars who Serbs claim wrongfully took Serb land). Past expulsions and dispersions feed diaspora-intolerance: if others created the diaspora, it is argued, then others should pay the price for restoring the diaspora to the nation by making territorial concessions.

The scope of the dangers posed by past crimes is a function, in part, of whether these crimes are remembered, and whether victims can attach responsibility for crimes to groups that are still present. Crimes that have faded in the victims' memories have a less corrosive effect on intergroup relations; thus mayhem that occurred before written records poses fewer problems than more recent crimes that are better recorded.[35]

Crimes committed by groups still on the scene pose more problems than crimes committed by vanished groups. This, in turn, is a matter of interpretation: who committed the crime in question? Can inherited blame be attached to any present group? Thus the Ukrainians can assess responsibility for Stalin's vast murders of Ukrainians in several ways.[36] Were they committed by a crazed Georgian? This interpretation is benign: it points the finger at a single man who is long gone from the scene. Were they committed by that now-vanished tribe, the Bolsheviks? This interpretation is also benign: those responsible have miraculously disappeared, leaving no target for violence. More ominously, were these the crimes of the Russian empire and the Russian people? This interpretation would guarantee bitter Russian-Ukrainian conflict, because the crimes in question were so enormous, and many of the "criminals" live in Ukraine, making ready targets for hatred and setting the stage for a Russian-Ukrainian conflict-spiral.[37] Such a spiral is more likely because Russians would not accept the blame assigned them: they count themselves among the victims, not the perpetrators, of Bolshevism's crimes, and they would view others' demands that they accept blame as a malicious outrage.

The chances that violence will break out over past crimes also depend on the criminal group's later behavior. Has the group apologized or otherwise shown contrition? Or has it shown contempt for its victims' suffering? Nazi Germany's crimes were among the greatest in human history, but Germany has reestablished civil relations with its former victims by acknowledging its crimes and showing contrition. Postwar German leaders have made public apologies and symbolic acts of repentance. Conversely, Turkey has denied the great crimes it committed against the Armenian people during World War I.[38] This display of contempt has sustained an Armenian hatred that is still expressed in occasional acts of violent anti-Turkish retribution.

A final significant factor lies in the degree of coincidence of power and victimhood. Are the groups with the greatest historic grievances also the groups with the greatest power today? Or is past victimhood confined to today's weaker groups? Things are more dangerous when power and aggrievement coincide, since this combination brings together both the motive and the capacity to make trouble; when power and aggrievement are separated, grievances have fewer effects. On this count the past crimes of the Russian and Bolshevik states leave a less dangerous legacy than the crimes committed in the former Yugoslavia during World War II, because the strongest group in the former Soviet Union (the Russians) is the least aggrieved; in contrast, in former Yugoslavia the strongest group (the Serbs) is the most aggrieved.

(2) Current Conduct

Are minority rights respected? As noted earlier, nations are less accepting of a diaspora if others abuse the rights of that diaspora; such abuse magnifies the impulse to incorporate the territory of the diaspora by force. Thus Serbia's 1991 attack on Croatia was spurred partly by Croatian threats against the Serbian minority.[39] Likewise, Russia's attitude toward the Russian diaspora will be governed partly by the treatment of the Russian diaspora in their new homelands. Oppressive policies will provoke wider Russian aims.[40]

Perceptual Factors

The effects of nationalism depend heavily on the beliefs of nationalist movements, especially their self-images and their images of their neighbors. Nations can coexist most easily when these beliefs converge—when they share a common image of their mutual history, and of one another's current conduct and character. This can be achieved either by common convergence of images on something close to the "truth," or by convergence on the same distortion of the truth. Relations are worst when images diverge in self-justifying directions. This occurs when nations embrace self-justifying historical myths, or adopt distorted pictures of their own and others' current conduct and character that exaggerate the legitimacy of their own cause. Such myths and distortions can expand a nation's sense of its right and its need to oppress its minorities or rescue its diaspora. If carried to extremes, such myths can also transform nationalism from symmetrical to asymmetrical—from a purely self-liberating enterprise into a hegemonistic enterprise.[41]

Chauvinist mythmaking is a hallmark of nationalism, practiced by nearly all nationalist movements to some degree.[42] These myths are purveyed through the schools, especially in history teaching,[43] through literature, or by political elites. They come in three principal varieties: self-glorifying, self-whitewashing, and other-maligning. Self-glorifying myths incorporate claims of special virtue and competence, and false claims of past benefi-cence toward others.[44] Self-whitewashing myths incorporate false denial of past wrongdoing against others.[45] Both types of myths can lead a nation to claim a right to rule others ("we are especially virtuous, so our expansion benefits those we conquer"). They also lead a nation to view others' com-plaints against them as expressions of ungrateful malice ("we have never harmed them; they slander us by claiming we did"). This can produce conflict spirals, as the nation responds to others' legitimate complaints with hostility, believing that the claimant knows its claims are illegitimate and will back down if challenged.[46] The targets of this hostility, in turn, will take it as further evidence of the nation's inherent cruelty and injustice. Self-glorifying myth, if it contains claims of cultural superiority, can also feed false faith in one's capacity to defeat and subdue others, causing expansion-ist wars of optimistic miscalculation.

Myths that malign others can incorporate claims of others' cultural in-feriority, false blame of others for past crimes and tragedies, and false claims that others now harbor malign intentions against the nation.[47] Such myths support arguments for the righteousness and necessity of denying equal rights to minorities living in the national territory, and for subjugating peo-ples farther afield. These minorities and distant peoples are perceived as imperiling the nationalistic country if they are left unsuppressed; moreover, their suppression is morally justified by their (imagined) misconduct, past and planned.

Self-whitewashing myths are probably the most common of these three varieties.[48] The dangers they pose are proportional to the gravity of the crimes they whitewash. If small crimes are denied, their denial is seen as disrespect that victims can choose to overlook. The denial may even spring from simple ignorance; if so, it conveys little insult. If great crimes are denied, however, their denial conveys contempt for the victims' very human-ity. The denial cannot be ascribed to unintended ignorance (if truly great crimes are forgotten, the forgetting is willful), hence it conveys greater insult. And being willful, the denial implies a dismissal of the crime's wrong-ness, which in turn suggests an ominous willingness to repeat it. As a result, the denial of great crimes provokes greater hostility from the victims than the denial of minor crimes.[49] Thus Croatian historians and politicians who whitewashed the Croatian Ustashi's vast murders of Serbs during World War II were playing with especially powerful dynamite.[50] The crimes they denied were enormous, hence their denial had serious ramifications, feeding Serb hostility that led to the Serbo-Croatian war of 1991–92. Likewise, the question of historical responsibility for Stalin's crimes in the former Soviet Union is especially explosive because the crimes in question are so vast.

Why are myths purveyed? They emanate largely from nationalist political elites, for whom they serve important political functions. Some of these functions also serve the nation as a whole, while others serve only the narrow interests of the elite. Self-glorifying belief-systems encourage citizens to contribute to the national community—to pay taxes, join the army, and fight for the nation's defense. These purposes are hard to fault, although the myths purveyed to achieve them may nevertheless have pernicious side-effects. Myths also bolster the authority and political power of incumbent elites: self-glorifying and self-whitewashing myths allow elites to shine in the reflected luster of their predecessors' imagined achievements and the imagined glory of the national institutions they control. Myths that malign others enhance the authority of elites by supporting claims that the nation faces external threats, thus deflecting popular hostility away from national elites and toward outsiders. Myths that serve only these purposes injure intercommunal relations without providing countervailing benefits to the general community.

Although mythmaking is ubiquitous among nationalisms, the scope and character of mythmaking varies widely across nations. National myths flourish most when elites need them most, when opposition to myths is weakest, and when publics are most myth-receptive. Four principal factors govern the level of infection by nationalist myth.

(1) *The legitimacy of the regime.* In cases where the national movement remains stateless, this factor concerns the legitimacy of the movement's leaders. As just noted, nationalist myths can help politically frail elites to strengthen their grip on power. The temptation for elites to engage in mythmaking is therefore inversely proportional to their political legitimacy: the less legitimate their rule, the greater their incentive to resort to myths.

A regime's legitimacy in turn depends on its representativeness, its competence and efficiency, and the scope of the tasks that face it. Unrepresentative regimes face challenges from underrepresented groups, and the regime sows myths to build the support needed to defeat this challenge.[51] This motive helped fuel the extreme nationalism that swept Europe in the late nineteenth century: oligarchic regimes used chauvinist myths, often spread through the schools, to deflect demands from below for a wider sharing of political and economic power.[52] Corrupt regimes or regimes that lack competence due to underinstitutionalization will likewise deploy chauvinist myths to divert challenges from publics and elites. This is a common motive for mythmaking in the Third World. Finally, regimes that face overwhelming tasks—such as economic or social collapse, perhaps caused by exogenous factors—are often tempted to use myths to divert popular impatience with their inability to improve conditions. For example, the Great Depression fueled nationalist mythmaking in some industrial states during the 1930s.[53]

These factors correlate closely with the ebb and flow of nationalist mythmaking through history. Nationalist mythmaking reached high tide in Europe when the continent's regimes had little legitimacy, during 1848–1914. Recourse to myth then fell dramatically as these regimes democratized and their societies became less stratified, which greatly lessened popular challenge to elites.[54]

(2) *The scope of the demands posed by the state on its citizenry.* The more the regime asks of its citizens, the harder it must work to persuade its citizens to fulfill these demands. This equation increases the temptation to deploy nationalist myths for purposes of social mobilization. Regimes at war often use myths to motivate sacrifice by their citizens and to justify their cruelties against others.[55] These belief-systems can live on after the war to poison external relations in later years. Mass revolutionary movements often infuse their movements with mythical propaganda for the same reason; these myths survive after the revolution is won.[56] Regimes that are forced by external threats to sustain large peacetime military efforts are likewise driven to use myths to sustain popular support. This is especially true if they rely on mass armies for their defense.[57] Finally, totalitarian regimes place large demands on their citizens, and use correspondingly large doses of chauvinist stories to induce their acquiescence.

(3) *Domestic economic crisis.* In societies suffering economic collapse, mythmaking can take scapegoating form—the collapse is falsely blamed on domestic or international malefactors. Here the mythmaking flourishes because of the increased receptivity of the audience. The public is more willing to believe that others are responsible for their pain when they are, in fact, suffering; when that pain is new and surprising, they search for the hand of malevolent human agents. Germany in the 1930s is the standard example.[58]

(4) *The strength and competence of independent evaluative institutions.* Societies that lack free speech traditions, a strong free press, and free universities are more vulnerable to mythmaking because they lack "truth squads" to counter

the nationalist mythmakers. Independent historians can be an antidote to official historical mythmaking; an independent press is an antidote to official mythmaking about current events. The absence of academic freedom and free media is a permissive condition for nationalist mythmaking.[59] Wilhelmine Germany illustrates: the German academic community failed to counter the official myths of the era, and scholars often helped purvey the propaganda.[60]

Several conclusions follow from this discussion. Democratic regimes are less prone to mythmaking, because such regimes are usually more legitimate and are free-speech tolerant; hence they can develop evaluative institutions to weed out nationalist myth. Absolutist dictatorships that possess a massive military superiority over their citizens are also less prone to mythmaking, because they can survive without it. The most dangerous regimes are those that depend on some measure of popular consent, but are narrowly governed by unrepresentative elites. Things are still worse if these governments are poorly institutionalized, are incompetent or corrupt for other reasons, or face overwhelming problems that exceed their governing capacities. Regimes that emerged from a violent struggle, or enjoy only precarious security, are also more likely to retain a struggle-born chauvinist belief-system.

PREDICTIONS AND PRESCRIPTIONS

The hypotheses set out in this chapter can be used to generate forecasts; applied to Europe, they predict that nationalism will pose little risk to peace in Western Europe but will endanger peace in Eastern Europe.

Most of the nationalisms of the West are satisfied, having already gained states. Western diasporas are few and small, reflecting the relative homogeneity of Western national demography, and Western minorities are relatively well treated. The historic grievances of Western nationalities against one another are also small—many of the West's interethnic horrors have faded from memory, and the perpetrators of the greatest recent horror—the Germans—have accepted responsibility for it and reconciled with their victims. The regimes of the West are highly legitimate, militarily secure, and economically stable; hence chauvinist mythmaking by their elites is correspondingly rare. The West European nationalisms that caused the greatest recent troubles, those of Germany and Italy, are now clearly benign, and the conditions for a return to aggressive nationalism are absent in both countries. Outsiders sometimes fear that outbreaks of anti-immigrant extremism in Germany signal the return of German fascism, but the forces of tolerance and decency are overwhelmingly dominant in Germany, and the robust health of German democracy and of German academic and press institutions ensures they will remain strong. As a result nationalism should cause very little trouble in Western Europe.

In the East the number of stateless nationalisms is larger, raising greater risk that future conflicts will arise from wars of liberation. The collapse of Soviet dominance shifted the balance of power toward these nationalisms, by replacing the Soviet state with weaker successor states. This shift has produced secessionist wars in Georgia and Moldova, and such wars could multiply. The tangled pattern of interethnic intermingling across the East creates large diasporas. East European societies have little tradition of respect for minority rights, which steps up the likelihood that these diasporas will face abuse; this in turn may spur their homelands to try to incorporate them by force. The borders of many emerging East European nations lack natural defensive barriers, leaving the state exposed to attack; some borders also lack legitimacy, and correspond poorly with ethnic boundaries. Some new East European regimes, especially those in the former Soviet Union, lack legitimacy and are underinstitutionalized, intensifying the probability that they will resort to chauvinist mythmaking to maintain their political viability. This risk is heightened by the regional economic crisis caused by the transition from command to market economies. Evaluative institutions (free universities and a free press) remain weak in Eastern Europe, raising the odds that myths will pass unchallenged. Under Bolshevism the Soviet regime committed vast crimes against its subject peoples; this legacy will embitter relations among these peoples if they cannot agree on who deserves the blame.[61]

The East European picture is not all bleak. The main preconditions for democracy—high levels of literacy, some degree of industrial development, and the absence of a landed oligarchy—exist across most of the East. As a result, the long-term prospects for democracy are bright. Moreover, the East's economic crisis is temporary: the conditions for prosperous industrial economies (a trained workforce and adequate natural resources) do exist, so the crisis should ease once the market transition is completed. These relatively favorable long-term prospects for democracy and prosperity dampen the risk that chauvinist mythmaking will get out of hand.[62] The fact that the new East European states managed to gain freedom without violent struggles also left them with fewer malignant beliefs, by allowing them to forgo infusing their societies with chauvinist war propaganda. The power and ethnographic structure of Eastern Europe, while dangerous, is less explosive than that of Yugoslavia: historic grievances and military power coincide less tightly (there is no other East European equivalent of Serbia, having both military superiority and large historical grievances); and ethnographic patterns create less imperative for a diaspora-rescue operation by the state most likely to attempt such a rescue (i.e., Russia.)

All in all, however, conditions in Eastern Europe are more bad than good; hence nationalism will probably produce substantial violence there over the next several decades.[63]

What policy prescriptions are in order? The Western powers should move to dampen the risks that nationalism poses in the East, by moving to channel manipulable aspects of East European nationalism in benign directions. Some aspects of East European nationalist movements are immutable (e.g., their degree of intermingling, or the history of crimes between them). Other features, however, can be decided by the movements themselves (e.g., their attitude toward minorities, their vision of history, and their willingness to reach final border settlements with others); these can be influenced by the West if the movements are susceptible to Western pressure or persuasion. The Western powers should use their substantial economic leverage to bring such pressure to bear.

Specifically, the Western powers should condition their economic relations with the new Eastern states on these states' conformity with a code of peaceful conduct that proscribes policies that make nationalism dangerous. The code should have six elements: (1) renunciation of the threat or use of force; (2) robust guarantees for the rights of national minorities, to include, under some stringent conditions, a legal right to secession;[64] (3) commitment to the honest teaching of history in the schools,[65] and agreement to refrain from the propagation of chauvinist or other hate propaganda; (4) willingness to adopt a democratic form of government, and to accept related institutions—specifically, free speech and a free press;[66] (5) adoption of market economic policies, and disavowal of protectionist or other beggar-thy-neighbor economic policies toward other East European states; and (6) acceptance of current national borders, or agreement to settle contested borders promptly though peaceful means. This list rests on the premise that "peaceful conduct" requires that nationalist movements renounce the use of force against others (element 1), and also that they agree to refrain from policies that the hypotheses presented here warn against (elements 2–6).

Table 8.1 summarizes the hypotheses. Hypothesis I.4 warns that the risk of war rises when nationalist movements oppress their minorities; hence the code of peaceful conduct requires respect for minority rights (element 2). Hypothesis II.6 cautions that divergent beliefs about mutual history and current conduct and character raise the risk of war; hence the code asks for historical honesty and for curbs on official hate propaganda (element 3). Hypothesis II.6.a warns that illegitimate governments have a greater propensity to mythmake, and hypothesis II.6.d maintains that chauvinist myths

Table 8.1. Hypotheses on Nationalism and War: Summary

I. Immediate Causes
   1. The greater the proportion of state-seeking nationalities that are stateless, the greater the risk of war.
   2. The more that nationalities pursue the recovery of national diasporas, and the more they pursue annexationist strategies of recovery, the greater the risk of war.
   3. The more hegemonistic the goals that nationalities pursue toward one another, the greater the risk of war.
   4. The more severely nationalities oppress minorities living in their states, the greater the risk of war.
II. Causes of These Causes and Conditions Required for Their Operation
   Structural Factors
   1. Stateless nationalisms pose a greater risk if they have the strength plausibly to reach for freedom and the central state has will to resist their attempt.
   2. The more densely nationalities are intermingled, the greater the risk of war.
      a. The risks posed by intermingling are larger the more local (house-by-house) rather than regional (province-by-province) the pattern of intermingling.
      b. The risks posed by intermingling are larger if the rescue of diasporas by homelands is difficult but possible; smaller if rescue is either impossible or easy.
   3. The greater the defensibility and legitimacy of borders, and the greater the correspondence between these political borders and communal boundaries, the smaller the risk of war.
      a. The less secure and defensible the borders of emerging nation-states, the greater the risk of war.
      b. The greater the international legitimacy of the borders of emerging nation-states, the smaller the risk of war.
      c. The more closely the boundaries of emerging nation-states follow ethnic boundaries, the smaller the risk of war.
   Political/Environmental Factors
   4. The greater the past crimes committed by nationalities toward one another, the greater the risk of war.
      a. The better these crimes are remembered by the victims, the greater the risk of war.
      b. The more that responsibility for past crimes can be attached to groups still on the scene, the greater the risk of war.
      c. The less contrition and repentance shown by the guilty groups, the greater the risk of war.
      d. The greater the coincidence of power and victimhood, the greater the risk of war.
   5. The more severely nationalities oppress minorities now living in their states, the greater the risk of war. (This restates Hypothesis I.4; I list it twice because it operates as both a direct and a remote cause of war.)
   Perceptual Factors
   6. The more divergent are the beliefs of nationalities about their mutual history and their current conduct and character, the greater the risk of war.
      a. The less legitimate the governments or leaders of nationalist movements, the greater their propensity to purvey mythical nationalist beliefs, hence the greater the risk of war.
      b. The more the state must demand of its citizens, the greater its propensity to purvey mythical nationalist beliefs, hence the greater the risk of war.
      c. If economic conditions deteriorate, publics become more receptive to scapegoat myths, hence such myths are more widely believed, hence war is more likely.
      d. If independent evaluative institutions are weak or incompetent, myths more often prevail, hence war is more likely.

---

prevail more often if independent evaluative institutions are weak; hence the code asks that movements adopt democracy (to bolster legitimacy) and respect free speech and free press rights (to bolster evaluation) (element 4). Hypothesis II.6.c warns that economic collapse promotes chauvinist mythmaking; hence the code asks movements to adopt market reforms, on the grounds that prosperity requires marketization (element 5). Hypothesis II.3.b posits that the risk of war rises if the borders of emerging nation-states lack legitimacy; hence the code requests movements to legitimize their borders through formal settlement (element 6).[67]

The Western powers should enforce this code by pursuing a common economic policy in dealings with the states of the East: observance of the code should be the price for full membership in the Western economy, while nonobservance should bring exclusion and economic sanctions.[68] This policy should be married to an economic aid package to assist marketization, also conditioned on code observance.

The Bush and Clinton administrations have adopted elements of this policy but omitted key aspects. In September 1991 Secretary of State James Baker outlined five principles that incorporate most of the six elements in the code of conduct outlined here (only element 3—honest treatment of history—was unmentioned), and he indicated that American policy toward the new East European states would be conditioned on their acceptance of these principles.[69] During the spring and summer of 1992 the Bush administration also proposed a substantial economic aid package (the Freedom Support Act) and guided it through Congress.

However, Baker's principles later faded from view. Strangely, the Bush administration failed clearly to condition release of its aid package on East European compliance with these principles. It also failed to forge a common agreement among the Western powers to condition their economic relations with the East European states on these principles. The principles themselves were not fleshed out. Most important, the minority rights that the East European states must protect were not detailed, leaving these states free to adopt a watered-down definition. The Bush administration also recognized several new East European governments (e.g., Azerbaijan's) that gave Baker's principles only lip service while violating them in practice.[70] The Clinton administration has largely followed in Bush's footsteps: it continued Bush's aid program, but omitted clear political conditions.[71]

There is still time for such a policy, but the clock is running out. A policy resting on economic sticks and carrots will be too weak to end major violence once it begins; hence the West should move to avert trouble while it still lies on the horizon.

9

Ethnic Nationalisms and Implications for U.S. Foreign Policy

Henry Bienen

The breakdown of empires, the creation of new states, and transformations in existing political systems always raise new foreign policy issues for neighboring states and for large powers. Thus, the collapse of the Soviet Union, far-reaching political changes in Eastern Europe, and fundamental alterations in the relations among the East European countries and Russia have created new opportunities and problems for Western Europe and for the United States. There are, no doubt, lessons to be learned for U.S. foreign policy from the histories of Europe in the aftermath of the French and Russian revolutions, the breakdown of the Austro-Hungarian and Ottoman empires, and the creation of new states after World War II. However, U.S. policy responses to the profound post-1989 changes in the international system in Europe and in Central Asia must follow from an understanding and redefinition of our national interest as well as from an assessment of the dangers posed by new and old nationalisms set loose by the loss of Soviet control in Eastern Europe, the disappearance of the Soviet Union itself, and the end of the Cold War.

Pundits and policymakers have been preoccupied by the awful bloodletting in the former Yugoslavia. For many people, the optimism stemming from change in East Europe and the USSR has given way to fears that the experiences of Yugoslavia will be repeated in other Eastern European countries and perhaps in Russia itself on an even greater scale and that not only civil war but interstate wars may occur. These seem possible because newly independent states have arisen out of the old Soviet Union and are already engaging in cross-border conflict in the Caucasus, as is happening in the successor states to Yugoslavia.

158

West European countries and the United States, confronted by the crisis in Bosnia, search for policies and employ historical analogies to try to capture the present situation. Were we so unprepared for the post–Cold War world that we underestimated enduring ethnically based enmities that remind us of a situation better described as pre–World War I than a New World Order? Does the disunity of the West and its failure to stop ethnic cleansing in Bosnia and Croatia presage a post-Munich Europe? Or is there a failure of leadership and a withdrawal of U.S. power from Europe that can be captured by images of American isolationism and the breakdown of collective security in the 1920s and 1930s?

Those who entertain these images add to them the idea that if conflict is not stopped in the former Yugoslavia it will spread north to Hungary and south and east through the Balkans. They anticipate demonstration and contagion effects: if the aggressor can get away in Bosnia with rape, murder, genocide, the forcible change of territorial boundaries, and the effective destruction of an independent state, what is to stop others in Eastern Europe, Russia, and perhaps in Western Europe from playing the nationalism card and creating instability in the very heart of Europe?

The dilemmas for policymakers are not new ones. The nationalist demands made by some ethnic groups in the former Yugoslavia and the former Soviet Union already have resulted in the creation of new states. But these demands also have been resisted by those who did not want the breakup of the old order. Moreover, they have been resisted by ethnic communities that once were majorities and now have become minorities in the new state: for example, Serbs in Bosnia, and Russians in the Baltics.

The questions raised for U.S. policymakers are old ones. How much self-determination is a good thing? How shall ethnic minority rights be protected? How destabilizing will be demands made by ethnic groups for secession or for amalgamation? These questions have been answered in various ways since Woodrow Wilson argued for relatively unconstrained self-determination in 1918.

The United States usually supported nationalist movements after World War II in Asia, Africa, and the Middle East. Later, for the most part, it supported maintaining the territorial integrity of states in these areas. The United States did not support the breakup of Nigeria; it has not wanted to see the dissolution of Iraq or the creation of a new Kurdish state. In Europe, it has not supported secessionist movements in Spain. The Bush administration, while rhetorically committed to the independence of the Baltic States from the Soviet Union, did not push for the breakup of the USSR. The United States did agree to the independence of Eritrea from Ethiopia and, well after German recognition of Croatia, it supported the creation of new states from the old Yugoslavia. But U.S. policymakers have been more concerned with stability of the state system, more concerned about creating viable economic structures, more concerned about not opening the Pandora's box of ethnically based demands for new nation-states, than they have been concerned to support self-determination everywhere as a principle.

The policy argument that follows is that the United States should not favor secessionist movements in Europe except in the extreme case of persecution of a community which makes life intolerable within present state borders. Normatively, one could argue the value of self-determination pro and con. Practically, large-scale movements of peoples to create homogeneous states usually is very difficult to bring about except through war and forced migration, the very processes that we see today in the former Yugoslavia. Instead, we should encourage the viability and strength of multi-ethnic states by working with our NATO allies and with others to provide carrots—access to markets, assistance, and association and eventual entrance into the European Community—to states that obey norms of tolerance and maintain the rights of minorities. We should make clear our commitment to democratic processes, pluralism, and institutional safeguards to ensure the welfare of ethnic minorities inside states.

Europe must use the same carrots in Eastern Europe that it used when linking entry into the European Community for Spain, Greece, and Portugal with the willingness of those countries to pursue democratic practices. If the West is protectionist toward East European goods and exclusionist toward East European labor, it will give up critical policy tools to effect change positively. We should affirm our commitments to the present borders of Europe and guarantee those borders through formal pacts and agreements and by associating East European countries with NATO.

These are important policies to consider.[1] And they do not exhaust the list of things the United States can continue to do or to do with more vigor in order to moderate nationalist tensions and work to stabilize fluid interstate relations in Eastern Europe. However, an underlying assumption of this chapter is that ethnically based nationalisms in Europe do not threaten U.S. national security. While ethnically based nationalisms run against the grain of many things we wish and hope for, and while they often violate our values and sometimes harm our interests, they are not likely to be profoundly destabilizing or harmful to *vital* interests.[2]

NATIONAL SECURITY AND NATIONAL INTERESTS

It is possible for leaderships and for segments of populations to make mistakes in their evaluation of security threats. Not every one agreed, of course, that German nationalism or Nazism posed a threat to American interests in the late 1930s. Isolationists of various stripes saw no threats posed to American interests or to national security by events in Europe. Later, how threatening the Soviet Union was to America was perhaps more debatable *after* than during the Cold War. While a strong consensus existed that there was a threat, whether this threat stemmed from Soviet ideology, Russian nationalism, or Soviet Great-Power status was much debated among foreign policy and Soviet experts.

The current debate about American intervention in the former Yugoslavia has been especially interesting because it takes place in the context of an incipient debate about how to define national interests and national security in the aftermath of the Cold War. At the same time, there exists a widely shared concern to refocus American priorities on the domestic agenda. There is a consensus, from neo-isolationists to those who want to end American unilateralism and who want to bring into being a New World Order under the auspices of international agencies, that more attention should be paid to domestic concerns. For some, putting the U.S. domestic house in order is a prerequisite for having a strong foreign policy. For others, the domestic concerns are themselves paramount and have been neglected by a Cold War focus on defense and on the Soviet Union. Of course, views are mixtures of these positions.

Many issues raised in this incipient debate are old ones. Should the national interest, and a derivative idea of national security, be narrowly conceived to mean the preservation of territorial integrity and independence of decision-making by national elites? And if so, what are the bounds of the territory and who are the elites? Is the preservation of national values part of security, and, if so, what are the values and should they be promulgated abroad? The idealist/realist debates engaged many of these concerns. Now, the argument is made by some that we need an expanded idea of security. It is maintained not only that fostering democracy abroad will lead to a more stable and peaceful international system and thus is a security concern for the United States, but that the national interest can be defined in terms of increasing the number of democratic states. This is a good in and of itself. It is also maintained that preservation of both the U.S. environmental quality and, more broadly, international environments should be understood in realist terms as essential to the maintenance of life and welfare in the United States.[3] If this argument were taken literally, it could lead to major new U.S. commitments abroad.

On the other hand, the argument is heard that America must now be a more "normal" country.[4] Part of this argument is a thrust against American exceptionalism, against the idea of American hegemony. Security, it is said, should be more narrowly defined and economic welfare should be emphasized more than military concerns since military threats are less likely with the end of the Cold War. The America that threw a security umbrella over Europe, Japan, and Korea after World War II, the America that was willing to open markets to competitors, must now worry about its own trade competitiveness and its savings rate and productivity. For some analysts of the post–Cold War period, neither the idealism of the left nor the right's concern for Great Power status or for making unilateral determinations about global security issues make much sense in a world of trading states.[5]

There are those who insist that the U.S. must not let genocide occur again in Europe. I stress *Europe* because few, if any, voices have been raised for American military intervention in the Sudan, where ethnic conflict is a large component of long-standing and bloody struggles. Nor has anyone argued, to my knowledge, that U.S. military power should be brought to bear to help resolve conflicts and to stop violence in Kashmir or Afghanistan, where, again, ethnicity intersects with regional and factional struggles as well as religious and ideological ones.

For those who believe that the U.S. should intervene in the former Yugoslavia, perhaps unilaterally if necessary, on human rights grounds, the old frightful faces of pre–World War II European nationalisms have been important in thinking about post–Cold War nationalisms. Serbian or Georgian nationalisms are perceived as having possible demonstration effects. The argument is: stop ethnic cleansing now before it spreads elsewhere in the Balkans, Eastern Europe, the old Soviet Union, and perhaps Western Europe as well. The specter of Nazism is raised; the vulnerability of ethnic minorities is emphasized; and the fact that some of the old nasty players seem with us again almost fifty years later in Croatia and elsewhere is not irrelevant to the debate. We now have a new contagion theory of the spreading effects of nationalism and nationalist-based conflicts tied to the Munich metaphor. If we do not stop ethnic cleansing and the ugly nationalisms in the former Yugoslavia, we will see extreme nationalist behavior emulated elsewhere in Europe.

For those who move beyond human rights arguments for intervention in Bosnia, the appeals of nationalist separatist groups seem to provide a challenge to principles of state sovereignty, territorial integrity, and the inviolability of borders.[6] Thus, the perception of ethnic conflict and nationalism as threatening to U.S. national interests and to national security has entangled ethnic conflict and nationalism, themselves not the same thing, with national interest and national security, themselves not the same thing.

Typically, there is much less consensus over what constitutes the national interest at any given time than there is consensus over what constitutes national security. As noted earlier, there is a general sense in the country that more attention should be paid to domestic concerns than has been the case. When we come to economic agreements, Congress is heavily involved and there is even less consensus about the national interest writ large. For example, whether the North American Free Trade Association was good or bad for U.S. national interest was hotly debated. There has been support for specific interventions, such as sending U.S. troops to Somalia, until the intervention(s) turned sour. There is support for promoting human rights abroad. But there is no reason to believe that support would be forthcoming for many interventions such as that in Somalia. I will argue that these dispositions are sound ones.

If Americans could wave a magic wand and stop the killing in Angola or in Rwanda, to name only two examples, and turn those countries into paragons of stability and democracy, few would be against the wave of the wand. But relatively few Americans would be in favor of major commitments to try to bring about those outcomes. Few would see the national interest served by so doing or national security threatened by turning away from the task. And here the majority is correct.

POLICY PRESCRIPTIONS

I do not share the assumptions stated elsewhere in this volume that ethnicity and national identity will be the central forces shaping Europe in the next decades—although they will be important. United States relations with Europe and intra-European relations are more likely to pivot on economic questions of trade and finance. More traditional power politics having to do with Great and Middle Power status and relative influence may bedevil relations among European states more than the virulent ethnic conflicts we see now in the former Yugoslavia.

Moreover, when ethnically based conflicts do emerge, the U.S. will find it difficult to influence them, just as it has found its ability to affect change to its liking in Serbia, Bosnia, and Croatia to be limited, to say the least. I am extremely skeptical that we can modify antipathies via educational processes, or that we can provide models from the West for how people should cooperate in Eastern Europe or in Russia. I am even skeptical of the idea that we can blame much of the ethnic conflict in the Balkans, Eastern Europe, Russia, and the Caucasus on parlous economic conditions and on the difficulties of the transitions from state to market economies. Yes, world economic conditions are not propitious for democratic transitions. But good times can exacerbate ethnic tensions too. Some groups do better than others; some take advantage of access to new markets; some lose preferred positions they had through control of the instruments of the state. Status reversal occurs between ethnic groups. Class and status relations are not irrelevant to ethnic tensions.

It may be very difficult to create smoother relations among peoples in Eastern Europe who exist in less homogeneous states than those of Western Europe (although we often exaggerate the homogeneity of the latter). This said, I do not anticipate chaos and ethnic conflict everywhere. For one thing, arguments stating that Western weakness in the face of genocide in Bosnia will have demonstration and contagion effects seem dubious to me. Every leadership that contemplates using force to work its will internally on some segment of its own population or thinks about the use of military force across its own borders makes a judgment as to whether neighboring or large outside powers will themselves intervene. The past behavior of the potential intervenor will be measured against a perception of its present interests. Contemporary leaders do not give great weight to the past behavior of states. Leaders always make judgments about the importance of their specific concerns and those interests that they represent and the utility of military force in attaining them. That the U.S. engaged in World War II did not persuade the North Koreans not to invade South Korea. The United States-led alliance which forced Iraq out of Kuwait in 1991 did not persuade Slobodan Milošević and company to stay their hands in Croatia and Bosnia.

I do not contest that the conditions exist for the spread of ethnic conflict and for elites to use nationalism and ethnicity to create new political bases. These phenomena are occurring across Eastern Europe, in the Baltics and Balkans and in Central Asia as they did in Africa, Asia, and the Middle East with the creation of new states after World War II.[7] This is not because of emulation or demonstration effects. It is because the withdrawal of Soviet power creates new conditions within Russia, Eastern Europe, and the successor states of the USSR. Indeed, ethnic conflicts had broken out within and between republics of the Soviet Union before Mikhail Gorbachev's fall from power in 1990–91. It had become clear already that the Soviet leadership was not willing to commit sufficient military force to end outbreaks of ethnically based fighting within the empire. Moreover, the collapse of communist parties requires old elites to find a new base of power in societies that are very much in flux. Appealing to ethnic communities and to national sentiments is an old formula for constituting or reconstituting a base of power.

THE ISSUE OF INTERVENTION

The historical images of appeasement and comparisons of the breakdown of collective security arrangements are conjured up by those who want American military intervention, or, at the least, want U.S. leadership of NATO intervention in Bosnia. The views expressed stem from a concern for a loss of stability in Europe and from a fear that the Western alliance as we have known it since World War II will break apart as West European nations take their own stances toward the states of Eastern Europe and the former Soviet Union.

Interventionist proclivities are also voiced by those concerned above all with human rights violations and with the consequences of turning a blind eye to violations of UN resolutions. Here, some of the strongest opponents of U.S. intervention in Vietnam call for U.S. involvement in Bosnia—albeit usually under United Nations auspices. For what is left of the left, and this represents only a segment of those who call for intervention, the idea is to tame American power by embedding it within international agencies.

Opposition to intervention comes from those who argue from a range of positions. At one extreme are the neo-isolationists who argue that no U.S. interests, security or otherwise, are at stake in the former Yugoslavia or in Eastern Europe. For them, this has always been an area of dirty and messy conflicts, more a part of the Third World than the First, and best left to its ugly and ancient hatreds. Less sweeping in their commitment to nonintervention are those who argue that either it is too late to intervene with ground troops in Bosnia or that the U.S. would get bogged down with hundreds of thousands of troops in Bosnia and Croatia and perhaps in Serbia as it did when it confronted Vietnamese nationalism more than two decades ago.

Whether old or new nationalisms in Europe pose security threats for the U.S. depends on an evaluation of nationalisms within their geopolitical contexts. It depends also on evaluations of the U.S. national interest and a *conception* of U.S. national security. Americans have long debated the meaning of security and whether specific challenges were threatening or not. We will now debate whether various nationalisms are threatening to our security.

My own view is that changes in Eastern Europe and the breakup of the Soviet Union do, indeed, constitute a fundamental alteration in the international system. However, the United States has lived with instability stemming from ethnic conflict in many parts of the world and it can do so in Eastern Europe. Ethnic conflict usually, but not always, will be contained within states. More dangerous than majorities dealing badly with ethnic minorities, as deplorable as this is, more dangerous even than civil wars in the Balkans and in the successor states of the Soviet Union, would be large-scale conflict among these states. However, even in a situation of open military conflict between the two most important successor states, Ukraine and Russia, U.S. military involvement would be extremely unlikely. After all, despite all the talk of rolling back the Iron Curtain under John Foster Dulles's stewardship of U.S. foreign policy, the U.S. did not intervene when the Soviet Union deployed its military power in Hungary in 1956 or in Czechoslovakia in 1968; nor did we do so when the USSR earlier intervened in Poland and in East Germany.

Of course, foreign policy should be aimed at forestalling situations where no good options exist. Thus, if possible, the West should work to prevent such situations from arising. The issue is; what options do exist? To create options short of military intervention requires Western unity just as military intervention so requires. Effective embargoes, improved trade relations, foreign aid, these are all foreign policy instruments that would be more effectively deployed by a unified West. However, it is not likely that we can expect a unified Western approach to ethnic clashes in Europe any more than such unity has existed as the West has faced ethnic violence and nationalism outside of Europe. We have already seen a split among Western countries over the recognition of Slovenia and Croatia, with Germany in favor of early recognition and the United States originally opposed. Subsequently, Germany, Britain, France, and the United States were unable to provide cohesive support along the lines of the plans developed by former British foreign secretary David Owen and former secretary of state Cyrus Vance for a political settlement based on territorial and political realignment in 1991, or to agree to the lifting of the arms embargo against Bosnia. Managing Western divisions over potential and actual conflict in Eastern Europe and in the former Soviet Union will be difficult.

We can predict that there will be very little disposition in the U.S. for unilateral interventions in war or civil war situations in Eastern Europe. This disposition is a sound one. Nor will the United States engage in large-scale crisis management in advance of the crises. We can envision limited placement of trip-wire military forces in a few places, such as occurred in Macedonia. But since the ethnic conflicts in Eastern Europe are and will be intricate and since the U.S. will look first and foremost to domestic problems, both domestic political constraints and sound analyses will work against the United States becoming Eastern Europe's gendarme, holding the fort against all possible ethnic division in Europe and in the former Soviet Union.

To try to make the United States Europe's policeman would not be wise policy even if it were feasible policy. If the concern is to protect innocent lives from havoc wrought by ethnic conflict, why are Bosnian lives more precious than Angolan or South African or Sri Lankan ones? If the argument is that we should save lives where we can, I agree. But this takes us to an argument about what is feasible, not an argument that the United States should through its policies and its commitments anticipate ethnic antagonisms and new nationalisms by committing itself to combat them in advance or when they become virulent. If limited air power can accomplish agreed-on goals in Bosnia, the costs may well be commensurate with the gains.

The issue is, as always, what are the costs and benefits of actions? Which bad consequences can be prevented or mitigated and where? How threatening to U.S. interests are specific conflicts? How destabilizing are specific antagonisms? But these are old, not new questions and they can be answered within our understandings of national security and national interests. True, it will be critical for Western policymakers to stake out in advance potential crises to see whether problems in policy coordination can be anticipated. But, again, this is not a new phenomenon.

Surely, the idea that every area of potential civil unrest stemming from internal ethnic conflict threatens fundamental U.S. national interests is not a sustainable one. As long as Germany remains firmly anchored in the Western alliance, the security of Central and Western Europe will be preserved. Of course, the United States has a great concern for and national interest in orderly transitions in the east and in Russia especially. But aside from open interstate conflict between major powers, conflict that might turn nuclear under the worst case scenarios, U.S. national security is not at stake.

Indeed, this does not mean that the United States should not strive mightily for peaceful resolution of both intrastate and interstate disputes. And we should not forgo the use of military pressure as well as political and economic pressure to bring about changes in policies of aggressors where we can be effective. Military pressure might well have been useful against Serbia earlier and it still might be if we could deploy arms in concert with allies and selectively so. The use of force, however, can be considered only in specific circumstances. It makes no sense to see every ethnic conflict within and between countries as one that has the potential to lead to widespread conflict and as one threatening to fundamental U.S. security interests.

Also, we should not entertain the idea that we can micromanage ethnic conflicts. The evolution of the relations among ethnically and religiously based communities in Switzerland, Belgium, Britain, and Canada, not to say the United States, makes clear how complicated is the creation of constitutional and political formulas for managing ethnic disputes and allocating power based on the ways that communities differentiate themselves.

It has been difficult enough to impose economic conditionality on countries via broad economic targets such as lowering deficits and rates of inflation and floating exchange rates. The idea that outsiders can weaken virulent nationalisms through political conditionality requires a number of conditions to be present before we could hope for success. Sanctions policies can impose costs, as they did in Rhodesia, South Africa, and Iraq to name only three situations. But sactions rarely are decisive; they may require a significant amount of time before they bend others to one's will. And they can have unintended effects, such as occurred when Serbs rallied around Milošević. Cooperation of the sanctioning states needs to be established for sanctions to work at all. Sanctions work best when aimed, like economic conditionality, at effecting specific but flexible policy goals. Thus, sanctions, or the carrots of foreign aid, can be deployed to try to stop human rights violations more effectively than they can be used to influence negotiations over constitutional procedures or legal stipulations to protect minorities.

Of course, it is fully within our right to define our national interest to include the projection of values that affirm human and specifically minority rights, democracy, and peaceful resolution of disputes. Nonetheless, we must distinguish between our national interests, which include the projection of values, from what we consider to be essential national security concerns. The distinction between national security and national interest is not always accepted. Nor is it easy to agree on the content of either concept. But as we face new situations, especially in a context of the diffusion of economic power in the world and a perception in the United States that our resources are constrained and that domestic needs are very pressing, we must make distinctions as to what is threatening to us, what we desire, and what we can attain.

In order to make this argument fuller, we must understand and disentangle ethnic conflict and come to grips with nationalism.

ETHNICITY AND NATIONALISM

Ethnicity is the phenomenon of belonging and community, based on various criteria. Typically, the ethnic group is one where belonging is based on tracing of descent, oftentimes a fictive tracing of a people that involves a significant amount of mythmaking. Language and territory are usually significant in defining the ethnic group but not always. Ethnic groups are often spread around or across countries. Broadly speaking, communal associations refer to those of language, race, lineage, religion, culture. Ethnic associations are a subset of communal ones with the focus on lineage (descent) and language. But even language may be not very differentiating, as in the case of Serbo-Croatian. (For example, one may be an Italian-American or a German-American without being able to speak Italian or German.) Religious affiliation or territorial occupation may come to be the critical components that distinguish groups from each other.

It is not true that ethnic affiliations are simply those acquired at birth. Just as people change religions (although this is easier for an American to do by marriage or by movement than it is to do for a Muslim in a Middle Eastern state who may violate religious and civil law by leaving Islam), people can and do change ethnic affiliations. They sometimes accomplish this by marriage or by changing their self-definition. Indeed, societies are differentiated in interesting and important ways by how fluid are individual and group attachments. Societies are also differentiated by whether state formulas such as Nuremberg laws exist for defining membership in a group, whether the membership is desired or not.

The process of ethnic identification involves first-person identification (how one identifies oneself), second-person identification (whether others accept you into the group), and third-person identifications (the formal definitions made by the state and sometimes coded in law or constitution).[8] For example, Christian Serbs have a hard time seeing Bosnian Muslims who speak Serbian dialects as Serbs or perhaps even as Slavs. But third parties to the dispute do see them as Slavs and perhaps even as Serbs. Third parties may be outside the direct arena of conflict, but they may make identifications that are consequential for the outcomes of the conflict. For example, how do Russians see "Slavs" or "Serbs" in Serbia and Bosnia?

These complicated processes of identification involve interactions among groups and interactions between masses and elites. There are many different possible models for national integration and group identification in any given nation, and these may exist simultaneously or they may be held differentially by various groups. The assimilationist model states that all should incorporate some dominant cultural group's modes. For example, there may be insistence in a state that all should speak English or be Muslims in order to be good citizens. The melting pot model can be thought of as a melding together to forge a new identity or as a "stew" with distinguishable components that tolerate each other. In the hyphenated identity model, one can be a Catholic-American, a Polish-American, an African-American. The models and realities of individual and group identifications may be hard to specify and they may be fluid, but they are hardly irrelevant for assessing the potential for conflict within and between nations. An assessment leads us to the nexus of the relationship between ethnicity and nationalism which Paul Goble and George Schöpflin take up in this volume.

Nationalism, a political ideology that specifies loyalty to the nation and glorifies the nation, may or may not be based on a particular ethnic group. The Manifest Destiny of the United States did not single out a particular ethnic group but stressed the new community that had been created by Americans. The "new Soviet man" was not per se a Russian but supposedly was a new creature.

In this volume, Stephen Van Evera asks us to distinguish among nationalisms that pose much or little danger in Europe, making a distinction between benign and malignant nationalisms in part, but stressing more the structure of different situations in terms of potentials for violence. His criteria for deciding whether nationalisms are dangerous have to do with whether they exist in situations where statehood is largely attained or not; whether the nationalisms seek to incorporate a diaspora via expansion; whether other nations' rights to independence are respected, which seems to me a very fluid matter; and how internal minorities are treated within a nation, which also is a highly contingent phenomenon.

Van Evera suggests that if we can decide where to place specific nationalisms in terms of the criteria given, we can assess risks to peace and stability. But Van Evera takes as given rather than explains why individuals give primary loyalty to their own culture or ethnic group and why they seek states for these groups. I believe the reasons are crucial if we are to assess conflict possibilities.

Without getting inside the "black box," it may be difficult to evaluate whether or not economic downturns or foreign policy reverses will provide shocks to the existing nationalisms, transforming them into something even more virulent. Only by getting inside the black box can we assess whether searches for scapegoats will take place and which particular groups will be singled out. Historical identities and the ideological content of nationalisms matter, as does the content of ethnicity.[9]

It is true, however, as Van Evera states, that we must also examine the structure of situations. It is also true, as Steven Burg notes, that "the violence of ethnic-based conflicts is easily escalated by individual acts of brutality into widespread death and destruction."[10] This is not necessarily so because nationalism or ethnically based conflicts make for stronger emotions or more hatred than class-based conflicts or even factional ones. Colombians had no qualms in the mid-twentieth century killing each other over a person's party membership; Vietnam's and China's brutal civil wars were not ethnically based. And during the Cultural Revolution in China of the 1960s, a person's status and education provided sufficient reasons to degrade, torture, and kill. Millions of people in Russia were killed for putatively being "kulaks" in the 1930s.

The potential for escalating violence in ethnic conflicts may be more a function of the fact that, as in Bosnia today, ethnic communities live cheek by jowl in villages or towns and are very vulnerable to attack and counterattack. Language and location may make individuals and groups easily identifiable targets. There may be a security dilemma for ethnic groups who fear that they must strike first given their geographic and military vulnerabilities. But whether ethnically based nationalisms have a greater potential for eroding the cohesiveness of the state than class or factional conflicts is an open question.

Similarly, the question whether national expansion that is ethnically based is more destabilizing internationally than national expansion that stems from ideological imperatives or territorial imperatives, or from a sense of the need to preserve security by striking first, also seems open. Of course, a particular state's expansionism may stem from a combination of a sense of virulent national superiority, irredentism, ideology, and the security dilemma—as in Nazi Germany. But there was little irredentism in postrevolutionary France's policies or in Japan's in the 1930s, although nationalism figured in both cases.

Analysts of conflict in Russia and Eastern Europe have posed civic nationalism, defined as nationalism based on equal and universal citizenship rights within a territory, as a contrast to ethnic nationalism, defined as being based on the consciousness of a shared identity within a group, an identity rooted in shared culture and a belief in common ancestry.[11] These distinctions may be posed much too sharply as "good" (civic) and "bad" (ethnic) nationalisms, with civic nationalism as the nationalism of developed countries and ethnic nationalism as the nationalism of developing countries. We have many examples, however, of industrial democracies with their fair share of ethnic nationalisms, the salience of which has waxed and waned as in Quebec in Canada; Wales and Scotland in the United Kingdom; Flemish language issues in Belgium; continued separatist movements in the Basque Country and Catalonia in Spain. Indeed, it has been argued that industrialism has stimulated nationalism rather than sweeping it away by forcing a particular culture and language on populations within states.[12] It also has been argued that whatever the functional needs for homogeneity, European countries, including France, supposedly the centralized nation par excellence, had persisting localisms of language and culture well into the late nineteenth century.[13]

It is true that in many developing countries national identities within states are weak and there is a lack of commitment to the nation. Or, at least, the focus of identity for millions of people is a unit that is smaller than the nation-state whether that focus is tribe, clan, or language group. At the same time, the unit that draws loyalties may be larger than the nation-state when ethnic affines live beyond the borders of the state.[14] But this may hold for many people who live in industrial societies too, although the focus of identity is likely to be on subnational units rather than on larger transnational ones.[15]

For U.S. foreign policies to be soundly based, the dichotomies that we might well reject reach beyond good and bad nationalisms, beyond civic and ethnic ones. There is reason to believe that history counts but that it is much too simple to say that, as in the former Yugoslavia, ancient hatreds govern. Old grievances may be reformulated, disappear, rise again. New situations and struggles over scarce resources may define quite different tensions than existed in the past. Class and ethnicity often intersect. At least part of the conflict in the former Yugoslavia seems to be related to land grabbing and resource appropriation by one community from another. It may well be that Serbs want land corridors for security purposes to link Serbian communities in Serbia, Bosnia, and Croatia. But it also may be that Serbian peasants or recent migrants to cities resent Bosnian Muslims on class grounds as well as or more than on religious and ethnic ones.

Class differentiations have status and lifestyle implications. These may be acquired at birth just as communal distinctions are acquired at birth. What differs from context to context in conflict situations are the amounts and kinds of resources that are available for competition and the structures through which people compete. It is the form of the struggle and the relative weight of the factors that lead us to describe conflict as class or communally based.

Thus, while nationalism is a subject that requires analysis and reanalysis as to its content, fluidity, and impact, if we have recourse to the lessons of both pre-twentieth-century national construction in Europe, and in Asia and the Middle East too,[16] and if we examine the actions of new nations after World War II, it seems an exaggeration to say, as Jack Snyder does, that "nationalism is one of the gravest but least understood issues facing the international community today."[17] We know something about state formation, about the impact of ethnic conflict on nationalism and national conflict, and about the impact of economic decline on nationalism and inter-state conflict.[18]

What differentiates those who see little or large scope for deploying American power abroad? In the first place, the "little scopers" doubt that much can happen to threaten U.S. territorial integrity or its leaders' ability to make relatively unconstrained judgments and take actions down the line to preserve future independence of actions. Second, those with a narrow view of national security do not believe that most outcomes which are negative for the U.S. national interest are threats to national security. A nasty dictator coming to power who murders his own people on grounds of ethnic differences, or even does brutal things to neighboring states, does not necessarily threaten U.S. national security. Milošević's policies have been brutal in Kosovo and murderous in Bosnia but even as these policies violate American values, they do not threaten American security.

Would a Greater Serbia necessarily threaten U.S. national security? How destabilizing in Europe would be a Greater Serbia? What would be its claims? Does it want to annex parts of Hungary? Expel Hungarian speakers from Serbia? Take back Slovenia? Would any or all of these goals provoke a wider war in Central Europe? At what point, if any, would U.S. security interests be threatened?

To ask these questions is to take us back to the realm of rather traditional security concerns which do not depend primarily on assessing either ethnic conflict or Serbian ethnic nationalisms—although answers to them do require some assessment of the content of Serbian nationalism. In order to evaluate answers to these questions we need to evaluate both Serbian motives and aims and also Serbs' capacity to be an expansive Middle Power in Europe. Our judgments might lead us to want to guarantee some of the borders of Serbia's neighbors. The cast of the argument is different from one that suggests that any violation of human rights or United Nations resolutions in the former Yugoslavia per se is a threat to the security of the United States. Nor does casting the issue this way suggest that a breakdown of order in one place leads to an inevitable breakdown of collective security arrangements in Europe.

THE COLLAPSE OF EMPIRES

We know that the dissolution of empires creates boundary problems, new interstate rivalries and alliances, and new nationalisms.[19] The collapse of empires is relevant today with the dissolution of the Soviet Union and Yugoslavia. Barry Posen refers to the collapse of imperial regimes as a problem of "emerging anarchy."[20] New states must worry about their security. Some are large and strong; others are weak and small. Some have minorities within their new borders and these minorities may belong to a majority somewhere else, for example, Russians in the Baltic States, Ukraine, or Uzbekistan. Russia well may be able to protect Russians outside its new borders. But minorities may be greatly at risk in new entities. When the Ottoman Empire collapsed, Armenians, who had been relatively protected in the empire, were harmed grievously. Bosnian Muslims are at risk with the collapse of Yugoslavia.

In all these situations, particular policies themselves have been consequential. We cannot go back and change history but we can speculate as to what might have occurred if Germany, followed by others, had not recognized Croatia and Slovenia or if Bosnia's Muslim leadership had not declared its own independent state, or if communist leaders had not sought a new political base through hypernationalism. Perhaps the outcomes would have been the same for many of the reasons Posen and others give: with the collapse of central authority in multiethnic empires, a classic security dilemma arises among groups as it does among states. Rather than focus on the specific characteristics of groups or on the short-term incentives for new leaders to play "the nationalist card," Posen argues that we should focus on uneven state structures with different opportunities and vulnerabilities and on the conditions that make it hard to distinguish offensive from defensive capabilities.[21]

However, not all collapsed empires led to conflict among new states. Ataturk led Turks to seek their political future as Turks, and in so doing they turned their backs on Islamic solidarity and on the idea of a reconstituted Arab-Turkish Ottoman Empire.[22] Would a different brand of nationalism have led to attempts to reintegrate the empire from Istanbul or did structural conditions preclude this? Other successor states of the Ottoman Empire have had their conflicts and sometimes have gone to war with each other. But the Middle East has not been characterized by persistent and bloody inter-Arab state warfare in the twentieth century though inter-Arab wars have occurred. (The Iraq-Iran conflict was not an inter-Arab war.) Perhaps the content of Arab nationalism and Pan-Arabism did have a force here.

In other words, the collapse of empires points us to the problems that Posen and others address, but we still need to examine specific nationalisms in particular contexts as integrating or conflictual elements within and among states. Nationalisms can be destabilizing or stabilizing in any regional or subregional context and we can make deductions about their consequences. These deductions need to be tested against the empirical realities.

That is, the structural conditions and the specific nationalisms must be evaluated together to grasp their implications for U.S. foreign policy. While the numbers of states that exist, their relative sizes and power, and whether minorities are cut off from their core group when it is located in a different state all can be presumed to be consequential, it is often the waning of a central power rather than the creation of new states per se that allows ethnic conflict to break out or to escalate.

It is necessary also to understand whether ethnic, and national, identifications are relatively durable or fluid, whether ethnic ties are primordial or situational and newly created or recreated as elites seek to maintain their power.[23] Without such understanding, it is difficult to know whether sanctions will influence elites and masses or whether bargains can be struck over specific territorial and political disputes. Thus we ask ourselves whether the hatreds in Yugoslavia are ancient or newly manufactured by former communist party leaders who seek a new base of power in ethnicity and nationalism.

The answer, not surprisingly, is probably that there is a combination of ancient grievances and manipulation by elites. True, once sentiments are whipped up and certainly once bloodletting has occurred, it may be difficult for elites to put the genie of ethnic nationalism back in the bottle. But where, as in Serbia, elites have been strategic in their use of nationalism, it suggests that there is room for negotiation with outsiders over goals. This does not mean that outsiders, such as the United Nations or Western countries, can manipulate the strength of nationalisms directly. It seems to me very difficult for outsiders to be able to directly affect the form and content of nationalisms. Rather, the comparative advantage of outsiders is to make clear to nationalists the advantages and disadvantages of pursuing various goals by various means. They can negotiate with elites or even hold out for new players, with all the difficulties of that course being clear in U.S. dealings with Haiti and with Central American countries and with Iraq. Nationalisms rarely are directly malleable from abroad no matter how fluid are ethnic identifications and how torturous and changeable the course of nationalism under conditions of economic decline, power reversals, and status reversals within and between countries.

THERE are lessons to be learned for U.S. foreign policies in Central and Eastern Europe from the ways that the United States often has dealt with Asia, Latin America, and the Middle East since World War II. American foreign policy has been dominated by globalists more than by regionalists. Globalists, that is, those who focused primarily on Soviet-United States competition and global security issues, saw conflicts in Asia, Africa, Latin America, and the Middle East as largely derivative of that competition. They structured the outcome of foreign policy debates. National Security Advisors, Directors of the CIA, Secretaries of Defense, usually Secretaries of State, and, broadly speaking, members of the national security establishment can be labeled "globalists." These groups have been more influential than those who can be called "regionalists" and who argued that conflicts must be understood on the ground in all their specifics. The regionalists have asserted that without understanding local contexts, U.S. foreign policy would be built on sand.

Regionalists typically have been area experts in the academic community, sometimes country desk officers or regional assistant secretaries in the State Department or even national intelligence officers for regions in the CIA. They have argued against seeing all factional and ethnic conflicts as Cold War struggles even though these may have been affected by Soviet-American competition (more than they ever had implications for the balance of power in that competition). Regionalists argued, for example, against trying to persuade a military regime in Argentina that common British, American, and Argentinian defense of the South Atlantic against potential Soviet threats was more important than Argentina's claims on the Falklands. Globalists downplayed a rather traditional type of nationalism expressed in Argentina and whipped up by a military elite who feared loss of its power and was looking to consolidate that power by appealing to nationalist feelings. It was not that these facts were completely unknown to policymakers with a globalist bent. Rather, they let their concerns and predilections weigh too heavily on their assessment of likely Argentine actions.

There is a lesson for Europe here. Listen to the regionalists. Countries in Asia, Africa, Latin America, and the Middle East have had (and will have) disputes which are territorial and fueled by nationalism of a rather traditional type and which owe little or nothing to ethnic conflict and to diasporas. Further, the nationalisms we must worry about in Eastern Europe also may not look at all like the nationalisms that arise from the breakdown of multiethnic empires.

In Asia, for example, territorial disputes are still very much alive and they involve large as well as small powers. Japan wants the return of its northern islands from Russia. The latter needs Japanese assistance but domestic politics so far have not permitted the return of these islands, which are sparsely inhabited by Russians. Territorial disputes are possible between Russia and China; China and India; Laos and China; India and Pakistan; China and Vietnam; China and Burma; China and Taiwan; Malaysia and the Philippines, to name only some. The struggles are over resources and/or borders that raise security issues.[24]

Conflicts can be envisioned among East European states and those successors to the Soviet Union over water resources, trade, and immigration flows. These potential conflicts well may become intertwined with ethnic ones. Traditional disputes over economic and natural resources and flows of people may themselves attain symbolic content and engage the strong national feelings of large numbers even without the ethnic component and thus may fuel nationalisms. We can envision national pride infusing disputes over access to Danube water or admission to economic organizations. Greece's unhappiness with the creation of a state called Macedonia is a combination of its concern with ministates on its borders and territorial disputes plus its sense of proprietary right to the name Macedonia.

United States policymakers need to be able to gauge the nationalist components in a dispute in order to understand not only what is negotiable and under what terms but what issues have the potential for destabilizing national politics and allowing nationalist movements to grow.

Once we make judgments about nationalisms old and new and their effects on stability, the hard questions for U.S. policies still remain, as Bosnia makes evident. If senior U.S. policymakers decide in favor of American intervention, they need some level of consensus within the foreign policy apparatus and they need to build support for their judgments in the country. In the case of the former Yugoslavia, unilateral U.S. action without European support has proved impossible politically within the United States and perhaps logistically as well in the Balkans. For where there is conflict based on ethnicity and where ethnic groups are spread out in checkerboard fashion, as in Bosnia, it is very hard for outsiders to try to micromanage conflict. Local elites tend to have a lot of autonomy, especially where military commands are highly decentralized. It is this very situation that has given Europeans so much pause with respect to their military intervention in the former Yugoslavia.

It needs to be shown that conflict in the Balkans and in Eastern Europe calls into question U.S. national security. Analyses that are stronger than analogies to pre–World War I conditions must be made. Where is the large state with territorial and Great Power ambitions such as Germany had prior to World War I? Are we seeing a Russia reborn with new demands whose own nationalism is fueled by instability on its western and southern borders? The point of raising these questions is to suggest that the fact of ethnic rivalries cannot decide our judgments about American strategic interests.

A NATO statement of 1991 noted: "Risks to allied security are less likely to result from calculated aggression against the territory of the allies" than from "the adverse consequences of instabilities that may arise from the serious economic, social and political difficulties, including ethnic rivalries and territorial disputes, which are faced by many countries in central and eastern Europe."[25] It is difficult to quarrel with this statement. That the chance of territorial aggression against NATO allies is low, however, should not lead us to search for other reasons to deploy force or ipso facto to treat all local and subregional or regional instabilities, ethnic conflicts, aggressions, and warfare as threatening to American security.

Of course, we may well decide that murder and carnage in the Balkans is no threat to our security but we may still define our national interest in terms of preventing these outcomes if we can. Needless to say, Americans will want some estimate of the costs of prevention and the possibilities of being effective and withdrawing at some time in the future.

If we intervene on human rights grounds, can we do so selectively? It is not in our power to intervene everywhere that large-scale human rights violations take place. I believe that we should do so when we can intervene at fairly low costs, as in Somalia, even though no plausible argument can be made that there are large national security risks in not intervening because of demonstration effects or the increased probability of interstate warfare. But our interventions will be relatively few. And they are not likely to be in Eastern Europe where relatively large armies exist and where civilian combatants can be well armed. The cost of intervention will be too high when weighed against the gains to be achieved.

Can we create a typology for intervention in nationalist conflicts? I doubt if we can single out these conflicts as ones of a special type. Concrete interests will rub up against principles sometimes congruently, sometimes not. Allies will have their own calculations to make. We can say that ethnic-nationalist conflicts are difficult ones to engage in when they mobilize significant numbers of armed civilians who can fight guerrilla-style against the intervenors or peacekeepers. Here, as elsewhere, the content of nationalist ideology may give us clues. But we would have to know how widely accepted are the ideology's claims. Could leaders make peace with those who intervene and themselves survive? I think that checklists of such questions will be more effective than elaborate typologies to guide intervention decisions.

It is the very awareness of U.S. limitations at the end of the Cold War that has turned U.S. policymakers with new vigor to international agencies' peacemaking and peacekeeping capabilities. Spreading risks and costs of intervention makes sense for U.S. policy. However, as events in Cambodia, Somalia, Angola, not to say Bosnia, already make clear, it will be exceedingly difficult for the United Nations to manage ethic conflict. In many instances, neither the local knowledge nor the requisite force will exist to sustain peacekeeping activities. For, as John Chipman points out, ethnic conflict management requires both a comprehensive and a tailor-made approach. Often, territorial change will be necessary, requiring amalgamations and secessions. At the same time, internal redistributions of power and resources may occur within a state.[26]

The United States will now think about its involvements abroad in the context of greater concern for American domestic welfare, trade competition, and the use of U.S. resources. While it is not likely that there will be radical new definitions of the national interest, there may be less willingness to link American security to those who are seen as free riders and/or economic competitors. Thus it is very possible that the only superpower remaining will have more, not less, reluctance to intervene militarily in situations of conflict. At the same time, disagreements will exist over U.S. interventions because the end of the Cold War makes possible a foreign policy less constrained by a countervailing superpower and less subject to defining the national interest narrowly in security terms.

No doubt we will hear the argument in the future that national security in any case should be understood to mean not only being able to avoid threats to the core values of the United States but that these values, including a concern for democracy and human rights, should be projected abroad. Or, national security may come to mean the preservation and enhancement of domestic welfare more modestly conceived in economic terms. Whether Americans see their country as "bound to lead" or in decline will affect the ways that national security and national interest are defined and will affect the ways that Americans understand ethnic nationalisms and respond to them.

My own view is that we should retain a narrow definition of national security precisely so that we can make assessments about the depths of the instabilities that ethnic nationalist conflicts in Europe will entail and so that we can gauge their ability to spread and create havoc for a range of U.S. interests. When we do this, we will see that the dangers from ethnic nationalism are primarily moral and political, as William Pfaff has argued.[27] To predict that we are unlikely to intervene militarily in Europe and that our security interests are not likely to be threatened by conflicts in Europe is not to minimize the potential of ethnic nationalisms for wreaking grievous harm on large numbers of people and for weakening attempts to build a liberal order. At the same time, we should expect traditional national rivalries to perhaps be less bloody in Europe but to also rear their heads. And we will be forced, in any case, to make cost/benefit judgments for U.S. actions once we assess the content of the nationalisms we face and the structure of the conditions in which they wax and wane.

10

Conclusion

Charles A. Kupchan

Of necessity, the following conclusions represent more of an initial assessment based on select examples than a definitive summary based on rigorous comparison of the cases examined in this book. As is no doubt evident, the authors in this volume are not of a single mind about either the causes or the effects of nationalism. Furthermore, each was given considerable flexibility in addressing the assigned topic; I did not require the authors to adhere exclusively to the typology or conceptual packaging laid out in the first chapter. These conclusions draw on their labor, but they represent my own assessment of what is an admittedly contestable set of issues.

THE MOBILIZATION OF STATE-CLAIMING ETHNIC NATIONALITIES

The causes of ethnic mobilization vary widely. Indeed, all the factors pointed to in the first chapter—loss of state capacity, treatment of minorities, historical rivalries, contagion, and identity formation—have contributed to the intensification of ethnic sentiments. Nevertheless, it is possible to distinguish between the principal causes of ethnic mobilization and those of second-order significance.

Social change and its impact on identity formation are the single most prevalent and potent causes of state-claiming ethnic nationalism in Europe's east. Communist rule throughout the Soviet bloc deliberately took aim at political identities that would compete with allegiance to the party and its doctrine. Coercive governance, alienation from the state, and the

180

absence of political participation ensured that civic identities and values did not take root. As George Schöpflin eloquently argues, the collapse of communism left an ideological and political vacuum in which ethnicity naturally emerged as an attractive and available foundation for the formation of a newly defined political community. Absent were both the political institutions and the political sophistication needed to balance ethnicity's allure and ensure that it became only one of several anchors of identity in the midst of change. Whether in southeastern Europe, Central Europe, or Central Asia, ethnicity served as a new source of legitimacy, community, and identity in a political landscape left barren by the collapse of the Soviet empire.

That this search for new identities has so often singled out ethnicity was clearly affected by contagion and the relegitimation of ethnic politics that occurred with the Cold War's end. German reunification could be justified only on ethnic grounds. The international community readily accepted the split of Czechoslovakia, effectively sanctioning new divisions along ethnic lines. Yugoslavia's breakup and the international recognition of Croatia and Slovenia furthered the widespread legitimation of ethnic politics and helped to ensure that ethnic groups came to see statehood as the logical endpoint of claims to nationhood. Ethnicity's allure lay not only in its ability to fill the identity vacuum, but also in its relegitimation as a building block for dilapidated states.

The treatment of minorities in Eastern Europe has affected the timing and pace of ethnic mobilization, although it appears to be more a symptom than a cause of the emergence of state-claiming strains of nationalism. Minority groups tend to be mistreated or excluded when ethnicity becomes a pressing issue for the polity as a whole. Once political dividing lines have been drawn on the basis of ethnicity, the ethnic mobilization of minorities becomes far more likely. But Czechs, Slovaks, Slovenes, and Croatians sought independent nation-states because ethnic identities came to dominate the post–Cold War political landscape, not because they were persecuted at home or abroad. As Aleksa Djilas makes clear, Serbs living in Croatia were indeed mistreated by Croatian nationalists, but such mistreatment was by no means a necessary condition for the emergence of strong currents of nationalism in Serbia. Similarly, the resurgence of ethnic politics in Central Europe could well lead to the persecution of the large Hungarian population living outside Hungary, fueling a nationalist response among Hungarians inside and outside the country. But should this occur, the mistreatment of minorities—though a precipitating cause of Hungarian nationalism—would be a symptom of a broader ethnicization of politics in the region.

In similar fashion, historical rivalries and hatreds have been elicited by, but have not been a major cause of, the mobilization of state-claiming nationalism. To be sure, historical tension between Slovaks and Czechs played a role in precipitating the split of their country. So too did memories of past injustices intensify violence during the breakup of Yugoslavia. But in both these cases, historical claims and counterclaims need not have dominated the political discourse. Czechs and Slovaks, and Croats, Serbs, and Muslims had lived together for decades—and not just because a coercive regime forced them to do so. These groups had willingly intermingled and intermarried. Historical tensions were rekindled by a new focus on ethnicity as a key component of political identity, and especially by politicians who sought to better their fortunes by drawing on the past to generate nationalist myths and fuel ethnic rivalries. Past injustices indeed played a role in intensifying nationalist sentiments, but historical memories were more the tool of the propagandist than the original source of ethnic rivalry.

The loss of state capacity appears to have had little impact on the mobilization of ethnic nationalism. Elites in Eastern Europe, supported by their electorates, chose to create new nation-states in spite of, not because of, the effect of secession on the new state's ability to provide public goods.[1] Slovaks separated from Czechoslovakia even though continued union offered a brighter economic future. Slovene and Croatian decisions for independence had little to do with efforts to strengthen state capacity; the breakup of Yugoslavia was a manifestation of nation-building, not of state-building. That some former Soviet republics are rebuilding economic ties to Russia— at a cost to their autonomy—suggests that elites see secession as degrading, not enhancing, their state's ability to provide public goods. Only in Western Europe, where the European Union has begun to compete with the state as a provider of goods and services, has ethnic mobilization occurred in step with changes in state capacity. And, as Ezra Suleiman points out, the strength of national identities in Western Europe may well prevent the EU from implementing policies that ultimately benefit all member states. In Europe's east, ethnic mobilization is primarily the result of a search for political identity, not of a search for new ways to provide collective goods of a more material nature.

THE EMERGENCE OF AGGRESSIVE, STATE-EXPANDING NATIONALISM

War-causing strains of nationalism are the product of all three of the factors identified in the first chapter: state structure, transitions in state structure, and perceptions of insecurity. The principal cause of the re-emergence of aggressive strains of nationalism in Europe has been the dislocation that accompanies large-scale political and economic transformation. Individuals in societies undergoing deep-rooted change—such as those in Europe's east—often experience disaffection and disillusionment. Disaffection results from the economic deprivation that accompanies the dismantlement of command economies and the emergence of markets. Disillusionment results from unfulfilled expectations about the benefits of democracy and its ability to erect a just and orderly society. These conditions provide fertile ground for populist ideologues and opportunistic elites hoping to use nationalist rhetoric to gain political power. Their programs usually include identifying internal scapegoats (often minorities) responsible for the nation's problems, exaggerating external threats, and calling for the mobilization and centralization of resources to do battle against the nation's internal and external enemies. In the context of widespread social malaise and the search for alternatives that such malaise triggers, these illusory programs for national renewal find a receptive audience. It is principally this causal mechanism that has given rise to pockets of virulent nationalism throughout the former communist bloc. As both Paul Goble and Schöpflin point out, this problem is particularly acute in states that lack a middle class—a social group whose stake in preserving the status quo acts as a moderating influence.

The extent to which aggressive strains of nationalism spread within a polity is heavily influenced by state structure. Intensification occurs most readily in nondemocratic societies where elites, because of their control over the media and the dissemination of information, are able to propagate their ideas without interference. In the absence of alternative sources of information and public debate, extremist strains of nationalism take hold among elites and masses alike. Slobodan Milošević enjoyed such success in whipping up Serb nationalism because he hermetically sealed the country and prevented opponents either inside or outside Serbia from broadcasting or disseminating alternative points of view. Zhirinovsky's efforts to build an ultranationalist movement in Russia have met with less success at least in part because more open media and free public debate have exposed for many the fallacies and dangers of his program.

Vulnerability, whether perceived or real, also plays an important role in the formulation and intensification of aggressive strains of nationalism. The existence of an external threat to the nation's territory or its nationals living elsewhere provides a solid foundation for nationalist platforms. In Central Europe, the war in the Balkans and the perception of a security vacuum in the region continue to undercut reformers and bolster conservative nationalists. In Russia, concern about the welfare of Russians living in the Baltics and other parts of the former Soviet Union fuels nationalist sentiments. In instances in which no clear threat exists, one can be conveniently concocted to rally the public around national causes and to justify the mobilization and centralization of the state apparatus.[2]

As Stephen Van Evera details in his chapter, elites facing both external and domestic threats often resort to nationalist mythmaking to deal with their predicament. Milošević built support for his brand of Serbian nationalism by propagating the mythical notion that the well-being of Serbia was imminently threatened by its neighbors. Despite the fact that Hungarians living outside the country are generally well treated, Hungarian nationalists repeatedly conjure up inflated stories of the persecution of their brethren in the region. So too do Russian nationalists seek to intensify public fears about the dire threat posed to Russia by the loss of empire and the affinity of reformers for strategic cooperation with the West. In all three of these cases, irresponsible elites exaggerated external threats and propagated myths of imminent conflict in order to facilitate the spread of aggressive strains of nationalism and further their own political fortunes.

POLICY IMPLICATIONS

In responding to the upsurge of nationalism in post–Cold War Europe, the international community should be guided by one overriding objective: to nurture civil societies in Europe's east in which ethnicity is only one of several competing sources of identity. I am not arguing that ethnic identity is an evil that needs to be eradicated. On the contrary, ethnicity and ethnic nationalism are likely to remain key components of political cohesion and legitimacy in the new democracies. The bonds of language and common history and descent (whether real or imagined) serve a vital function in the process of state-building. But unless ethnic identification becomes only one of several sources of legitimacy and political affiliation, the prospects for multiethnic society in Europe's east look quite bleak. In addition, the international community will continue to find itself faced with the stark, unattractive choice that has confounded it in Yugoslavia: tolerating ethnic violence or intervening militarily.

Primary responsibility for building civil society rests with the people of Europe's east. The task is long-term; especially after decades of alienation from the state, it will take generations to cultivate the habits and attitudes of civic participation. Furthermore, a vicious circle of sorts complicates the struggle. The painful political and economic transition needed to lay the foundation for civil society is precisely what creates social conditions conducive to the mobilization of ethnic sentiments and to upsurges in aggressive nationalism. In light of these formidable obstacles, the international community must do what it can to facilitate the emergence of civic culture in the eastern half of Europe. It is clearly in the West's interest to do so; addressing the underlying causes of destabilizing forms of nationalism is far preferable to responding to their unwelcome effects.

The European Union

The EU has played a key role in embedding competing political identities among the peoples of Western Europe. That political and economic integration continues to proceed despite the end of the Cold War confirms that the Union rests firmly on interdependence and the construction of a European identity, not just on an expedient framework erected in response to an external threat. Inasmuch as the EU's unraveling would precipitate the renationalization of Western Europe—and consequently call into question the integrity of the transatlantic relationship—its well-being is as important to the United States as it is to EU member states.

Despite its ambitious plans for deepening political and economic integration among current members, the EU can no longer afford to focus primarily on its internal agenda. No single institution is better prepared than the EU to facilitate reform and the emergence of civil society in the east. Association with, and eventual membership in, the Union will help build a European identity among the people of Central and Eastern Europe and satisfy their yearning for entry into the "West." Ethnic and national affiliations will no longer dominate political identities. Entry into the EU will be accompanied by the institutionalization of legal codes, human rights conventions, and measures to protect minorities—all important components of civic culture. In the meantime, increasing commerce with Western Europe—the east's natural market—will do much to ease the underlying conditions of social and economic duress that continue to inflame nationalistic passions in the former communist bloc. Expansion to the east must be the EU's top priority, even if such expansion comes at the expense of Western Europe's near-term aspirations for deepening monetary and political union. Suleiman's skepticism about the feasibility of the EU's ambitious internal agenda and his concern about its ability to fuel a nationalist backlash in Western Europe also argue in favor of orienting eastward the Union's momentum.

Economic and Technical Assistance

The importance of economic and technical assistance to the process of reform is widely accepted among scholars and policymakers alike. Outside assistance is constrained by limited resources, not by doubts about its value. Whether and to what extent the international community should condition the provision of economic and technical assistance on the fulfillment of specified criteria, however, remains a contentious issue.[3] Most analysts agree that target countries should meet a minimum set of economic criteria before receiving aid; otherwise, transferred funds will be wasted on an economy with no promise. Tying assistance to political criteria is more problematic. On the one hand, contingent aid provides a clear incentive for states to adhere to accepted norms of behavior. On the other hand, it may be unrealistic to expect nascent nation-states going through painful transitions to ensure freedom of the press, protect the rights of minorities, and uphold other norms considered to be integral to the functioning of liberal democracy. To withhold assistance from struggling democracies may well deprive them of the resources needed to build stable institutions and stave off the disaffection and disillusionment that erode legitimacy and provide inroads for irresponsible elites pandering to nationalistic ideologies.

To deal with this dilemma, the international community should distinguish between two phases of democratic transition. During the first phase, when states are struggling to build democratic institutions and the foundations of a market economy, aid should be contingent on the fulfillment of only a minimum base-line of political criteria.[4] During the second phase, which would begin after states have enjoyed several years of democratic rule and transition to a market economy, they would be held to much higher standards. Although privatization and stabilization funds may no longer be needed at this point, other economic incentives can be used to encourage adherence to the norms of civil society. The proposed EU Security Pact, which holds out the prospect of quickened accession to the Union for those states that sign agreements guaranteeing the rights of minorities (among other stipulations), is a case in point. The offer of integration into other Western institutions and markets could be similarly used as a material inducement.

Treatment of Minorities

As nation-building progresses in Europe's east, ethnicity will continue to serve as the most potent source of political identity. Even if most of the new democracies embark on ambitious projects to build robust civic institutions and instill civic values, the accompanying identities will emerge only slowly. In the meantime, the centrality of ethnicity in defining political community will continue to spell trouble for minority populations. Dominant ethnic groups may discriminate against those of different ethnicity. Even if they do not, minorities are likely to feel excluded from the political mainstream, increasing the chances that ethnic mobilization will lead to new claims of statehood.

For these reasons, the international community should put particular emphasis on protecting the rights and welfare of minorities throughout the former communist bloc. In both bilateral and multilateral forums, third parties should stress to elites in Europe's east the importance of ensuring the well-being of minorities—and hold them accountable when persistent persecution occurs. International tribunals have a significant role to play in this respect. Even if it proves difficult to bring perpetrators of war crimes and persecutions to justice, the prospect of accountability should serve as a deterrent. It may not be enough to isolate only those responsible for violating human rights. As I have argued earlier, elites who propagate nationalist propaganda are the principal instigators of virulent strains of nationalism. The international community should therefore consider publishing a "blacklist" of irresponsible elites to erode their public credibility and legitimacy.

The international community can, through multilateral institutions and nongovernmental organizations, also help the new democracies create institutions and pass legislation to protect minorities. These steps would moderate insecurity among minorities and dampen separatist tendencies. Equally important are efforts to promote tolerance among dominant populations. No matter how protective of minorities are legal codes or other institutionalized safeguards, the viability of multiethnic states depends first and foremost on the attitudes and values of dominant groups. Only as these groups develop political loyalties and identities that complement ethnicity will the welfare of minority groups and the durability of multiethnic nation-states be ensured.

For both ethical and pragmatic reasons, measures to protect minorities must ensure them full political rights as well as considerable cultural autonomy (including the right to use their own languages and freely engage in their own cultural rituals). (For further discussions of minority rights and fair minority representation, see Van Evera's chapter.) The experience of Western Europe strongly suggests that accommodating calls for increased autonomy satisfies rather than fuels separatist tendencies. Across Western Europe, minority groups that enjoy a substantial degree of cultural freedom live comfortably inside states dominated by other ethnic groups. The case of Quebec, where increased autonomy may not succeed in quenching separatist yearnings, is a clear exception. And one needs to keep in mind the counterfactual—namely, that efforts to repress Quebec nationalism may well have led to a more strident and perhaps violent separatist movement.

Education and Social Programs

Outside assistance in promoting reform in Europe's east has focused primarily on privatization and other economic tasks. Efforts to deepen the underpinnings of civil society through education and social programs have been limited and tentative; there is considerable room for exploration in this area.[5] Especially because nationalism engages the realm of ideas and emotions, more direct efforts to shape public attitudes and values may have substantial payoffs. Programs are needed in three specific areas: local institution-building, educational reform, and media reform.

Even though many of the states in the former communist bloc have functioning democratic institutions, they lack the deeply embedded participatory values and habits that are the foundation of democratic society. Especially after decades of estrangement between the state and society, special attention must be devoted to nurturing civic values and identities. Accordingly, opportunities for political participation need to be expanded, particularly by developing local government and social programs at the community level. Town councils, business organizations, local chapters of national organizations (I have in mind bodies similar to Planned Parenthood or the American Civil Liberties Union)—these all contribute to building the infrastructure of democratic society. The United States and Western Europe have the expertise and personnel to lend a helping hand. And in doing so, they will help build the communal ties and participatory values needed to nurture political identities that can complement ethnicity as bases for allegiance and legitimacy.

The international community could also work through national education systems to promote civic values. Helping local school districts develop courses on democratic governance would lay the groundwork for a next generation of voters and leaders better prepared for the responsibilities of democracy. Seminars on ethnic tolerance should be developed and offered both through the school system and through organs that reach the adult population, such as churches, unions, and business organizations. Of particular consequence in this respect is the accuracy of the texts and other materials used to teach national history. All too often, nationalists resort to a selective or distorted presentation of the historical record to suit their political needs.[6] The availability of outside funds to print new textbooks and of independent boards to evaluate the accuracy of historical interpretations in those texts helps counter nationalist propaganda.

The media—both national and foreign—also have considerable influence over the content and intensity of nationalism. Print and broadcast media can serve as important vehicles for promoting ethnic tolerance and civic values. At the same time, they are powerful weapons in the hands of nationalist elites seeking to polarize ethnic groups inside a given state or to rally nationalist sentiments against an external enemy.

Three objectives should guide international efforts to help reform the media. First, national governments should be prevented from monopolizing the dissemination of information. Independent newspapers and radio and television stations are essential in fostering critical evaluation of information and exposing policies to public scrutiny. Pressure should be brought to bear on governments that infringe on freedom of the press. Funds and equipment should be made available to support the establishment of independent newspapers and radio and television stations. Second, more resources should be devoted to training a professional cadre of journalists. Too many media outlets in Europe's east are affiliated with political parties; journalists tend to take sides and serve as advocates, not as defenders of the public's right to unbiased information. Participation in training programs in the United States and Western Europe and the establishment of more media training centers in the east might remedy this problem. Third, the international community should take steps to thwart any government seeking to seal its country off from outside sources of information. The rights of foreign journalists must be strictly protected. Foreign broadcasts must continue, both as a counter to distorted information propagated by state-controlled organs and as a yardstick against which listeners can measure the quality and independence of their own national stations.

Military Measures

Under even the most optimistic of scenarios, progress toward democracy and civil society in Europe's east will be punctuated by bouts of intrastate ethnic conflict and, quite possibly, interstate war. Events in Bosnia, Nagorno-Karabakh, Abkhazia, and other areas of the former communist bloc have revealed the West's reluctance to engage militarily. But they have also illuminated the costs associated with such reluctance.

Making the international community better prepared to address ethnic conflict entails distinguishing between violence emanating from separatist struggles (civil wars) and conflict associated with virulent and predatory strains of nationalism (wars of aggression). From both a political and military perspective, the violence associated with the breakup of multiethnic states represents the most intractable problem. To intervene on behalf of the existing state is to flout principles of self-determination. To intervene on behalf of the state-claiming nationality is to violate a state's right to territorial integrity. In either case, military involvement is likely to require the engagement of ground troops in the midst of low-intensity, intracommunal warfare. For these reasons, the international community should focus its attention on improving its ability to deploy forces in a preventative and peacekeeping mode. Creating buffers between hostile parties, protecting pockets of minority populations, enforcing ceasefires while negotiations proceed—these are the new military missions for which multilateral institutions and national militaries should prepare.

Wars of aggression carried out by states charged with nationalist fervor, although more demanding militarily, lend themselves more easily to the direct use of force by outside powers. The aggressor and the victim become readily apparent when one party is engaging in territorial conquest and ethnic cleansing. Low-cost military options that would be inappropriate in the midst of intercommunal warfare—such as punitive airstrikes against combat units as well as military infrastructure—become available. Recent events in the Balkans suggest that preventive deployments and deterrent warnings (in Macedonia and Kosovo, respectively) have a valuable role to play in containing conflicts of this type. The war in Bosnia and the responsiveness of the Serbs to punitive strikes also demonstrate that the international community, as long as it is prepared to stand behind its commitments, can effectively use threats and the limited application of force to stop aggression. Had the UN and NATO acted earlier to counter Serb aggression, thousands of lives—and possibly a multiethnic Bosnia—might have been saved.[7] Once a state has been seized with virulent strains of nationalism and has embarked on the path of war, there is little other than preponderant force that can stop it.[8]

At the same time that it addresses how to deal with the symptoms of nationalist conflict, the international community should also help address its causes by incorporating the new democracies into a meaningful security framework. As discussed earlier, perceptions of vulnerability fuel the intensification of nationalism. These perceptions of vulnerability continue to be exacerbated by the fact that security institutions for the new Europe have yet to take shape. This delay has resulted in large part from the conflicting needs of different states. The Central Europeans want to become full members of NATO to gain reassurance against a resurgent Russian threat. Russia opposes expansion of NATO, arguing that it will create new dividing lines and threaten Russia's security and status. By offering military cooperation to all former Warsaw Pact members and putting off the question of NATO expansion, NATO's Partnership for Peace has enabled NATO members to avoid directly confronting these issues. But the Partnership for Peace is not enough.[9] Whether through NATO, the EU, the Organization for Security and Cooperation in Europe (OSCE) or a structure that does not yet exist, Europe's new democracies must be incorporated into a new security order.

Recognizing New States

The international community should be predisposed toward honoring existing borders and preserving the territorial integrity of existing states.

The emergence of new states, even if they ultimately lead to more stable political communities, is disruptive and destabilizing. Furthermore, new precedents and norms are being set in post–Cold War Europe; these norms should favor the maintenance of ethnically heterogeneous, pluralist societies, not homogeneous, majoritarian states. Nevertheless, at least some states in Europe will continue to fall prey to the powerful centrifugal forces unleashed by the collapse of the Soviet empire. The international community must therefore develop common understandings about and clear standards for the recognition of new states.

A thorough discussion of the conditions under which the international community should recognize new states goes beyond the scope of this volume.[10] The events surrounding the breakup of Yugoslavia, however, merit discussion of three important lessons. First, the timing of recognition has serious consequences for how an attempted secession reverberates in the affected region. Had Germany not rushed forward with recognition of Slovenia and Croatia, Bosnia might well have delayed its own decision to declare independence. This delay might have provided time for concerned parties to deploy peacekeepers, broker a settlement, or take other steps to prevent the bloodletting that followed Bosnia's claim to independent statehood. The international community needs to develop a more circumspect and coordinated approach to recognition.

Second, states should not be recognized until political and legal mechanisms are in place to protect minorities. Especially if secession is driven by the desire of a specific ethnic group to establish its own nation-state, minorities living in the territory of that state are likely to become targets of persecution. Withholding recognition until adequate safeguards are in place provides the international community leverage over a critical issue and increases the chances that the process of nation-building will occur peacefully.

Third, the international community should recognize a new state only after that state has established effective control over its territory and arrangements are in place to provide for its security. In some cases, states have to build the capabilities required for self-defense. Where this is not possible, regional arrangements—alliances, security pacts, UN or OSCE-sponsored protectorates—will be needed. Unless the international community addresses the security needs of new states prior to recognition, it is likely to find itself repeatedly confronted with the dilemma it has faced in Bosnia—namely, having to come to the rescue of communities that it has just sanctioned as independent, sovereign states.

EUROPE'S east is in the midst of a historic transformation. Newly emergent nation-states are poised uneasily between stable, market-oriented democracy and continued turmoil—if not return to more authoritarian ways. The content and intensity of nationalism play a critical role in shaping outcomes. Sentiments capable of merging nation and state are needed to relegitimate state structures discredited by decades of coercive rule. Yet these same sentiments, if not channeled toward constructive ends, can trigger continued fragmentation and violence.

At this critical historical juncture, the international community must act with urgency to help consolidate democratic reform in Central and Eastern Europe and the former Soviet republics. A window of opportunity remains open, but it will not remain open indefinitely. The more prolonged the economic duress and political uncertainty, the more likely it is that ethnic mobilization will lead to the breakup of existing states and that virulent strains of nationalism will take root.

The key challenge for the international community is to help build the underlying political and economic conditions that foster the emergence of civil society and civic identities. Not until ethnicity becomes just one among many competing elements of political identity—as it is in Europe's west—will nationalism become a source only of cohesion and stability, and not also of fragmentation and conflict.

Notes

1 INTRODUCTION: NATIONALISM RESURGENT

1   A rich literature exists on the rise of modern nationalism during the eighteenth and nineteenth centuries. It examines the relationship between the birth of the idea of the nation-state and contemporaneous social and political developments—industrialization, increasing social and labor mobility, and the emergence of citizen armies. See, for example, John A. Armstrong, *Nations before Nationalism* (Chapel Hill: University of North Carolina Press, 1982); Anthony D. Smith, *The Ethnic Origins of Nations* (Oxford: Basil Blackwell, 1986); Eric Hobsbawm, *Nations and Nationalism since 1780* (Cambridge: Cambridge University Press, 1990); Ernest Gellner, *Nations and Nationalism* (Ithaca: Cornell University Press, 1983); Liah Greenfeld, *Nationalism* (Cambridge: Harvard University Press, 1992); Elie Kedourie, *Nationalism* (Cambridge, Mass.: Blackwell, 1993); Rogers Brubaker, *Citizenship and Nationhood in France and Germany* (Cambridge Harvard University Press, 1992); Benedict Anderson, *Imagined Communities*, rev. ed. (New York: Verso, 1991); John Breuilly, *Nationalism and the State*, 2d ed. (Chicago: University of Chicago Press, 1994); Michael Mann, *The Sources of Social Power* (Cambridge: Cambridge University Press, 1986).

2   Few works have systematically addressed the causes of the resurgence of nationalist sentiment in Europe's east since 1990 and the effect of this resurgence on Europe's evolving strategic landscape. The growing body of literature on this subject includes "Reconstructing Nations and States," *Daedalus* 122 (Summer 1993); Michael E. Brown, ed., *Ethnic Conflict and International Security* (Princeton: Princeton University Press, 1993); William Pfaff, *The Wrath of Nations: Civilization and the Furies of Nationalism* (New York: Simon and Schuster, 1993); Michael Ignatieff, *Blood and Belonging: Journeys into the New Nationalism* (New York: Farrar, Straus and Giroux, 1994); Misha Glenny, *The Fall of Yugoslavia: The Third Balkan War* (New York: Penguin, 1994); Allan Buchanan, *Secession* (Boulder, Colo.: Westview Press, 1991); John McGarry and Brendan O'Leary, *The Politics of Ethnic Conflict Regulation* (New York: Routledge, 1993).

193

3   Nationalism is commonly defined in academic literature as an ideology claiming that political boundaries should parallel ethnic ones. See, for example, Gellner, *Nations and Nationalism,* p. 1. This definition is inadequate because, as discussed later, it is important to draw a clear distinction between civic and ethnic nationalism. Disparate ethnic groups can and do unify around a common notion of nationality when nationhood is defined in terms of citizenship, not common ethnicity or culture. The nation-state can very comfortably cut across ethnic and cultural boundaries as long as national sentiments and identities do so as well. Defining nationality in terms of identity rather than in terms of ethnicity or culture resolves this problem.

4   I accept that contemporary national identities in many instances draw on the attributes of traditional ethnic, cultural, and linguistic groupings. But I view these attributes as providing a reservoir of images and symbols from which modern national identities are constructed. Furthermore, the claim that the boundaries of such traditional groupings should coincide with political boundaries is a quite recent invention. For an extensive discussion of whether nationalism is primordial or modern see Armstrong, *Nations before Nationalism.*

5   Nationalism itself says nothing about the distribution of political power among actors inside the nation-state. Thus, while nationalism can instill ideas that facilitate the functioning of democracy, it can also serve as an ideological foundation for authoritarian regimes.

6   See Alexander Motyl, *Dilemmas of Independence* (New York: Council on Foreign Relations Press, 1993); and Charles Kupchan, "What Ukraine Especially Needs Now Is a Little More Nationalism," *Los Angeles Times,* November 27, 1994.

7   On the distinction between civic and ethnic nationalism, see Greenfeld, *Nationalism,* and Smith, *The Ethnic Origins of Nations.*

8   Prior to 1948, Jews recognized themselves—and were recognized by others—as a distinct national grouping even though Israel did not exist. Similarly, the Palestinians today are widely accepted as a national grouping despite remaining stateless.

9   The United States is a prime example of a country in which civic forms of nationalism predominate.

10   See Jack Snyder, "Nationalism and the Crisis of the Post-Soviet State," in Brown, ed., *Ethnic Conflict,* pp. 85–86.

11   The two phenomena may also be causally linked: intensifying nationalism among the dominant group in a nation-state can threaten minority groups in that state, thereby intensifying nationalism among threatened minority groups.

12   Consider how British and French imperialism during the twentieth century contrasts with that of Germany and Japan during the interwar period and World War II, respectively. Britain and France were exploitative and extractive, but sought to incorporate their colonial territories into imperial structures that were intended to promote the political and economic welfare of the inhabitants—while, of course, benefiting the metropole. In contrast, Germany and Japan, whose imperial aspirations were tinged with racism and claims of ethnic superiority, sought primarily to subjugate conquered territories and extract resources for their war efforts.

13   For further discussion of differing notions of nationhood in Western Europe, see Brubaker, *Citizenship and Nationhood in France and Germany.*

14   This argument is succinctly laid out by Snyder in "Nationalism and the Crisis of the Post-Soviet State," pp. 79–101.

15   Kathleen Newland, "Ethnic Conflict and Refugees," in Brown, ed., *Ethnic Conflict,* pp. 143–163.

16   On Quebec's gradual distancing from the state, see Hudson Meadwell, "The Politics of Nationalism in Quebec," *World Politics*, 45 (January 1993), 203–241.

17   This view is particularly prevalent in journalistic accounts of the current nationalist upsurge in Europe. See, for example, Serge Schmemann, "Ethnic Battles Flaring in Former Soviet Fringe," *New York Times*, May 24, 1992.

18   See, for example, Anderson, *Imagined Communities*, especially chs. 5 and 6.

19   For discussion of how industrialization and modernization break down traditional identities and foster nationalism, see Gellner, *Nations and Nationalism*.

20   For a more general discussion of the links between state structure and foreign policy, see Michael Doyle, "Liberalism and World Politics," *American Political Science Review*, 80 (December 1986), 1151–1169; and Jack Snyder, *Myths of Empire* (Ithaca: Cornell University Press, 1992).

21   See, for example, Breuilly, *Nationalism and the State*, ch. 15.

22   See Charles Kupchan, *The Vulnerability of Empire* (Ithaca: Cornell University Press, 1994).

23   Perceptions of vulnerability usually stem from threats to the nation-state's territory, but they could also stem from threats to its nationals living abroad. For further discussion of threats posed to nationals living outside the national territory, see Stephen Van Evera's chapter in this volume.

24   External threats strengthen hard-liners by bolstering their claims that the nation-state needs to build up its military forces and stand firm in dealings with an array of hostile powers. See Kupchan, *The Vulnerability of Empire*, ch. 2.

25   See Barry Posen, "The Security Dilemma and Ethnic Conflict," in Brown, ed., *Ethnic Conflict*, pp. 104–124.

2   REFLECTIONS ON THE IDEA OF THE NATION-STATE

1   Jean-Jacques Rousseau, *Political Writings: Containing "The Social Contract, Considerations on the Government of Poland, Constitutional Project for Corsica, Part I,"* trans. Frederick M. Watkins (Madison: University of Wisconsin Press, 1986). *The Social Contract* transposed the Greek and Roman city-state to eighteenth-century Geneva. But Rousseau also explicitly applied his state model to modern nations, in particular to the submerged Poland of the eighteenth century. For the international implications, see Rousseau's "Abstract and Judgment of Saint-Pierre's Project for Perpetual Peace (1756)," in Stanley Hoffmann and David P. Fidler, *Rousseau on International Relations* (Oxford: Clarendon Press, 1991), pp. 53–100.

2   For a broad discussion of the republican tradition, see Paul A. Rahe's monumental *Republics Ancient and Modern: Classical Republicanism and the American Revolution* (Chapel Hill: University of North Carolina Press, 1992). For a particularly stimulating account of the rise of the modern democratic national state, see Frederick M. Watkins, *The Political Tradition of the West: A Study in the Development of Modern Liberalism* (Cambridge: Harvard University Press, 1948).

3   Johann Gottfried von Herder, *Ideen zur Philosophie der Geschichte der Menschheit* (Riga: Johann Friedrich Hartknoch, 1786–1792); abridged English translation *Reflections on the Philosophy of the History of Mankind*, intro. Frank E. Manuel (Chicago: University of Chicago Press, 1968). See also Herder's *God: Some Conversations*, trans.

Frederick H. Burkhardt (Indianapolis: Bobbs-Merrill, 1962). For comprehensive studies of Herder's ideas, see Robert R. Ergang, *Herder and the Foundations of German Nationalism* (New York: Octagon Books, 1966), Frederick M. Barnard, *Herder's Social and Political Thought: From Enlightenment to Nationalism* (Oxford: Clarendon Press, 1965), and Isaiah Berlin, *Vico and Herder: Two Studies in the History of Ideas* (London: Hogarth, 1976).

4   I use the terms "Enlightenment" and "Romanticism" to denote two broadly contrasting world-views with pervasive influence in religion, philosophy, science, the arts, politics, economics, and so on. For my own attempt to justify this practice and to acknowledge its limitations, and also to give a working definition of "Romanticism," see David P. Calleo, *Coleridge and the Idea of the Modern State* (New Haven: Yale University Press, 1966), ch. 2.

5   Bernhard Suphan, ed., *Herder's "Sämtliche Werke,"* 33 vols. (Berlin: 1877–1913), 17:211–212.

6   Ibid., 13:339.

7   Bernard Bosanquet, *The Philosophical Theory of the State*, 4th ed. (1923) (rpt. New York: St. Martin's Press, 1966), *Psychology of the Moral Self* (London: Macmillan, 1897), and *Social and International Ideals: Being Studies in Patriotism* (London: Macmillan, 1917).

8   Bosanquet, *The Philosophical Theory of the State*, p. 57.

9   Bosanquet, *Psychology of the Moral Self*, p. 18.

10   Ibid., p. 67.

11   Ibid., pp. 94, 43.

12   Bosanquet, *Philosophical Theory of the State*, p. 186.

13   Bosanquet, *Social and International Ideals*, p. 300.

14   Ibid., pp. 292, 287.

15   Ibid., pp. 300–301.

16   Giuseppe Mazzini, *The Duties of Man, and Other Essays*, trans. Thomas Jones (New York: Dutton, 1966). The most recent Italian edition is *Dei Doveri dell'Uomo* (Genoa: Costa i Nolan, 1990).

17   See Isaiah Berlin, "The Naiveté of Verdi," in William Weaver and Martin Chusid, eds., *The Verdi Companion* (New York: Norton, 1979), pp. 1–12; George Martin, *Aspects of Verdi* (New York: Dodd, Mead, 1988), pp. 3–28; and David R. B. Kimbell, *Verdi in the Age of Italian Romanticism* (Cambridge: Cambridge University Press, 1981).

18   In Burke's famous formulation a state was "not a partnership in things subservient only to the gross animal existence of a temporary and perishable nature. It is a partnership in all science; a partnership in all art; a partnership in every virtue, and in all perfection. As the ends of such a partnership cannot be obtained in many generations, it becomes a partnership not only between those who are living, but between those who are living, those who are dead, and those who are to be born." Edmund Burke, "Reflections on the Revolution in France," *Works*, vol. 3 (Boston: Little, Brown, 1865), p. 359. Samuel Taylor Coleridge, *On the Constitution of Church and State*, ed. John Colmer (Princeton: Princeton University Press, 1976), and Essays 10, 13, and 14 in *Volume II* of *The Friend: A Series of Essays in Three Volumes to Aid in the Formation of Fixed Principles in Politics, Morals, and Religion with Literary Amusements Interspersed*, ed. Barbara E. Rooke (Princeton: Princeton University Press, 1969), 1:263–275, 289–312. See also Calleo, *Coleridge and the Idea of the Modern State.*

19   Such was the view of, for example, the British Fabian socialists Beatrice and

Sidney Webb. See Sidney Webb's essay "Historic," in George Bernard Shaw, ed., *Fabian Essays in Socialism* (c. 1889) (rpt. Gloucester, Mass.: Peter Smith, 1967), pp. 46–83; and Sidney and Beatrice Webb, *The Decay of Capitalist Civilization* (c. 1923; New York: Greenwood Press, 1969). See also A. M. McBriar, *Fabian Socialism and English Politics, 1884–1918* (Cambridge: Cambridge University Press, 1962).

20 Joseph Arthur, comte de Gobineau, *Essai sur l'inegalité des races humaines (1853–1855)* (Paris: Firmin-Didot, 1922), English translation *Essay on the Inequality of the Human Races (1853–1855)*, in Michael D. Biddiss, ed., *Gobineau: Selected Political Writings* (London: Cox & Wyman, 1970), pp. 37–176; Houston Stewart Chamberlain, *Die Grundlagen des neunzehnten Jahrhunderts* (Munich: F. Bruckmann, 1907), English translation *Foundations of the Nineteenth Century* (New York: John Lane, 1913). For Wagner, see Michael M. Harrison, "Richard Wagner as a Political Artist," published in the 1984 Bayreuth Festival program book. See also Ernest Newman, *The Life of Richard Wagner,* 4 vols. (Cambridge: Cambridge University Press, 1976). Wagner's essays on art and national identity can be found in W. A. Ellis, ed., *Richard Wagner's Prose Works,* 8 vols. (New York: Broude Brothers, 1966). Of particular relevance here are "The Revolution" (1849), vol. 8, pp. 232–238; "Art and Revolution" (1849), vol. 1, pp. 21–65; "Opera and Drama" (1850–1851), vol. 2; "Judaism in Music" (1850), vol. 3, pp. 75–122; "What Is German" (1865), vol. 4, pp. 149–170; and "German Art and German Policy" (1867), vol. 4, pp. 35–148.

21 Richard Cobden, "The Balance of Power" in *The Political Writing of Richard Cobden* (New York: Kraus Reprint, 1969), pp. 194–216.

22 Samuel Taylor Coleridge, *A Lay Sermon Addressed to the Higher and Middle Classes on the Existing Distresses and Discontents,* in R. J. White, ed., *Lay Sermons* in *The Collected Works of Samuel Taylor Coleridge* (Princeton: Princeton University Press, 1972), p. 223.

23 See Mazzini's "Duties to Country" chapter in his *The Duties of Man,* pp. 51–59.

24 Friedrich List, *The National System of Political Economy,* trans. Sampson S. Lloyd (London: Longmans, Green, 1885), (rpt. New York: Augustus M. Kelley, 1966).

25 Clarence K. Streit, *Union Now: A Proposal for a Federal Union of the Democracies of the North Atlantic* (New York: Harper & Brothers, 1939). See Cordell Hull, *The Memoirs of Cordell Hull* (New York: Macmillan, 1948). For a rich development of hegemonic economic ideas, see also Charles P. Kindleberger's *The World in Depression, 1929–1939* (Berkeley: University of California Press, 1986), and his chapter "Systems of International Economic Organization" in David P. Calleo, ed., *Money and the Coming World Order* (New York: New York University Press, 1976), pp. 15–39. For a general discussion, see David P. Calleo and Benjamin M. Rowland, *America and the World Political Economy: Atlantic Dreams and National Realities* (Bloomington: Indiana University Press, 1973), Parts 1 and 2.

26 See Kindleberger, *The World in Depression,* and his chapter in Calleo, ed., *Money and the Coming World Order,* pp. 15–39; also Paul Kennedy, *The Rise and Fall of the Great Powers* (New York: Random House, 1988).

27 See David P. Calleo, *Beyond American Hegemony: The Future of the Western Alliance* (New York: Basic Books, 1987), ch. 8.

28 A brilliant and balanced German view can be found in Ludwig Dehio, *The Precarious Balance: Four Centuries of the European Power Struggle* (1948), trans. Charles Fullman (New York: Knopf, 1962). For my own survey of historiographical perspectives and the issues of German aggression, see *The German Problem Reconsidered: Germany and the World Order, 1870 to the Present* (New York: Cambridge University Press,

1978). For a critical analysis of Britain's interwar position on free trade, see Edward H. Carr, *The Twenty Years' Crisis, 1919–1939: An Introduction to the Study of International Relations* (New York: Harper & Row, 1964), especially chs. 4, 5, 8.

29 Richard Coudenhove-Kalergi, *Weltmacht Europa* (Stuttgart: Seewald Verlag, 1972). See also Calleo and Rowland, *America in the World Political Economy*, ch. 4. For the postwar European movement, see Richard Mayne, *The Recovery of Europe* (New York: Harper & Row, 1970); and François Duchêne *The First Statesman of Interdependence: Jean Monnet* (New York: Norton, 1994); and David P. Calleo, *Europe's Future: The Grand Alternatives* (New York: Horizon Press, 1965), chs. 1–3.

30 Karl Marx, *Capital: A Critical Analysis of Capitalist Production*, trans. Samuel Moore and Edward Aveling, ed. Frederick Engels (London: S. Sonnenschein, Lowrey, 1887); also Robert L. Heilbroner, *Marxism, For and Against* (New York: Norton, 1980).

31 V. I. Lenin, *Imperialism, the Highest Stage of Capitalism: A Popular Outline* (New York: International Publishers, 1939).

32 See note 22, also Calleo, *Coleridge and the Idea of the Modern State*, ch. 1.

33 John Maynard Keynes, *The General Theory of Employment, Interest and Money* (New York: St. Martin's Press, 1973). See also Robert Skidelsky, *John Maynard Keynes: A Biography*, 2 vols., 2d ed. (London: Macmillan, 1993).

34 Richard N. Gardner, *Sterling-Dollar Diplomacy in Current Perspective: The Origins and the Prospects of Our International Economic Order* (New York: Columbia University Press, 1980), chs. 5 and 15. See also Roy Forbes Harrod, *The Life of John Maynard Keynes* (New York: Avon, 1971), pp. 681–692.

35 For my own early breakdown of federalist and Gaullist visions, see Calleo, *Europe's Future*. For a more recent attempt to analyze the structure of the European Community see my *Beyond American Hegemony*, ch. 10.

36 For de Gaulle's prewar views on the inevitability of interdependence and its constraints, see Charles de Gaulle, *Vers l'armée de metier* (Paris: Berger-Levrault, 1944), pp. 87–88. For his later views on Europe, see his *Memoirs of Hope: Renewal and Endeavor* (New York: Simon and Schuster, 1971), pp. 163–198.

37 For an authoritative statement of Gaullist notions of sovereignty in an interdependent world, see Maurice Couve de Murville, *Une politique étrangère* (Paris: Plon, 1971), pp. 292–299.

38 David P. Calleo and Claudia Morganstern, eds., *Recasting Europe's Economies: National Strategies in the 1980s* (Lanham, Md.: University Press of America, 1990), chs. 1, 2, and 6.

39 For a recent analysis of that relationship from differing perspectives, see Patrick McCarthy, ed., *France—Germany, 1983–1993: The Struggle to Cooperate* (New York: St. Martin's Press, 1993).

3   NATIONALISM AND ETHNICITY IN EUROPE, EAST AND WEST

1 Some of the arguments in this chapter appear in George Schöpflin, "Nacionalizmus a posztkommunista rendszerekben," *Vilagossag*, 33 (July–August 1991), 481–491.

2 Joseph Rothschild, *Ethnopolitics* (New York: Columbia University Press, 1981).

3   John Armstrong, *Nations before Nationalism* (Chapel Hill: University of North Carolina Press, 1982).

4   Anthony Smith, *The Ethnic Origins of Nations* (Oxford: Blackwell, 1986).

5   Charles Tilly, ed., *The Formation of National States in Western Europe* (Princeton: Princeton University Press, 1975).

6   John Keane, "Nations, Nationalism and the European Citizen," *Filozofski Vestnik/ Acta Philosophica* (Ljubljana) 14 (1993), 35–55.

7   Olwen Hufton, *Europe: Privilege and Protest, 1730–1789* (London: Fontana, 1980).

8   Andrew Orridge, "Varieties of Nationalism," in Leonard Tivey, ed., *The Nation-State: The Formation of Modern Politics* (Oxford: Martin Robertson, 1981), pp. 39–58.

9   Linda Colley, *Britons: Forging the Nation, 1707–1837* (London: Pimlico, 1992).

10 Anthony D. Smith, *National Identity* (London: Penguin, 1991).

11 Maurice Keens-Soper, "The Liberal State and Nationalism in Post-war Europe," *History of European Ideas* 10 (1989), 698–703.

12 Istvan Bibo, "Reflections on the Social Development of Europe," in his *Democracy, Revolution, Self-Determination: Selected Writings* (Boulder, Colo.: Atlantic Research, 1991), pp. 421–526.

13 James Mayall, *Nationalism and International Society* (Cambridge: Cambridge University Press, 1990).

14 Michael Keating, "Spain: Peripheral Nationalism and State Response," in John McGarry and Brendan O'Leary, eds., *The Politics of Ethnic Conflict Regulation* (London: Routledge, 1992), pp. 204–225.

15 Quebec should also come into this category, though the level of violence there has been low and it is, of course, outside Europe.

16 Anthony E. Alcock, *The History of the South Tyrol Question* (London: Michael Joseph, 1970).

17 There are others, such as assimilation and integration, cantonization, federalism, and arbitration. See John McGarry and Brendan O'Leary, "Introduction: The Macro-Political Regulation of Ethnic Conflict," in McGarry and O'Leary, *Politics of Ethnic Conflict*, pp. 1–40.

18 Consociationalism has nothing to do with the minority treaties of the interwar period, which sought to guarantee certain protection to national minorities, and generally failed, because the state—dominated by the majority nation—rejected these attempts. Consociationalism deals with a situation where the majority accepts that the minority must play an active role in the political life of the state and should do so on the same terms as itself.

19 The classic exposition of consociationalism is Arend Lijphart, *Democracy in Plural Societies: A Comparative Explanation* (New Haven: Yale University Press, 1977). See also G. Bingham Powell, Jr., *Contemporary Democracies: Participation, Stability and Violence* (Cambridge: Harvard University Press, 1982), pp. 212–218.

20 This topic has an enormous literature devoted to it. See *inter alia* Daniel Chirot, ed., *The Origins of Backwardness in Eastern Europe* (Berkeley: University of California Press, 1989); Jeno Szucs, "The Historical Regions of Europe," in John Keane, ed., *Civil Society and the State* (London: Verso, 1988) pp. 291–332; and George Schöpflin, *Politics in Eastern Europe, 1945–1992* (Oxford: Blackwell, 1993), ch. 1.

21 Walter Kolarz, *Myths and Realities in Eastern Europe* (London: Drummond, 1946).

22 George Steiner, *In Bluebeard's Castle* (London: Faber, 1971).

23 Zygmunt Bauman, "Intellectuals in East-Central Europe: Continuity and Change," *Eastern European Politics and Society* 1 (Spring 1987), 162–186.

24 My own views are set out in "Nationalism, Politics and the European Experience," *Survey* 28 (1974), 67–86.

25 Roman Szporluk, *Communism and Nationalism: Karl Marx versus Friedrich List* (Oxford: Oxford University Press, 1988).

26 Anthony Giddens, *The Consequences of Modernity* (Cambridge: Polity Press, 1990), p. 38.

27 See the argument in Patrick Dunleavy and Brendan O'Leary, *Theories of the State: The Politics of Liberal Democracy* (London: Macmillan, 1987).

28 See the perceptive analysis by Isaiah Berlin, "The Bent Twig: On the Rise of Nationalism," in *The Crooked Timber of Humanity* (London: Murray, 1990).

29 I have explored some of these themes in greater detail in "Nationalism and National Minorities in Central and Eastern Europe," *Journal of International Affairs* 45 (Summer 1991), 51–66.

30 David I. Kertzer, *Ritual, Politics and Power* (New Haven: Yale University Press, 1988).

31 On boundaries, see Fredrik Barth, ed., *Ethnic Groups and Boundaries: The Social Organization of Culture Difference* (London: Allen & Unwin, 1969).

32 In many national ideologies, there are elements of self-perception that claim particular democratic virtue for the nation in question; however, these are contingent and are in no way necessarily connected with the definition of nationhood.

33 Florence Beauge, "La Belgique en ses habits fédéraux," *Le Monde Diplomatique*, February 6, 1994. The population of Belgium is divided roughly 5:4 in favor of the Flemings (who speak a language that in its written form is identical with Dutch). Flanders, having been largely controlled by French speakers until World War II, has become much more prosperous than Wallonie since the 1960s. Despite or because of this increase in wealth, the Flemings have demanded greater access to the symbolic goods of the state, especially recognition of their language by the Francophone Walloons, while the latter have responded with alarm at what they see as the rise of a Flemish antagonism that threatens their own future as a community.

34 *Financial Times*, September 16, 1991.

35 See several of the essays in Soledad Garcia, ed., *European Identity and the Search for Legitimacy* (London: Pinter, 1993).

36 My own views of the problems of postcommunism are set out in "Central and Eastern Europe over the Last Year: New Trends, Old Structures," *Report on Eastern Europe* (Munich: RFE/RL Research Institute) 2, No. 7 (February 15, 1991), pp. 26–28; and "Postcommunism: Constructing New Democracies in Central Europe," *International Affairs* 67 (April 1991), 235–250; and in ch. 10 of *Politics in Eastern Europe*.

37 Project on Ethnic Relations (Princeton, N.J.), *The Ethnic Situation in Bulgaria* (Sofia: Club '90, 1993).

38 Ken Jowitt, *New World Disorder: The Leninist Extinction* (Berkeley: University of California Press, 1992).

39 The Hungarian political scientist Attila Agh has called this "political inflation." See his "A kiabrandulas kora" [The era of disenchantment], *Valosag* 36 (October 1993), 62–73.

4 IS DEMOCRATIC SUPRANATIONALISM A DANGER?

1 Edgar Morin, "Maastricht, espoirs et peurs d'Europe," *Le Monde,* July 10, 1993.

2 *Financial Times,* September 16, 1992, p. 3.

3 See the poll published in the *Economist,* May 15, 1993, p. 55.

4 Council of the European Communities, Commission of the European Communities, *Treaty on European Union* (Luxembourg: Office for Official Publications of the European Communities, 1992).

5 On the EMU see Articles 102–109 of the Treaty on European Union.

6 On some of these issues see Wayne Sandholtz, "Choosing Union: Monetary Politics and Maastricht," *International Organization* 47 (Winter 1993), 1–39.

7 European Communities, *Treaty on European Union,* Protocol on the excessive debt procedure, p. 183. The treaty, however, leaves the door open to a political evaluation of the convergence criteria: *Treaty on European Union,* Article 104c (2a).

8 Lionel Barber, "EC Ministers Allow for EMU Delay," *Financial Times,* February 16, 1993, p. 1.

9 See Paul de Grauwe, *The Economics of Monetary Integration* (Oxford: Oxford University Press, 1992).

10 Martin Feldstein, "The Ultimate Opt-out," *Financial Times,* December 9, 1992, p. 12.

11 The actual "Yes" vote in France was only 49.3 percent because more than 900,000 ballots were invalid. Given the turnout of 69.7 percent, only 34.4 percent of those eligible to vote supported the treaty. See Peter Bohley, "Europäische Einheit, föderatives Prinzip und Wahrungsunion: Wurde in Maastricht der richtige Weg beschritten?" *Aus Politik und Zeitgeschichte* B 1/93 (January 1, 1993), 34–45.

12 Only 24 percent of the German population support the monetary union. See *Suddeutsche Zeitung,* September 18–19, 1992, p. 8.

13 Germany ratified the treaty in 1993 after the constitutional court declared that the treaty did not violate the Constitution.

14 For accounts of the French referendum debate see Andrew Appleton, "Maastricht and the French Party System: Domestic Implications of the Treaty Referendum," *French Politics and Society* 10 (Fall 1992), 1–18; Alec Stone, "Ratifying Maastricht: France Debates European Union," *French Politics and Society* 11 (Winter 1993), 70–88; Byron Criddle, "The French Referendum on the Maastricht Treaty, September 1992," *Parliamentary Affairs* 46 (April 1993), 228–238.

15 Shirley Williams, "Sovereignty and Accountability in the European Community," in Robert Keohane and Stanley Hoffmann, eds., *The New European Community: Decisionmaking and Institutional Change* (Boulder, Colo.: Westview Press, 1991), p. 162.

16 Robert Keohane and Stanley Hoffmann, "Institutional Change in Europe in the 1980s," in *The New European Community,* p. 13.

17 Ibid.

18 Williams, "Sovereignty and Accountability in the European Community," p. 159.

19 For an evaluation of the democratic deficit in the Maastricht Treaty see George Ross, "After Maastricht: Hard Choices for Europe," *World Policy Journal* 9 (Summer 1992), 487–513.

20   Edward Mortimer, "A Cause without Delors," *Financial Times*, February 11, 1993, p. 10.

21   Neill Nugent, "The Deepening and Widening of the European Community: Recent Evolution, Maastricht and Beyond," *Journal of Common Market Studies* 30 (September 1992), 326.

22   For a critical evaluation of the principle of subsidiarity see Markus Jachtenfuchs, "Die EG nach Maastricht: Das Subsidiaritätspringzip und die Zukunft der Integration," *Europ-Archiv* 10 (1992), 279–287. See also A. G. Todt, "The Principle of Subsidiarity in the Maastricht Treaty," *Common Market Law Review* 29 (1992), 1079–1105; and D. Z. Cass, "The Word that Saves Maastricht? The Principles of Subsidiarity and the Division of Powers within the European Community," *Common Market Law Review* 29 (1992), 1107–1135.

23   See Bohley, "Europäische Einheit, föderatives Prinzip und Wahrungsunion," pp. 34–45. Charles Jeffery and John Yates, "Unification and Maastricht: The Response of the Lander Government," *German Politics* 1 (December 1992), 58–81; Uwe Leonardy, "Federation and Lander in German Foreign Relations: Power-Sharing in Treaty-Making and European Affairs," *German Politics* 1 (December 1992), 119–135; Thomas Christiansen, "The Lander between Bonn and Brussels: The Dilemma of German Federalism in the 1990s," *German Politics* 1 (August 1992), 239–263.

24   See Daniel Wincott, "The European Central Bank: Constitutional Dimensions and Political Limits," *International Relations* 11 (August 1992), 111–126.

25   Jean-Louis Quermonne, "Trois lectures du Traité de Maastrict," *Revue Française de Science Politique* 42 (October 1992), 815.

26   Williams, "Sovereignty and Accountability in the EC," pp. 173–74.

27   Ibid., p. 175.

28   The case of Italy is especially notable; see Enzo Mingione, "Divided Italy: The Resurgence of Regionalism," *International Affairs* 69 (April 1993), 305–318.

29   *Time* magazine, December 29, 1992, p. 21.

30   See Stanley Hoffmann, "Goodbye to a United Europe?" *New York Review of Books*, May 27, 1993, pp. 27–31; and Wolfgang Danspeckgruber, "Balkan Web: Unraveling a Region's Tangled History," *Washington Post*, May 9, 1993.

31   The French accusation of "social dumping" vis-à-vis the British government in the case of the relocation of a Hoover plant from France to Great Britain is likely to be only a first taste of these coming struggles.

32   *Le Nouvel Observateur*, December 28, 1992.

33   Pierre Hassner, "L'Europe et le spectre des nationalismes," *Esprit* 175 (October 1991), 16.

34   "Delors amid the Ruins," *Economist*, August 14, 1993, p. 7. See also "Maastricht c'est fini," *Le Nouvel Economiste*, May 21, 1993.

35   See the discussion of Jacques Delors with three French intellectuals on this issue in "La Communauté européenne et les chocs de l'histoire," *Esprit* 176 (November 1991), 28–29.

36   "Europe Falls to Earth," *Economist*, August 7, 1993, p. 6. See also Alexander J. Motyl, "The Modernity of Nationalism: Nations, States and Nation-States in the Contemporary World," *Journal of International Affairs* 45 (Winter 1992), 307–323.

37   See "Europe's Skeptical South," *Economist*, May 15, 1993.

38   See Quermonne, "Trois lectures du Traité de Maastricht," pp. 809–817.

39   See Williams, "Sovereignty and Accountability in the European Parliament."

5   FEAR THY NEIGHBOR: THE BREAKUP OF YUGOSLAVIA

1   Reflecting the European experience, the *Oxford English Dictionary* defines a nation as a "distinct race or people, characterized by common descent, language or history."

2   The Croats from Dalmatia tend to be taller and darker than the Croats from Zagorje. More important, the two groups speak such different dialects that they have great difficulty communicating with each other. In their way of life the Dalmatian towns are very much a part of Mediterranean culture, while Zagorje is culturally more a part of Central Europe's Pannonian plain. The Croats from Dalmatia and Serbs and Muslims of eastern Herzegovina show no physical differences, are linguistically very close, and their peasantry has very similar customs and attitudes.

3   The fall of Constantinople to the Ottoman Turks in 1453 was one factor that moved Ferdinand and Isabella to reconquer Granada toward the end of that century and impose religious unity on Spain by expelling Muslims and Jews. This religious assertiveness and the subsequent sixteenth-century Catholic Counter-Reformation strengthened, in turn, the determination of the Ottoman Turks, who completed the conquest of Bosnia in 1463. In order to incorporate this principal borderland facing Catholic Central Europe permanently into their empire, they decided to make it Muslim.

In general, forced conversions in the Islamic world were rare. But in the case of Bosnia's nobility, the Turks applied some pressure: they also offered economic and political advantages. Most of the nobility converted. Those serfs who followed suit, whether under coercion or of their own choice, considerably improved their lot in comparison to those who did not.

See, *inter alia*, Branislav Djurdjev, "Bosna," *Encyclopedia of Islam*, 1954, vol. 1, pp. 1261–1275; Sima Ćirković, *Istorija srednjevekovne bosanske države* (Belgrade, 1964); Jaroslav Šidak, *Studije o "Crkvi bosanskoj" i bogumilstvu* (Zagreb, 1975); John V. A. Fine, "The Medieval and Ottoman Roots of Modern Bosnian Society," in Mark Pinson, ed., with a foreword by Roy P. Mottahedeh, *The Muslims of Bosnia-Herzegovina: Their Historic Development from the Middle Ages to the Dissolution of Yugoslavia* (Cambridge: Center for Middle Eastern Studies, Harvard University, 1994). It should always be kept in mind that there are serious disagreements among scholars about developments in Bosnia during the fifteenth and sixteenth centuries.

4   While there was no Serbian hegemony in economic affairs, Serbs predominated in the state administration, diplomatic corps, and the military. The dynasty was also Serbian, and the Serbian political parties almost always played a leading role in the government. See Stevan K. Pavlowitch, *Yugoslavia* (New York: Benn, 1971); Ivo Banac, *The National Question in Yugoslavia: Origins, History, Politics* (Ithaca: Cornell University Press, 1984); Aleksa Djilas, *The Contested Country: Yugoslav Unity and Communist Revolution, 1919–1953* (Cambridge: Harvard University Press, 1991), pp. 79–83, 128–149.

5   See Stipe Šuvar, *Nacionalno i nacionalističko* (Split, 1974); Ivan Perić, *Suvremeni hrvatski nacionalizam* (Zagreb, 1976); Dennison Rusinow, *The Yugoslav Experiment, 1948–1974* (London: C. Hurst, 1977); Dušan Bilandžić, *Historija Socijalističke Federativne Republike Jugoslavije—glavni procesi* (Zagreb, 1979); Zagorka Golubović, *Kriza identiteta savremenog jugoslovenskog društva: Jugoslovenski put u socijalizam vidjen iz*

različitih uglova (Belgrade, 1988); Leonard J. Cohen, *The Socialist Pyramid: Elities and Power in Yugoslavia* (Oakville, Ont.: Mosaic Press, 1989).

6   For an accurate portrait of Serbia's liberals by one of their leaders, see Latinka Perović, *Zatvaranje kruga; Ishod političkog rascepa u SKJ 1971/1972* (Sarajevo, 1991).

7   Josip Broz Tito became the general secretary of the Communist party of Yugoslavia in the late 1930s, and was the leader of the Yugoslav Partisans during the Second World War. From 1944 to 1945, when the communists came to power in Yugoslavia, until his death in 1980, Tito was the head of both the state and the party and the supreme commander of the armed forces. See Milovan Djilas, *Tito: The Story from Inside* (New York: Harcourt Brace Jovanovich, 1980); Pero Simić, *Kad, kako i zašto je Tito postavljen za sekretara CK KPJ* (Belgrade, 1989); Steven K. Pavlowitch, *Tito: Yugoslavia's Great Dictator* (London: C. Hurst, 1992).

8   Between 200,000 and 300,000 Serbs did, however, leave Kosovo during this period, primarily as a result of pressure from Albanian extremists.

9   For a chronology of Yugoslavia's disintegration, see Radmila Nakarada, Lidija Basta-Posavec, and Slobodan Samardžić, eds., *Raspad Jugoslavije: Produžetak ili kraj agonije* (Belgrade, 1991), pp. 127–146.

10   See Aleksa Djilas, "A Profile of Slobodan Milošević," *Foreign Affairs* 72 (Summer 1993), 81–96.

11   See Vladimir Goati, "Iskušenja demokratije u 'trećoj Jugoslaviji,'" *Republika* 5 (December 16–31, 1993).

12   See Vladimir Goati, Zoran Dj. Slavujević, and Ognjen Pribićević, *Izborne borbe u Jugoslaviji (1990–1992)* (Belgrade, 1993).

13   Croatian paramilitary units began to patrol Serbian villages, and the Croatian Guard, consisting only of Croats, was formed. The new Croatian constitution established Croatia as the Croatian national state, excluding those not belonging to the Croatian national group. See Robert M. Hayden, "Constitutional Nationalism in the Formerly Yugoslav Republics," *Slavic Review* 51 (Winter 1992), 203–223. On the deterioration of the Serbs in Croatia under Tudjman's government, see, *inter alia,* Misha Glenny, *The Fall of Yugoslavia: The Third Balkan War* (London: Penguin Books, 1992), 12–14; Stevan K. Pavlowitch, "Who Is 'Balkanizing' Whom? The Misunderstandings between the Debris of Yugoslavia and an Unprepared West," *Daedalus,* 123 (Spring 1994); Slavoljub Djukić, *Izmedju slave i anateme: Politička biografija Slobodana Miloševića* (Belgrade, 1994), pp. 178–192; Jovan Mirić, "Hrvatska demokracija i srpsko pitanje," *Republika* 6 (October 1–15, 1994), 15–31.

14   The new Croatian government belittled the genocide. See Robert M. Hayden, "Balancing Discussion of Jasenovac and the Manipulation of History," *East European Politics and Societies* 6 (1992), 207–212.

15   For an attempt to give objective estimates of Yugoslavia's World War II losses, see Bogoljub Kočović, *Žrtve Drugog svetskog rata u Jugoslaviji* (London, 1985).

16   From the moment it won the election, the Muslim party began to elevate Muslims to leading positions in Bosnia's political, economic, and cultural life, at the expense of Bosnian Croats and Serbs. In Sarajevo, for example, Muslims soon dominated the media. The leaders of the Muslim party often spoke of Bosnian Muslims as a part of the Islamic world, rather than as Bosnians, and contacts with Islamic countries were frequent. So were statements that Muslims would soon be the dominant majority in Bosnia because of their higher birth rate. The leaders of the Muslim party showed great interest in the predicament of Muslims in other parts of the

former Yugoslavia, and declared that the Bosnian state would struggle for their rights. At the same time, they insisted that Bosnian Croats and Serbs should not identify with Croatia and Serbia, but only with Bosnia. The Muslim party also promoted the view that only Bosnian Muslims were true Bosnians. Similarly to other political parties in the former Yugoslavia, it also engaged in a selective reading of history. It magnified the crimes committed against the Muslims (e.g., those of the Chetniks, the Serbian nationalist and monarchist guerrillas during World War II), while minimizing Muslim crimes (e.g., those of the Muslims who joined the Croatian Ustashas or those who fought in the Nazi-created Muslim SS division).

See Slobodan Inić, "Razbijeno ogledalo—Jugoslavia u Bosni i Hercegovini," in Nakarada, Basta-Posavec, and Samardžić, eds., *Raspad Jugoslavije;* Miroljub Jevtić, *Od islamske deklaracije do verskog rata u BiH* (Belgrade, 1993); Mervyn Hiskett, *Reflections on "the Unspeakable Serb"* (Birmingham: Lazanica Press, 1994).

I am not arguing here that the hegemonistic tendencies of the Muslim party justified a military response by the Bosnian Croats and Serbs. On the contrary, Croats and Serbs in Bosnia could have struggled effectively against Muslim hegemony with political means. The Muslim party did work to maintain a coalition government and did not arm itself.

17 Alija Izetbegović, *Islamska deklaracija* (Sarajevo, 1990), p. 22. See also Alija Izetbegović, *Islam izmedju Istoka i Zapada* (Sarajevo, 1990).

18 General Veljko Kadijević, former Yugoslav minister of defense, tries to defend the federal army's role in the Croatian-Serbian war, but actually reveals that it had accepted Milošević's policies. See Veljko Kadijević, *Moje vidjenje raspada: Vojska bez države* (Belgrade, 1993).

19 Glenny, *The Fall of Yugoslavia*, p. 123.

20 "Čičak: Srbi u Hrvatskoj su ugroženi," *Politika*, December 25, 1993, 7; also "Crnac u selu Kju kluks klana," *Borba*, April 12, 1994, 13.

21 For a well-documented analysis of the anti-Serbian bias of the Western media during the Croatian-Serbian and Bosnian wars, see Peter Brock, "Dateline Yugoslavia: The Partisan Press," *Foreign Policy* 93 (Winter 1993–94), 152–172.

22 See, *inter alia,* Dorothea Gräfin Razumovsky, *Chaos Jugoslawien* (Munich: Piper, 1992).

23 Glenny, *The Fall of Yugoslavia*, pp. 148–149. Tudjman and Milošević had met secretly in March 1991 to discuss the division of Bosnia. See Judy Dempsey, "Bosnian Carve-Up in the Making," *Financial Times,* July 8, 1992. It is also generally believed that in January 1992, Tudjman forced Stjepan Kljujić to resign as the leader of the main party of Bosnia's Croats. For Croatian and Serbian deals about Bosnia, see also Blaine Harden, "Serbs, Croats, Agree to Carve Up Bosnia," *Washington Post,* May 8, 1992.

24 See Nada Burić, Associated Press (November 27, 1991), and Stephen Kinzer, "Europe, Backing Germans, Accepts Yugoslav Breakup," *New York Times,* January 16, 1992.

25 This was especially true in the conservative newspapers *Frankfurter Allgemeine Zeitung* and *Die Welt.* See also Johann Georg Reißmüller, *Der Krieg vor unserer Haustür: Hintergründe der kroatischen Tragödie* (Stuttgart: Deutsche Verlags-Anstalt, 1992). For an attempt to give a balanced account of the Yugoslav disintegration, see Wolfgang Libal, *Das Ende Jugoslawiens: Chronik einer Selbstzerstörung* (Vienna: Europaverlag, 1991).

26   See Razumovsky, *Chaos Jugoslawien,* p. 170.

27   The United States did not follow suit, stating that peace should first be achieved and the rights of minorities protected.

28   Warren Zimmermann, former U.S. ambassador to Yugoslavia, claims in an interview ("Hounded by What the US Didn't Do in Yugoslavia," *New York Times,* June 14, 1992) that it was a mistake for the West to follow the German lead in recognizing Bosnia, since it triggered a war there.

29   In an interview with a Belgrade opposition daily, Warren Zimmermann, former U.S. ambassador to Yugoslavia, described his efforts to convince Izetbegović, after he had returned to Sarajevo from Lisbon, to respect the Lisbon agreement. However, Izetbegović was confident that Bosnia would be recognized even if he abandoned the agreement. See "Ne mrzimo Srbe već nacionalističku agresiju," *Nedeljna Borba,* April 30–May 3, 1994.

30   Among the more important incidents that led to the full-scale war were the following. On March 1, the second day of the referendum for independence, Muslim extremists shot the groom's father and wounded the priest at a Serbian Orthodox wedding in Sarajevo. Barricades were errected by Serbs and Muslims in and around Sarajevo, and twelve people were killed before the fighting ceased the next day. On March 3–4, at least twenty-seven people were killed in the towns of Bosanski Brod and Kupres. The fighting was between military forces from Croatia and Bosnian Serbs. On April 5, Serbian policemen attacked police stations, and Serbian extremists fired on thousands of peace marchers in Sarajevo. On May 2, regular Bosnian forces fired on a Yugoslav army column, retreating under the protection of the United Nations forces. This truce had been brokered after the Yugoslav army kidnapped President Izetbegović and then agreed to release him in return for safe passage. On May 27, in Vase Miskina Street in Sarajevo, an explosion killed sixteen people queuing for bread. There is still disagreement as to which side was responsible for the tragedy. See, *inter alia, War Crimes in Bosnia-Hercegovina: A Helsinki Watch Report* (New York: Human Rights Watch, 1992), 1:24–31.

31   On April 20, 1993, economic sanctions were stepped up, and the borders of Yugoslavia (consisting now only of Serbia and Montenegro) came under tight control. By the winter of 1993–94, experts claimed that it was the most successful economic blockade in history.

32   Many examples of such views can be found in Borisav Jović, *Komadanje Jugoslavije* (Belgrade: Politika, 1991).

33   See Svetozar Stojanović, *Autoritet bez vlasti: Dobrica Ćosić kao šef države* (Belgrade: Filip Visnjic, 1993), pp. 15–16.

34   For example, Lawrence S. Eagleburger, the acting U.S. secretary of state, declared that the United States was not going to recognize any results of "aggression" by Serbia and Croatia in Bosnia, and that the "fundamental objective" of U.S. policy was the restoration of the *status quo ante bellum.* See "US Worries Balkan War Could Spread," *New York Times,* August 22, 1992.

35   For the irreversibility of Bosnia's disintegration, see Aleksa Djilas, "The Nation That Wasn't," *New Republic,* September 21, 1992, 25–31.

36   See Aleksa Djilas, "What Should the West Do about Bosnia? Partition It into Three Units?" *Boston Globe,* April 26, 1993.

37   A number of distinguished political figures in the West (including Margaret Thatcher, the former British prime minister, and George Shultz, the former U.S.

secretary of state) had demanded the bombardment of Serbian positions. The culmination of these demands was the letter published under the title "What the West Must Do in Bosnia" in the *Wall Street Journal,* September 3–4, 1993.

38   See "Mir u Bosni još uvek, neizvestan," *Politika,* September 4, 1993; "U iščekivanju dobre vesti iz Ženeve," *Politika,* December 31, 1993–January 1, 2, 3, 1994; "Hronologija rata," *Politika,* February 7, 1994.

39   "Drašković: Srbiju treba pomiriti sa svetom," *Politika,* December 12, 1993.

40   See Robert M. Hayden, "The Constitution of the Federation of Bosnia and Herzegovina: An Imaginary Constitution for an Illusory 'Federation,'" *Balkan Forum* 2 (September 1994), 77–91.

41   "Muslimansko-hrvatska federacija etnički sve čistija," *Borba,* November 1, 1994.

6   NATIONALISM IN SOUTHEASTERN EUROPE

1   Francis Fukuyama, "The War of All against All," *New York Times Book Review,* April 10, 1994, p. 7.

2   Karl Marx and Frederick Engels, *The German Ideology* (Moscow, 1964), p. 37.

3   This was the age of erudite polyhistors, some rooted in the Renaissance (Vinko Pribojević), nearly all from the clerical estate (Pribojević, Mavar Orbin, Juraj Križanić) or petty nobility (Križanić, Pavao Ritter Vitezović), and among whom historians predominated. To these should be added the poets from the ranks of high nobility (Ivan Gundulić, Petar Zrinski).

4   Ivan Gundulić, "U slavu visine privedre Ferdinanda Drugoga, velikoga kneza od Toskane," *Pet stoljeća hrvatske književnosti,* vol. 12 (Zagreb, 1962), p. 153.

5   Juraj Križanić (1618–1683), himself a Catholic priest who joined the Dominican order by the end of his life, was a forerunner of modern ecumenism. He did not view the Orthodox Russians as schismatics and referred to the ecclesiastical organizations of Kiev and Moscow as "churches," both a singular departure from seventeenth-century Roman Catholic practice. On Križanić see esp. Ivan Golub, "The Slavic Idea of Juraj Križanić," *Harvard Ukrainian Studies* 10, no. 3/4 (1986), 438–491.

6   On Vitezović see Ivo Banac, "The Redivived Croatia of Pavao Ritter Vitezović," *Harvard Ukrainian Studies* 10, no. 3/4 (1986), 492–507.

7   On Branković see Jovan Radonić, *Đorđe Branković despot "Ilirika"* (Belgrade, 1929).

8   For an overview of Serbian ecclesiastical activities in the Habsburg lands see Ivo Banac, "The Insignia of Identity: Heraldry and the Growth of National Ideologies among the South Slavs," *Ethnic Studies* 10 (1993), 97–103.

9   Koço Bihiku, *A History of Albanian Literature* (Tirana, 1980), p. 14.

10   On Slovene controversies over Illyrianism see E. Petre, *Poizkus ilirizma pri Slovencih* (Ljubljana, 1939).

11   The best summary of the revivalist period in Croatia can be found in Jaroslav Šidak, "Hrvatski narodni preporod—ideje i problemi," *Studije iz hrvatske povijesti XIX stoljeća* (Zagreb, 1973), pp. 95–111.

12   There are no adequate interpretations of Karadžić's activities in most standard works. For an interpretation of his role see Ivo Banac, "Main Trends in the Croat Language Question," in Riccardo Picchio and Harvey Goldblatt, eds., *Aspects of the*

Slavic Language Question, vol. 1 (New Haven: Yale Russian and East European Publications, 1984), pp. 228–231.

13   On Garašanin and his activities among the Croats see Ivo Banac, "The Confessional 'Rule' and the Dubrovnik Exception: The Origins of the 'Serb-Catholic' Circle in Nineteenth-Century Dalmatia," *Slavic Review* 42, no. 3 (1983), 457–465.

14   Cited in Andrzej Walicki, *A History of Russian Thought from the Enlightenment to Marxism* (Stanford: Stanford University Press, 1979), p. 293.

15   Latinka Perović, "'Rusija i Evropa' N.J. Danilevskog i njeni odjeci u Srbiji," *Republika* 6, no. 8 (1994), 3–10.

16   On Starčević's ideology see Ivo Banac, *The National Question in Yugoslavia: Origins, History, Politics* (Ithaca: Cornell University Press, 1984), pp. 85–89.

17   On the League of Prizren and its consequences see Stavro Skendi, *The Albanian National Awakening, 1878–1912* (Princeton: Princeton University Press, 1967).

18   For an overview of Zbor's history see Mladen Stefanović, *Zbor Dimitrija Ljotića 1934–1945* (Belgrade, 1984).

19   On the ideology of "svetosavlje" see Geert van Dartel, *Ćirilometodska ideja i svetosavlje* (Zagreb, 1984), pp. 71–104; and Thomas Bremer, *Ekklesiale Struktur und Ekklesiologie in der Serbischen Orthodoxen Kirche im 19. und 20. Jahrhundert* (Wurzburg, 1992), pp. 112–252.

20   A leading Chetnik ideologist, Stevan Moljević, epitomized this program when he wrote of a "homogeneous Serbia that had to embrace the whole ethnic territory on which Serbs live." See Moljević, "Homogena Srbija," *Zbornik dokumenata i podataka o narodnooslobodilačkom ratu naroda Jugoslavije*, vol. 14, t. 2 (Belgrade, 1981), pp. 1–10.

21   Rossijskij centr za xranenija i izučenija dokumentov novejšej istorii, Moscow; fond 495, op. 70, d. 60: Aktuelna pitanja borbe protiv diktature (1929), p. 8.

22   On the Ustašas see Fikreta Jelić-Butić, *Ustaše i Nezavisna Država Hrvatska, 1941–1945* (Zagreb, 1977); Bogdan Krizman, *Pavelić i ustaše* (Zagreb, 1978); idem, *Pavelić između Hitlera i Mussolinija* (Zagreb, 1980); idem, *Ustaše i Treći Reich* (Zagreb, 1983) 2 vols.; idem, *Pavelić u bjekstvu* (Zagreb, 1986).

23   On the political history of socialist Yugoslavia see Dušan Bilandžić, *Historija Socijalističke Federativne Republike Jugoslavije: Glavni procesi, 1918–1985* (Zagreb, 1985).

24   For assessments of this period by the participants themselves see Miko Tripalo, *Hrvatsko proljeće* (Zagreb, 1990); and Latinka Perović, *Zatvaranje kruga: Ishod političkog rascepa u SKJ 1971/1972* (Sarajevo, 1991).

25   On this process see Ivo Banac, "The Fearful Asymmetry of War: The Causes and Consequences of Yugoslavia's Demise," *Daedalus* 121, no. 2 (1992), 141–174.

26   Montesquieu, *Lettres persanes* (Paris, 1835), pp. 68–69.

7   THREE FACES OF NATIONALISM IN THE FORMER SOVIET UNION

1   The telegram is contained in footnote 141 in V. I. Lenin, *Sochineniia*, 3d ed. (Moscow and Leningrad, 1931), 25:624. For an expansion, and for the source of my description of Stalin's more general approach, see his numerous comments in *Chetvertoie Soveshchanie TsK RKP s otvetstvennymi rabotnikami natsional'nykh respublik i oblastei* (Moscow: TsK RKP, June 1923). This stenographic report was classified "Top Secret" in Soviet times and has become available to researchers only recently.

2   See Albert Hirshmann, *Exit, Voice, Loyalty* (Cambridge: Harvard University Press,

1970). For a discussion of the applicability of his ideas to ethnic assertiveness, see Thomas Hylland Eriksen, "Ethnicity versus Nationalism," *Journal of Peace Research* 28 (1991), 263–279; and his "Ethnicity and Nationalism," *Bulletin of Peace Proposals* 23 (1992), 219–224.

3   On this phenomenon, see my "New States and Sudden Minorities," in Harlan Cleveland, ed., *New Strategies for a Restless World* (Minneapolis: University of Minnesota Press, 1993), pp. 31–36.

4   For a useful discussion of nationalism as a response to this lack of correspondence, see especially Group for the Advancement of Psychiatry, *Us and Them: The Psychology of Ethnonationalism*, Report 123 (New York: Brunner/Mazel, 1987).

5   For an extraordinary study that places these movements in precisely this perspective, see Marianna Butenien, *Estland, Lettland, Litauen—Das Baltikum auf dem langen Weg in die Freiheit* (Munich, 1992).

6   For a useful summary of this perspective, see Martha Brill Olcott, "Democracy and Statebuilding in Central Asia," *Demokratizatisya* 2(1994), 39–52.

7   See Irina Kobrinskaya, *Vnutrupoliticheskaya situatsiya i prioritety vneshnoy politiki Rossii* (Moscow: ROPTs, 1992), p. 7.

8   Vilen Ivanov, Anatoliy Kotov, and Irina Ladodo, "Mezhetnicheskaya napriazhennost' v Rossiiskoi Federatsii glazami sotsiologov," *Etnopolis* 1 (1993), 99–107, and esp. the table on p. 107.

9   For a discussion of why scholars have misunderstood Russian nationalism, see my "Sowjetstaat und russischer Nationalismus," in Andreas Kappeler, ed., *Die Russen, Ihr National bewusstein in Geschichte und Gegenwart* (Cologne, 1990), pp. 91–102; and my "Russia's Extreme Right," *National Interest* 1 (Fall 1993), 93–96.

10   For a useful discussion of this, see Marie Mendras, *Un état pour la Russie* (Brussels, 1993). Cf. my "Russia and Her Neighbors," *Foreign Policy* 90 (1993), 79–88.

11   On the spectrum of opinion, see my "Can We Help Russia Become a Good Neighbor?" *Demokratizatsiya* 2(1994), 3–8; and my "Russia as a Eurasian Power," in Stephen Sestanovich, ed., *Rethinking Russia's National Interests* (Washington, D.C.: CSIS, 1994), pp. 42–51. For examples of two contrasting Russian positions, see Vladimir Lukin, "Rossiya—v dalnikh i blizhnikh krugakh," *Segodnya*, September 3, 1993; and the report by scholars at the Gorbachev Foundation, "Russkiie v 'blizhnem zarubezhye,'" *Nezavisimaia gazeta*, September 7, 1993.

12   See, among many others, Leonid Mlechin's remarks in *Izvestiia* on January 29, 1994. He writes: "The restoration of the Russian Empire will relieve the West of having to worry about the peoples of the former Soviet Union and allow it to help others. Neither the United States nor NATO will fight for the independence of Ukraine or Lithuania and neither will break relations with Moscow for reincorporating Belorussia. After an initial emotional reaction, reasonable egotism and a belief in realpolitik will prevail. And what about Eastern Europe? Her fate will be delayed under the reconstitution of the empire or the [Soviet] Union. And until a new summit in Yalta."

13   See *Polis* 7 (1991), passim.

14   See his "'Hot Spots' in the CIS and International Law," *Mezhdunarodnaya zhizn'* 5 (May 1994), in FBIS-USR-94-094, August 29, 1994, p. 70.

15   For an exploration of these dilemmas, see my "Ethnicity as Explanation, Ethnicity as Excuse," in Robert Pfaltzgraff, Jr., and Richard Shultz, Jr., eds., *Ethnic Conflict and Regional Instability* (Carlisle Barracks, Pa.: U.S. Army War College, 1994), pp. 51–58.

8   HYPOTHESES ON NATIONALISM AND THE CAUSES OF WAR

1   A survey is Anthony D. Smith, *Theories of Nationalism*, 2d ed. (New York: Harper & Row, 1983). Prominent recent works include Ernest Gellner, *Nations and Nationalism* (Ithaca: Cornell University Press, 1983); Anthony D. Smith, *The Ethnic Origins of Nations* (Oxford: Basil Blackwell, 1986); E. J. Hobsbawm, *Nations and Nationalism since 1780* (New York: Cambridge University Press, 1990); Benedict Anderson, *Imagined Communities: Reflections on the Origin and Spread of Nationalism*, rev. ed. (London: Verso, 1991); Liah Greenfeld, *Nationalism: Five Roads to Modernity* (Cambridge: Harvard University Press, 1992); and Barry R. Posen, "Nationalism, the Mass Army, and Military Power," *International Security* 18 (Fall 1993), 80–124. However, the nationalism literature leaves ample room for more work on nationalism's causes: much of it fails to frame hypotheses clearly and much does not systematically test hypotheses against empirical evidence, hence many questions remain unresolved.

2   Thus Anthony Smith notes that "the prevailing image of nationalism in the West today is mainly negative," and Boyd Shafer states his "belief that nationalism, especially when carried to extremes, leads to war and destruction." Smith, *Theories of Nationalism*, p. 8; Boyd C. Shafer, *Faces of Nationalism* (New York: Harcourt Brace Jovanovich, 1972), p. xiii. Yet the entry under "Nationalism and War" in Louis Snyder's 435-page *Encyclopedia of Nationalism* fills only two pages, and its bibliography lists no works focused on the topic. Louis L. Snyder, *Encyclopedia of Nationalism* (New York: Paragon, 1990), pp. 248–250. Exceptions exist: a few scholars have held a less purely critical view of nationalism, arguing that it has the potential for both good and evil. See, for example, Carlton J. H. Hayes, *Essays on Nationalism* (New York: Macmillan, 1926), pp. 245–275; Hayes's views are summarized in Snyder, *Encyclopedia of Nationalism*, pp. 132–133. And the impact of nationalism on the risk of war is now receiving more attention: see especially Jack Snyder, "Nationalism and the Crisis of the Post-Soviet State," *Survival* 35 (Spring 1993), 5–26; and Barry R. Posen, "The Security Dilemma and Ethnic Conflict," *Survival* 35 (Spring 1993), 27–47.

3   My usage of "ethnic community" follows Anthony Smith, who suggests that an ethnic community has six characteristics: a common name, a myth of common ancestry, shared memories, a common culture, a link with a historic territory or homeland (which it may or may not currently occupy), and a measure of common solidarity. See Smith, *Ethnic Origins of Nations*, pp. 22–30. Summarizing Smith nicely is Michael Brown, "Causes and Implications of Ethnic Conflict," in Brown, ed., *Ethnic Conflict and International Security* (Princeton: Princeton University Press, 1993), pp. 4–5.

Smith's second criterion (myth of common ancestry) excludes immigrant societies of diverse origin that have developed the other five characteristics of ethnic community, such as the immigrant peoples of the United States, Cuba, Argentina, Chile, and Brazil. However, the common usage of "nation" and "nationalism" includes these groups as nations that can have a nationalism, e.g., "American nationalism," "Argentine nationalism," "Chilean nationalism." I define nationalism as a movement of a "national community" as well as an "ethnic community" in order to include these nationalisms. My usage of "national" follows the *Dictionary of the Social Sciences*, which defines "nation" as "the largest society of people united by a common culture and consciousness," and which "occupies a common territory." Julius Gould and William L. Kolb, eds., *A Dictionary of the Social Sciences* (New York: Free Press of Glencoe, 1964), p. 451.

4 The academic literature defines nationalism in an annoyingly wide range of ways. My definition follows no other exactly, but it amalgamates the more prominent definitions: these include at least one element of my definition—i.e., prime loyalty is owed to one's ethnic/culture group, and/or the group to which prime loyalty is given should have its own state. My usage most closely follows Rupert Emerson and Richard Cottam, who define nationalism (in Cottam's words) as "a belief on the part of a large group of people that they comprise a community, a nation, that is entitled to independent statehood, and a willingness of this group to grant their community a primary and terminal loyalty" (quoted in Shafer, *Faces of Nationalism*, p. 4). Similar is Hans Kohn, whose nationalists give "supreme loyalty" to their own nationality, and see "the nation-state as the ideal form of political organization" (ibid.). Also similar are E. J. Hobsbawm and Ernst Gellner, who define nationalism as "primarily a principle which holds that the political and national unit should be congruent": Hobsbawm, *Nations and Nationalism since 1780*, p. 9, quoting and adopting Gellner's definition. However, their definition, by describing nationalism as an idea holding that states and nationalities should be coterminous, omits the many nationalisms that would claim their own state while also denying the statehood aspirations of other nationalities, and also omits more modest nationalisms that are content to allow a diaspora beyond their state borders.

In his Introduction to this volume Charles Kupchan distinguishes "ethnic" and "civic" nationalism: the identity of "ethnic" nationalists is ethnocultural, the identity of "civic" nationalists is territorial. In this chapter I address only Kupchan's "ethnic" nationalism. (In fact, his "civic" nationalism is not a form of nationalism under my definition.)

5 A similar exercise whose example influenced my design is Robert Jervis, "Hypotheses on Misperception," in Robert J. Art and Robert Jervis, eds., *International Politics: Anarchy, Force, Political Economy, and Decision Making*, 2d ed. (Glenview, Ill.: Scott, Foresman, 1985), pp. 510–526. The article was originally published in 1968.

6 The text of this chapter identifies factors that govern the size of the risk posed by nationalism, and explains the proposed causal relationship. Table 8.1 reformulates these factors and explanations as hypotheses.

7 The dichotomy between stateless and state-possessing nationalist movements is analogous to the dichotomy in international relations between "satisfied" and "dissatisfied" powers; the latter disturb the peace in their effort to gain satisfaction, while the former cause less trouble.

8 Wars can result from having too many states, as well as too few. If states are too numerous, wars of national unification will result, as they did in Germany and Italy in the nineteenth century, and as they might someday in the Arab world. In Europe, however, the problem everywhere is an excess of demand for states over the supply.

9 Alan Thein Durning, *Guardians of the Land: Indigenous Peoples and the Health of the Earth*, Worldwatch Paper 112 (Washington, D.C.: Worldwatch Institute, December 1992), p. 9. Durning reports that measured by spoken languages the world has 6,000 cultures. Of these some 4,000–5,000 are indigenous and comprise some 10 percent of the world's population. See also Michael Krauss, "The Language Extinction Catastrophe Just Ahead: Should Linguists Care?" Paper presented at the 15th International Congress of Linguists, Quebec City, Quebec, Canada, August 10, 1992.

For another estimate see Gunnar P. Nielsson, "States and 'Nation-Groups': A Global Taxonomy," in Edward A. Tiryakian and Ronald Rogowski, eds., *New Nationalisms of the Developed West* (Boston: Allen & Unwin, 1985), pp. 27–56. Nielsson identifies a global total of 589 ethnic groups, most of which are stateless (p. 33). He also found that only 41 of 161 states surveyed were ethnically homogeneous (one ethnic group comprises over 95 percent of the state's population); see his table 2.1, pp. 30–31.

10 These figures are for 1979 and are calculated from John L. Scherer, ed., *USSR Facts and Figures Annual*, vol. 5 (Gulf Breeze, Fla.: Academic International Press, 1981), pp. 51–52. Of these stateless groups the ten largest are the Tatar (6.3 million), German (1.9 million), Jewish (1.8 million), Chuvash (1.8 million), Dagestan (1.7 million), Bashkir (1.4 million), Mordvin (1.2 million), Polish (1.2 million), Chechen (0.8 million), and Udmurt (.7 million).

11 The Chinese state has historically left the overseas Chinese to their own political devices. See John E. Wills, "Maritime Asia, 1500–1800: The Interactive Emergence of European Domination," *American Historical Review* 98 (February 1993), 83–105, at 87.

12 Calculated from Scherer, *USSR Facts and Figures Annual*, pp. 49–51.

13 Russia's extensive military meddling in the affairs of the other former Soviet republics during 1992–94 and the political rise of Vladimir Zhirinovsky in 1993 warns that a new Russian expansionism is already emerging. On this military meddling see Thomas Goltz, "Letter from Eurasia: The Hidden Russian Hand," *Foreign Policy* 92 (Fall 1993), 92–116.

14 On twentieth-century German nationalism see Louis L. Snyder, *German Nationalism: The Tragedy of a People*, 2d ed. (Port Washington, N.Y.: Kennikat Press, 1969); Louis L. Snyder, *From Bismarck to Hitler: The Background of Modern German Nationalism* (Williamsport, Pa.: Bayard Press, 1935); and Hans Kohn, *The Mind of Germany: The Education of a Nation* (New York: Harper & Row, 1960). On official ideas and perceptions in fascist Italy see Denis Mack Smith, *Mussolini's Roman Empire* (Harmondsworth: Penguin, 1977). On domestic currents in imperial Japan see Saburo Ienaga, *The Pacific War, 1931–1945* (New York: Pantheon, 1978); and Saburo Ienaga, "The Glorification of War in Japanese Education," *International Security* 18, (Winter 1993/94).

Nationalism is not, of course, the only possible source of claims against neighbors. These can also arise from non-nationalist expansionist political ideologies (communism), from hegemonistic religious ideas (the crusading Christianity of the Middle Ages), from safety concerns arising from the security dilemma, from economic greed, and so forth.

15 Thus the second and fourth attributes are related: if some states oppress their minorities this affects other states' propensity to pursue diaspora recovery.

16 On the war's origins, including the important role of Croatia's prewar threats against its Serb minority, see Misha Glenny, "The Massacre of Yugoslavia," *New York Review of Books*, January 30, 1992, pp. 30–31; and Misha Glenny, *The Fall of Yugoslavia: The Third Balkan War* (London: Penguin, 1992), pp. 12–14, 123. An account stressing international aspects of the war's origins is Morton H. Halperin and David J. Scheffer with Patricia L. Small, *Self-Determination in the New World Order* (Washington, D.C.: Carnegie Endowment, 1992), pp. 32–38.

17 On the greater peacefulness of a defense-dominant world, see Robert Jervis,

"Cooperation under the Security Dilemma," *World Politics* 30 (January 1978), 167–214.

18   Thus the evident power of nationalism helped dampen Soviet-American competition during the Cold War, by persuading some in the West that nationalism imposed a natural limit on Soviet expansion. These observers argued that the Western powers need not actively check Soviet expansionism at every point (because local nationalism could defeat it alone), or move actively to roll back Soviet gains (because these gains would eventually be rolled back by indigenous nationalism; and in the meantime nationalist resistance would bleed Soviet power). For example, George Kennan took a calm approach to containment partly because he believed that resistant local nationalism would check Soviet expansion in the short run, and would rend the Soviet empire in the long run. See John Lewis Gaddis, *Strategies of Containment: A Critical Appraisal of Postwar American National Security Policy* (New York: Oxford University Press, 1982), pp. 42–48. Other arguments for Cold War restraint that rested in part on the power of nationalism included Arthur M. Schlesinger, *The Bitter Heritage: Vietnam and American Democracy 1941–1968*, rev. ed. (Greenwich, Conn.: Fawcett, 1968), pp. 78–80; Jerome Slater, "Dominos in Central America: Will They Fall? Does It Matter?" *International Security* 12 (Fall 1987), 105–134, at 113; and Stephen M. Walt, "The Case for Finite Containment," *International Security* 14 (Summer 1989), 3–49, at 26–27. Had nationalism been weaker these arguments would have lost force, leaving a stronger case for more aggressive American policies.

19   If nationalism is unattainable it may not even appear: the captive nation will submerge the nationalist thought. Some realist scholars of international relations argue that imperialism is a function of capability: states imperialize simply when and where they can. Likewise, and conversely, nationalism is in part simply a function of capability: it emerges where it can.

20   We can scale up this logic from single states to regions by asking whether nations have states in proportion to their power. That is, does the state-to-nation ratio correspond with the state-to-nation power ratio? Or do nations have fewer states than their power justifies? If the former is the case, peace is more likely. But if nations have fewer states than their power would allow, trouble results in the form of wars of secession.

21   Overall, then, three variables matter: (1) the supply of states; (2) the demand for states; and (3) the capacity of submerged nations to acquire states. Peace is stronger when supply and demand are in equilibrium; or when supply and capacity are in equilibrium. In one case, nationalism is satisfied; in the other, it is dissatisfied but impotent. Dangers arise if both supply and demand, and supply and capacity, are not in equilibrium. We then have submerged nationalisms that both desire and can assert the demand for statehood.

22   The scope and structure of intermingling governs the acuteness of what might be called the "interethnic security dilemma": this dilemma is posed where one group cannot achieve physical security without diminishing the physical security of other groups. It is analogous to the interstate security dilemma of international relations, except the clashing units are ethnic or culture groups, not states.

23   Moreover, Yugoslavia's one easy secession—that of Slovenia—was easy because the Slovene population was not intermingled with others. An excellent ethnographic map of the former Yugoslavia that details this intermingling is Central Intelligence Agency, "Peoples of Yugoslavia: Distribution by Opstina, 1981 Census," Map 505956

9–83 (543994). A useful though less detailed ethnographic map covering all of Eastern Europe including former Yugoslavia is Central Intelligence Agency, "Ethnic Majorities and Minorities," in Central Intelligence Agency, *Atlas of Eastern Europe* (Washington, D.C.: U.S. Government Printing Office, August 1990), p. 6. A good ethnographic map of the former USSR is National Geographic Society, "Peoples of the Soviet Union," supplement to *National Geographic* 149 (February 1976), 144A; back issues of *National Geographic* containing this map are available from the National Geographic Society, Washington, D.C.

24 These include Hungarians in Romania, Slovakia, and Serbia; Poles in Lithuania, Belarus, Ukraine, and the Czech Republic; Germans in Poland and the Czech Republic; Turks in Bulgaria; Greeks in Albania; Albanians in Serbia and Macedonia; Croats in Bosnia-Herzegovina; and Serbs in Croatia and Bosnia-Herzegovina. Summaries include F. Stephen Larrabee, "Long Memories and Short Fuses: Change and Instability in the Balkans," *International Security* 15 (Winter 1990–91), 58–91; Istvan Deak, "Uncovering Eastern Europe's Dark History," *Orbis* 34 (Winter 1989), 51–65; Barry James, "Central Europe Tinderboxes: Old Border Disputes," *International Herald Tribune*, January 1, 1990, p. 5; and the CIA map cited above, "Ethnic Majorities and Minorities, 1990."

25 See the maps cited in note 23. Overall, 16 percent of the titular peoples of the fifteen successor states of the former Soviet Union, totaling 39 million people, live outside their home states (the term "titular peoples" refers to the peoples after whom republics are named, e.g., Armenians, Kazakhs, Russians, etc.). Calculated from Scherer, *USSR Facts and Figures Annual,* pp. 49–51. And, as noted earlier, another 10 percent of the former Soviet population (26 million people) are members of the eighty-nine smaller nationalities without titular home republics (a republic named after the nationality).

26 Making this argument is Posen, "The Security Dilemma and Ethnic Conflict," pp. 32–35.

27 See ibid., pp. 32–38.

28 The intensification of fighting between Armenia and Azerbaijan in 1991–92 had similar origins: Armenia moved to free Nagorno-Karabakh at a moment that Armenia's power relative to Azerbaijan's was at its peak.

29 See Central Intelligence Agency, "Peoples of Yugoslavia."

30 The new states may also be more defensible than their parent states because they can call upon nationalism as a mobilizing defensive force, as their multiethnic parent states could not.

31 Likewise, Germany has produced the most troublesome Western nationalism partly because German borders are relatively exposed.

32 On latent Hungarian revanchism see, for example, Judith Ingram, "Boys Impatient for 'Great Hungary' to Take Wing," *New York Times*, January 15, 1993, p. A4. On its official manifestations see Stephen Engelberg with Judith Ingram, "Now Hungary Adds Its Voice to the Ethnic Tumult," *New York Times*, January 25, 1993, p. A3.

33 See Bette Denich, "Unbury the Victims: Nationalist Revivals of Genocide in Yugoslavia," paper presented at the American Anthropological Association annual meeting, Chicago, Illinois, November 1991.

34 On the Baltic States' policies see Steven Erlanger, "Baltic Identity: Russians Wonder If They Belong: New Citizenship Rules May in Effect Expel the Ex-'Occupiers,'" *New York Times*, November 22, 1992, p. 1. This Baltic anti-Russian

discrimination reflects the great cruelties inflicted on the Baltic peoples by Stalin's government: during the years 1940–49 some 36 percent of the indigenous population of Latvia, 33 percent of the indigenous population of Estonia, and 32 percent of the indigenous population of Lithuania were killed, deported, or driven into exile. Dag Sebastian Ahlander, "Help Baltics Deal with Russian Minority," *New York Times* (letter to the editor), December 6, 1992, p. E18.

35 For example, Native Americans can coexist, albeit uneasily, with European immigrants partly because the enormous horrors that the Europeans inflicted on the natives have faded into the mists of history. On these horrors see David E. Stannard, *American Holocaust: Columbus and the Conquest of the New World* (New York: Oxford University Press, 1992). Stannard estimates that the native population of the Americas fell by roughly 95 percent—in absolute numbers by about 71–95 million people—after the European arrival in 1492 (p. 268). If so, this was the greatest human-caused human dying in world history.

36 On these murders see Robert Conquest, *The Harvest of Sorrow: Soviet Collectivization and the Terror-Famine* (New York: Oxford University Press, 1986). Stalin's other crimes are covered in Robert Conquest, *The Great Terror: A Reassessment* (New York: Oxford University Press, 1990).

37 Ukraine contains 10.5 million Russians, 21 percent of its total population. Calculated from Scherer, *USSR Facts and Figures Annual*, p. 49.

38 On Turkish denial of these murders see Roger W. Smith, "The Armenian Genocide: Memory, Politics, and the Future," in Richard G. Hovannisian, ed. *The Armenian Genocide: History, Politics, Ethics* (New York: St. Martin's, 1992), pp. 1–20; Vahakn N. Dadrian, "Ottoman Archives and Denial of the Armenian Genocide," in Hovannisian, *Armenian Genocide*, pp. 280–310; and Roger W. Smith, "Genocide and Denial: The Armenian Case and Its Implications," *Armenian Review* 42 (Spring 1989), 1–38. On the general disappearance of the Armenian people from Turkish historical writings, see Clive Foss, "The Turkish View of Armenian History: A Vanishing Nation," in Hovannisian, *Armenian Genocide*, pp. 250–279.

39 Glenny, "The Massacre of Yugoslavia," pp. 30–31; and Glenny, *The Fall of Yugoslavia*, pp. 12–14, 123.

40 Even moderate Russian officials have voiced deep concern over the rights of Russian minorities in nearby states. See, for example, Sergei Stankevich, "Russia in Search of Itself," *National Interest* 28 (Summer 1992), 49–51; and "Four Comments" in ibid., pp. 51–53. So far they have proposed solutions within the framework of international law and institutions: for example, Russian Foreign Minister Andrei Kozyrev suggested in 1992 that the UN establish a mechanism to protect the rights of Russians in non-Slavic former Soviet republics. Thomas Friedman, "Russian Appeals to U.N. to Safeguard Minorities," *New York Times*, September 23, 1992, p. A17. If the rights of these minorities remain unprotected, however, it seems likely that Russia will act on its own to protect them.

41 In the past I referred to such myth-poisoned nationalism as "hypernationalism." See Van Evera, "Primed for Peace," *International Security* 15 (Winter 1990–91), 7–57, ("Hypernationalism is artificially generated or magnified by chauvinist myths. Conflicts arising from hypernationalism thus derive from the beliefs of nations," not from their circumstances, at 47–48n). However, my usage is narrower than others: see, for example, John Mearsheimer, who defines hypernationalism as the belief that other nationalities are "both inferior and threatening" and an "attitude of contempt

and loathing" toward other nations. Mearsheimer suggests that these beliefs can arise from false propaganda or from real experience. John Mearsheimer, "Back to the Future: Instability in Europe after the Cold War," *International Security* 15 (Summer 1990), 21. Others use the term "hypernationalism" still more broadly to refer to any type of nationalism that spawns aggressive conduct and war. I avoid the term in this chapter because it has acquired these several meanings. I regret adding to the confusion, and suggest we settle on a single usage—probably Mearsheimer's, since it has seniority.

42   Indeed, the intellectual history of Western nationalisms is largely a record of false claims of special self-virtue and of overwrought blaming of others. See examples in Shafer, *Faces of Nationalism,* pp. 313–342. However, myth is not an essential ingredient of nationalism; nationalism can also rest on a group solidarity based on truth, and the effects of nationalism are largely governed by the degree of truthfulness of the beliefs that a given nationalism adopts; as truthfulness diminishes, the risks posed by the nationalism increase.

43   As Ernst Renan has said, "Getting its history wrong is part of being a nation." Quoted in Hobsbawm, *Nations and Nationalism since 1780,* p. 12.

44   World War I–era European nationalists provide abundant examples of such self-glorification. General Friedrich Bernhardi, the German army's main propagandist, proclaimed in 1912 that the Germans are "the greatest civilized people known to history," and have "always been the standard-bearers of free thought" and "free from prejudice." Friedrich von Bernhardi, *Germany and the Next War,* trans. Allen H. Powles (New York: Longmans, Green, 1914, first published in Germany in 1912), pp. 14, 72. In 1915 German economist Werner Sombart declared that the Germans were "the chosen people of this century," and that this chosenness explained others' hostility: "Now we understand why other people hate us. They do not understand us but they fear our tremendous spiritual superiority." Kohn, *Mind of Germany,* pp. 300–301. Richard Dehmel, a German writer, proclaimed in 1914: "We Germans *are* more humane than the other nations; we *do have* better blood and breeding, more soul, more heart, and more imagination." Klaus Schröter, "Chauvinism and Its Tradition: German Writers and the Outbreak of the First World War," *Germanic Review* 43 (March 1968), 126, emphasis in original. In Britain Thomas Macaulay wrote that the British were "the greatest and most highly civilized people that ever the world saw" and were "the acknowledged leaders of the human race in the causes of political improvement." Paul M. Kennedy, "The Decline of Nationalistic History in the West, 1900–1970," *Journal of Contemporary History* 8 (January 1973), 81. In the United States, Senator Albert Beveridge proclaimed in 1899 that "God . . . has made us the master organizers of the world . . . He has made us adept in government that we may administer government among savage and senile peoples . . . He has marked the American people as His chosen nation." Albert K. Weinberg, *Manifest Destiny: A Study of Nationalist Expansionism in American History* (Chicago: Quadrangle, 1963), p. 308. The Soviet government continued this tradition after 1918: the standard Soviet school history text of 1948 claimed that Russian scientists invented the telegraph, steam engine, electric lamp, and the airplane. E. H. Dance, *History the Betrayer: A Study in Bias* (Westport: Greenwood, 1960), pp. 67–68.

45   Innocence can be asserted by denying a barbarous action, or by reinterpreting

the action to put a benign "spin" on it. Post-1919 German textbooks illustrate whitewash-by-denial: Weimar German textbooks denied German responsibility for World War I, falsely claiming that "there was no wish for war in Berlin" in 1914, and that "today every informed person . . . knows that Germany is absolutely innocent with regard to the outbreak of the war, and that Russia, France, and England wanted the war and unleashed it." Dance, *History the Betrayer,* p. 62. Nazi-era texts likewise claimed that "England willed the war" in 1914 after having "set Japan on Russia" in 1904. Dance, *History the Betrayer,* p. 57.

Whitewash-by-spin is also common. When Nazi forces overran Norway and Denmark in 1940 the Nazi party newspaper announced the invasion, but its headline proclaimed "GERMANY SAVES SCANDINAVIA!" William L. Shirer, *The Rise and Fall of the Third Reich: A History of Nazi Germany* (New York: Simon and Schuster, 1960), p. 698n. Similarly, after Soviet forces invaded Afghanistan in 1979 Leonid Brezhnev admitted the action but told the Soviet public: "There has been no Soviet 'intervention' or 'aggression' at all." Rather, Soviet forces were sent to Afghanistan "at its government's request," to defend Afghan "national independence, freedom and honor." L. I. Brezhnev, "Interview for Pravda, January 13, 1980," from *SSHA: Ekonomika, Politika, Ideologiya,* 2 (February 1980), trans. Joint Publication Research Service, in *U.S.S.R. Report,* 75485 (April 14, 1980), p. 3. Japanese imperialists of the 1930s and 1940s claimed Japan was saving China from the "death grip" of the Comintern, and liberating Asia from Western imperialism. Robert J. C. Butow, *Tojo and the Coming of the War* (Stanford: Stanford University Press, 1969), p. 134; Ienaga, *Pacific War,* pp. 153–154. Earlier a French textbook proclaimed the philanthropy of the French North African empire—"France is kind and generous to the peoples she has conquered." Dance, *History the Betrayer,* p. 44.

46   Thus German self-whitewashing of German responsibility for World War I helped fuel German hostility toward Europe during the interwar years and laid the basis for popular German support for Nazi foreign policy. On the post-1918 German "innocence" campaign see Holger H. Herwig, "Clio Deceived: Patriotic Self-Censorship in Germany after the Great War," *International Security* 12 (Fall 1987), 5–44. A good account of Germany's actual pre-1914 conduct is Imanuel Geiss, *German Foreign Policy, 1871–1914* (Boston: Routledge & Kegan Paul, 1976).

47   For example, Wilhelmine and Nazi German nationalists often asserted the inherent inferiority of other groups. Kaiser Wilhelm II declared in 1913: "The Slavs were not born to rule but to serve, this they must be taught." Fritz Fischer, *War of Illusions: German Policies from 1911 to 1914,* trans. Marian Jackson (New York: W. W. Norton, 1975), p. 222. Historian Heinrich von Treitschke thought the English suffered from "cowardice and sensuality," and the French from "besottedness," while an earlier German textbook declared France was "a fermenting mass of rottenness." Snyder, *From Bismarck to Hitler,* p. 35; Antoine Guilland, *Modern Germany and Her Historians* (Westport: Greenwood Press, n.d., reprint of 1915 ed.), pp. 304, 154 quoting an 1876 text by A. Hummel. Writer Richard Dehmel described an England with "only practical talents but not 'culture.'" Schröter, "Chauvinism and Its Tradition," p. 125. Later, Hitler thought Russia was "ripe for dissolution" because it was ruled by the Jews, who were "a ferment of decomposition." Jeremy Noakes and Geoffrey Pridham, eds., *Naziism 1919–1945: A History in Documents and Eyewitness*

Accounts 2 (New York: Schocken, 1988), pp. 615–616. He likewise viewed the United States, in Gerhard Weinberg's paraphrase, as a "mongrel society, in which the scum naturally floated to the top," one that "could not possibly construct a sound economy." Gerhard L. Weinberg, "Hitler's Image of the United States," *American Historical Review* 69 (July 1964), 1010.

Wilhelmine German nationalists also falsely accused others of malign intentions. Pan-German nationalists wove an elaborate myth of "encirclement"—what Hermann Kantorowicz later termed a "fairy tale of encirclement"—that posited a British-French-Russian plot to destroy Germany. See Geiss, *German Foreign Policy,* pp. 121–127. Imperial Japanese nationalists likewise saw a mythical anti-Japanese "ABCD encirclement" by America, Britain, China, and the Dutch, with the USSR and Germany sometimes thrown in as co-conspirators. See Butow, *Tojo and the Coming of the War,* chap. 8, pp. 188–227. During the Korean War, Chinese writers demonized the United States as a "paradise of gangsters, swindlers, rascals, special agents, fascist germs, speculators, debauchers and all the dregs of mankind." President Truman and General Douglas MacArthur became "mad dogs," "bloodstained bandits," "murderers," "rapists," and "savages." At the same time MacArthur warned that China "has become aggressively imperialistic, with a lust for expansion." John G. Stoessinger, *Nations in Darkness: China, Russia, and America,* 5th ed. (New York: McGraw-Hill, 1990), pp. 50–51.

For an example of falsely blaming others for past tragedies see notes 45 and 46 on the German post-1918 innocence campaign: in making this claim of innocence Germans also blamed others for starting the war.

48 Conversely, denigration of others is less common than both self-whitewashing and self-glorification, but is often implicit in self-glorification (others suffer in comparison to the virtuous self-image: if one's own group is spotlessly virtuous, others look worse by comparison).

49 Moreover, the victims' charges will anger the criminal nation, since it believes itself innocent, hence it views the victims' charges as malicious slander.

50 After Germany and Italy conquered Yugoslavia in 1941 they established a puppet state, the Independent State of Croatia, under the leadership of the Croatian Ustashi, a nationalist Croat extremist-terrorist organization headed by Ante Pavelic. Without prompting from the Nazis the Ustashi then launched a mass murder campaign against other ethnic groups, killing by one estimate 500,000–700,000 Serbs, 50,000 Jews, and 20,000 Gypsies. Alex N. Dragnich, *Serbs and Croats: The Struggle for Yugoslavia* (New York: Harcourt Brace, 1992), pp. 96, 101–103. Dragnich reports that even the Germans were horrified by the nature and extent of the killings, and German officials protested to Pavelic (p. 103). On these murders see also Aleksa Djilas, *The Contested Country* (Cambridge: Harvard University Press, 1991), pp. 120–127; he endorses a smaller estimate by Bogoljub Koáoviá of 234,000 Serbs murdered (p. 126). For Croatian denials of the Ustashi's mass murders see Denich, "Unbury the Victims," pp. 5–6.

51 Such mythmaking has two targets: the public at large, and state instruments of coercion, who may need special motivation to carry out their tasks.

52 Regime illegitimacy provides the largest motive for elite mythmaking when the state cannot rule by pure force: mythmaking is then the elite's only means to preserve its rule. The proximate cause of mythmaking can therefore be sometimes found in the decline of the state monopoly of force, not the decline of elite legitimacy. This

was the case in Europe in the nineteenth century: nationalist mythmaking rose with the rise of mass armies and popular literacy, which diminished the capacity of the state to govern by pure coercion. Elites were therefore forced to resort to persuasion, hence to mythmaking. (Mass literacy in this context proved a double-edged sword for newly literate publics. Literacy enabled mass political mobilization by spreading social knowledge and ideas; this led to popular empowerment. Literacy also made publics easier to control from above, by enabling elites to purvey elite-justifying myths through the written word; this limited or reduced popular power.)

53   Snyder makes a similar argument, although he casts it in somewhat different terms, in "Nationalism and the Crisis of the Post-Soviet State," pp. 14–16.

54   On the fall of nationalistic history in Europe since the world wars see Kennedy, "Decline of Nationalistic History in the West."

55   See, for example, Omer Bartov, *Hitler's Army: Soldiers, Nazis, and the War in the Third Reich* (New York: Oxford University Press, 1991), pp. 106–178, describing the myths purveyed by the Nazi regime to motivate its troops on the Eastern Front.

56   Advancing this argument is Stephen M. Walt, "Revolution and War," *World Politics* 44 (April 1992), 321–368, esp. 336–340.

57   For this argument see Posen, "Nationalism, the Mass Army, and Military Power."

58   This hypothesis is widely accepted but has not been systematically tested; more empirical research exploring the relationship between economic downturns and scapegoating would be valuable.

59   The existence of a free press and free universities does not guarantee that myths will be scrutinized; these institutions also require a "truth squad" ethos—a sense that mythbusting is among their professional missions. This ethos is often missing among university faculties, who often pursue research agendas that have little relevance to the worries of the real world. A discussion that remains valuable is Robert S. Lynd, *Knowledge for What? The Place of Social Science in American Culture* (Princeton: Princeton University Press, 1939). For recent discussion see Russell Jacoby, *The Last Intellectuals: American Culture in the Age of Academe* (New York: Basic Books, 1987), pp. 112–237. On this problem in political science see Hans J. Morgenthau, "The Purpose of Political Science," in James C. Charlesworth, ed., *A Design for Political Science: Scope, Objectives, and Methods* (Philadelphia: American Academy of Political and Social Science, 1966), pp. 69–74.

60   A good survey of German historiography of this era is Snyder, *German Nationalism*, chap. 6 (pp. 123–152). An older survey is Guilland, *Modern Germany and Her Historians*. Also relevant are John A. Moses, *The Politics of Illusion: The Fischer Controversy in German Historiography* (London: George Prior, 1975), chap. 1 (pp. 7–26); and Snyder, *From Bismarck to Hitler*, chap. 3 (pp. 25–35). German academics also cooperated with official German mythmaking after World War I; on this cooperation see Herwig, "Clio Deceived."

61   The emerging nations of the former USSR now stand knee-deep in the blood of Stalin's victims, and in the economic ruin that Bolshevism left behind. If every nation blames only others for these disasters, civil relations among them will be impossible: each will hope to someday settle accounts. Civil relations depend, then, on a convergence toward a common history of the Bolshevik disaster. Things would be best if all converged on a version that blamed the Bolsheviks—who, having vanished, can be blamed painlessly. (Bolshevism would then usefully serve as a hate-soaker—its final, and among its few positive, functions in Soviet history.) Absent that, things

would be better if the successor nations agree on how to allocate blame among themselves.

62   However, in the East's heterogeneous interethnic setting, democracy is a mixed blessing: if it takes a strict majoritarian form it can produce majority tyranny and the oppression of minorities, as it has in the past in Northern Ireland and the American Deep South. To produce civil peace in a multiethnic setting, democracy must adopt nonmajoritarian principles of power-sharing, like those of Swiss democracy. On this question see Arend Lijphart, "Consociational Democracy," *World Politics* 21 (January 1969), 107–125; Arend Lijphart, *Democracy in Plural Societies: A Comparative Exploration* (New Haven: Yale University Press, 1977); Arend Lijphart, *Democracies: Patterns of Majoritarian and Consensus Government in Twenty-One Countries* (New Haven: Yale University Press, 1984); Arend Lijphart, "The Power-Sharing Approach," in Joseph V. Montville, ed., *Conflict and Peacemaking in Multiethnic Societies* (Lexington, Mass.: Lexington Books, 1990), pp. 491–509; Kenneth D. McRae, "Theories of Power-Sharing and Conflict Management," in Montville, *Conflict and Peacemaking,* pp. 93–106; Jurg Steiner, "Power-Sharing: Another Swiss 'Export Product'?" in Montville, *Conflict and Peacemaking,* pp. 107–114; Hans Daalder, "The Consociational Democracy Theme," *World Politics* 26 (July 1974), 604–621; Kenneth D. McRae, ed., *Consociational Democracy: Political Accommodation in Segmented Societies* (Toronto: McClelland and Stewart, 1974); and Vernon Van Dyke, "Human Rights and the Rights of Groups," *American Journal of Political Science* 18 (November, 1974), 725–741, at 730–740. See also James Madison, "The Same Subject Continued . . . " (Federalist 10), *The Federalist Papers,* intro. by Clinton Rossiter (New York: New American Library, 1961), pp. 77–84, which addresses the danger of majority tyranny and remedies for it; Madison discusses the risks that arise when "a majority is included in a faction" (p. 80) and the dangers of tyranny by "the superior force of an interested and overbearing majority" (p. 77). Also relevant is Robert M. Axelrod, *Conflict of Interest: A Theory of Divergent Goals with Applications to Politics* (Chicago: Markham, 1970), whose theory of winning coalition membership explains why majoritarian rules distribute power unequally in deeply divided societies.

63   Nationalism will probably engender substantial violence in the Third World, too, largely because a high nation-to-state ratio still prevails there; hence many secessionist movements and wars of secession are likely in the decades ahead. For a discussion of the policy issues raised by this circumstance see Halperin, Scheffer, and Small, *Self-Determination in the New World Order;* for a global survey of current self-determination movements, see pp. 123–160.

64   Minority rights should be defined broadly, to include fair minority representation in the legislative, executive, and judicial branches of the central government. The definition of minority rights used in most international human rights agreements is more restrictive: it omits the right to share power in the national government, and includes only the right to political autonomy and the preservation of minority language, culture, and religion. See Edward Lawson, *Encyclopedia of Human Rights* (New York: Taylor & Francis, 1991), p. 1070; and, on the general neglect of minority rights by Western political thinkers, see Vernon Van Dyke, "The Individual, the State, and Ethnic Communities in Political Theory," *World Politics* 29 (April 1977), 343–369.

When should minority rights be defined to include the right to secession and national independence? Universal recognition of this right would require massive redrawing of boundaries in the East, and would raise the question of Western recognition of scores of now-unrecognized independence movements worldwide. One solution is to recognize the right to secede in instances where the central government is unwilling to fully grant other minority rights, but to decline to recognize the right to secede if all other minority rights are fully recognized and robustly protected. In essence, the West would hold its possible recognition of a right to secede in reserve, to encourage governments to recognize other minority rights. A discussion of the right to secession is Vernon Van Dyke, "Collective Entities and Moral Rights: Problems in Liberal-Democratic Thought," *Journal of Politics* 44 (February 1982), 36–37. Also relevant is Halperin, Scheffer, and Small, *Self-Determination in the New World Order.*

65   States should not be asked to accept externally imposed versions of history in their texts, since no society can arbitrarily claim to know the "truth" better than others. But states could be asked to commit to international dialogue on history, on the theory that free debate will cause views to converge. Specifically, they could be asked to accept the obligation to subject their school curricula to foreign criticism, perhaps in the context of textbook exchanges, and to allow domestic publication of foreign criticisms of their curricula. Schemes of this sort have a long history in Western Europe, where they had a substantial impact after 1945. See Dance, *History the Betrayer,* pp. 127–128, 132, 135–150. This West European experience could serve as a template for an East European program.

66   These democratic governments should adopt consociational power-sharing rules, not majoritarian rules; otherwise ethnic minorities will be denied equal political power (see note 62).

67   Such a code could be applied more widely, and serve as the basis for an international regime on nationalist comportment; a nationalist movement's entitlement to international support would correspond to its acceptance and observance of the code.

68   The Western powers should also offer to help the Eastern powers devise specific policies to implement these principles, and offer active assistance with peacemaking if conflicts nevertheless emerge. Specifically, Western governments and institutions should offer to share Western ideas and experience on the building of democratic institutions; the development of political and legal institutions that protect and empower minorities; the development of market economic institutions; and the best means to control nationalism in education. (On this last point see Dance, *History the Betrayer,* pp. 126–150.) Finally, if serious conflicts nevertheless emerge, the West should offer active mediation, as the United States has between Israelis and Arabs.

69   For Baker's principles see "Baker's Remarks: Policy on Soviets," *New York Times,* September 5, 1991, p. A12. Baker reiterated these principles in December 1991; see "Baker Sees Opportunities and Risks as Soviet Republics Grope for Stability," *New York Times,* December 13, 1991, p. A24. Reporting Baker's conditioning of American recognition of the new Eastern governments on their acceptance of these standards is Michael Wines, "Ex-Soviet Leader Is Lauded by Bush," *New York Times,* December 26, 1991, p. 1.

70   See "Winking at Aggression in Baku," *New York Times* (editorial), February 14, 1992, p. A28.

71   In April 1993 the Clinton administration forged agreement among the Group of Seven (G7) states (Britain, France, Germany, Italy, Canada, Japan, and the United

States) on a $28 billion aid package for the former Soviet Union, and Congress approved a substantial aid package in September 1993. See Serge Schmemann, "Yeltsin Leaves Talks with Firm Support and More Aid," *New York Times,* April 5, 1993, p. 1; David E. Sanger, "7 Nations Pledge $28 Billion Fund to Assist Russia," *New York Times,* April 16, 1993, p. 1; Steven Greenhouse, "I.M.F. Unveils Plan for Soviet Lands," *New York Times,* April 21, 1993, p. A16; Steven A. Holmes, "House Approves Bill Including 2.5 Billion in Aid for Russians," *New York Times,* September 24, 1993, p. A6; and Steven Greenhouse, "I.M.F. Tosses Bouquet to Russia: $1.5 Billion," *New York Times,* April 21, 1994, p. A9. The aid was conditioned on Eastern moves toward marketization, but political conditions were omitted. President Clinton did declare that "we support respect for ethnic minorities," and "we stand with Russian democracy" as he announced the American aid pledge (Schmemann, "Yeltsin Leaves Talks"). However, press accounts do not mention explicit political conditions.

9   ETHNIC NATIONALISMS AND IMPLICATIONS FOR U.S. FOREIGN POLICY

1   They are, however, hardly new recommendations. See William Pfaff, "Invitation to War," *Foreign Affairs* 72 (Summer 1993), 97–110.
2   I am distinguishing between national interests and values that we pursue as a matter of course and those vital interests that contribute to national security.
3   See, for a critical discussion of these ideas, Daniel Deudney, "Geopolitics and Change," paper presented to the Seminar on International Relations, Princeton University, 1992.
4   See O. Harries, ed., *America's Purpose: New Visions of U.S. Foreign Policy* (San Francisco: ICS Press, 1991); Charles Krauthammer, "The Unipolar Moment," *Foreign Affairs* 70 (Winter 1991), 23–33; Strobe Talbott, "Post Victory Blues," *Foreign Affairs* 71 (Winter 1992), 53–69.
5   This discussion is from Henry Bienen, "America: The Firsters, the Decliners, and the Searchers for a New American Foreign Policy," in Richard L. Leaver and James Richardson, eds., *The Post–Cold War Order: Diagnoses and Prognoses* (Boulder, Colo.: Westview Press, 1994), pp. 160–167.
6   See Steven L. Burg, "Nationalism Redux: Through the Glass of the Post-Communist States Darkly," *Current History* 92 (April 1993), 162.
7   Crawford Young, *The Politics of Cultural Pluralism* (Madison: University of Wisconsin Press, 1976); Joseph V. Montville, *Conflict and Peacemaking in Multiethnic Societies* (Lexington, Mass.: Lexington Books, 1987); Donald Horowitz, *Ethnic Groups in Conflict* (Berkeley: University of California Press, 1985); Ernest Gellner, *Nations and Nationalism* (Ithaca: Cornell University Press, 1983).
8   Henry Bienen, "The State and Ethnicity: Integrative Formulas in Africa," in Donald Rothchild and Victor A. Olorunsola, eds., *States versus Ethnic Claims: African Policy Dilemmas* (Boulder, Colo.: Westview Press, 1983), pp. 100–126.
9   See Anthony D. Smith, *Nationalism in the Twentieth Century* (New York: New York University Press, 1979).
10   Burg, "Nationalism Redux," p. 162.
11   Jack Snyder, "Nationalism and the Crisis of the Post-Soviet State," *Survival* 35 (Spring 1993), 5–26.

12 Gellner, *Nations and Nationalism.*

13 Arthur Waldron, "Theories of Nationalism and Historical Explanation," *World Politics* 37 (April 1985), 427–428.

14 Uri Ra'anan, "The Nation-State Fallacy," in Montville, *Conflict and Peacemaking in Multiethnic Socities,* pp. 5–20.

15 See Ezra Suleiman's chapter in this volume for an exploration of European Community identifications.

16 See John K. Fairbank, *The United States and China* (Cambridge: Harvard University Press, 1983); Chalmers Johnson, *Peasant Nationalism and Communist Power: The Emergence of Revolutionary China, 1937–1945* (Stanford: Stanford University Press, 1962); Milton J. Esman and Itamar Rabinovich, eds., *Ethnicity, Pluralism, and the State in the Middle East* (Ithaca: Cornell University Press, 1988).

17 Snyder, "Nationalism," p. 5.

18 The work of Charles Tilly has been very useful on state formation. See his edited work, *The Formation of National States in Western Europe* (Princeton: Princeton University Press, 1975). Also see Eric Hobsbawm, *Nations and Nationalism since 1780* (Cambridge: Cambridge University Press, 1990).

19 See Rupert Emerson, *From Empire to Nation* (Cambridge: Harvard University Press, 1960); Cyril E. Black and L. Carl Brown, eds., *Modernization in the Middle East: The Ottoman Empire and Its Afro-Asian Successors* (Princeton: Darwin Press, 1992); S. N. Eisenstat, *The Political Systems of Empires: The Rise and Fall of the Historical Bureaucratic Societies* (New York: Free Press, 1969); Michael W. Doyle, *Empires* (Ithaca: Cornell University Press, 1986).

20 Barry Posen, "The Security Dilemma and Ethnic Conflict," *Survival* 35 (Spring 1993), 27.

21 Ibid., p. 29.

22 Black and Brown, *Modernization in the Middle East,* p. 174.

23 Clifford Geertz, ed., *Old Societies and New States* (Glencoe: Free Press, 1968); Young, *The Politics of Cultural Pluralism.*

24 This discussion is from Henry Bienen and Aaron Friedberg, "International Security and National Security: With a Focus on Multipolar Asia," paper for the Congress of Sasakawa Fellows, Beijing, August 1993.

25 Cited by Craig Whitney, "What Does Europe Want?" *New York Times,* May 16, 1993, p. E5.

26 John Chipman, "Managing the Politics of Parochialism," *Survival* 35 (Spring 1993), 166–167.

27 Pfaff, "Invitation to War," p. 107.

10 CONCLUSION

1 This conclusion parallels the findings of Donald Horowitz in his broad comparative study of ethnic conflict *Ethnic Groups in Conflict* (Berkeley: University of California Press, 1985)

2 For discussion of how war and preparation for war lead to the centralization of the state and to the intensification of nationalist sentiments, see Michael Mann, *The Sources of Social Power,* vol. 2 (Cambridge: Cambridge University Press, 1993).

3 For discussion of this issue, see David Gordon, "Debt, Conditionality, and Reform: The International Relations of Economic Restructuring in Sub-Saharan Africa," in Thomas Callaghy, ed., *Hemmed In: Responses to Africa's Economic Decline* (New York: Columbia University Press, 1993).

4 These criteria might include the holding of free elections and the protection of basic human rights.

5 I do not share Henry Bienen's skepticism about the value of such programs. The influential role that education played in building new societies in postwar Germany and Japan, the popularity in the communist bloc of Voice of America and Radio Free Europe, the value of civic education in established democracies—all provide good reason to make better use of education and social programs.

6 See Paul Kennedy, "The Decline of Nationalistic History in the West, 1900–1970," *Journal of Contemporary History* 8 (January 1973), 77–100.

7 My own assessment of the war in Bosnia differs somewhat from that of Aleksa Djilas. Djilas argues that Western analysts apportioned the Serbs too much blame for the war. I believe that one has to distinguish between the Bosnian civil war—for which all the parties are responsible and in which all the parties committed atrocities; and the war of aggression waged against Bosnia—for which the Serbs (and to a lesser extent the Croats) are principally responsible.

8 The experience of Wilhelmine Germany and interwar Japan suggests that even preponderant force cannot deter states charged with nationalistic fervor. Both Germany and Japan went to war despite military assessments suggesting that the chances of victory were slim. It took actual defeat in war, not just the prospect of it, to break the momentum provided by military establishments and societies running on the fuel of aggressive nationalism.

9 On the evolution of the Partnership for Peace and its strengths and weaknesses, see Charles Kupchan, "Strategic Visions," *World Policy Journal* 11 (Fall 1994), 112–122.

10 For one view of the criteria that should be used in recognizing new states see Morton Halperin and David Scheffer, with Patricia Small, *Self-Determination in the New World Order* (Washington, D.C.: Carnegie Endowment for International Peace, 1992), pp. 84–93.